The Human Tradition in the New South

The Human Tradition in America

CHARLES W. CALHOUN
Series Editor
Department of History, East Carolina University

Michael A. Morrison, ed., *The Human Tradition in Antebellum America* (2000)
Malcolm Muir Jr., ed., *The Human Tradition in the World War II Era* (2001)
Ty Cashion and Jesús F. de la Teja, eds., *The Human Tradition in Texas* (2001)
Benson Tong and Regan A. Lutz, eds., *The Human Tradition in the American West* (2002)
Charles W. Calhoun, ed., *The Human Tradition in America from the Colonial Era through Reconstruction* (2002)
Donald W. Whisenhunt, ed., *The Human Tradition in America between the Wars, 1920–1945* (2002)
Roger Biles, ed., *The Human Tradition in Urban America* (2002)
Clark David and David Igler, eds., *The Human Tradition in California* (2002)
James C. Klotter, ed., *The Human Tradition in the Old South* (2003)
Nina Mjagkij, ed., *Portraits of African Amerian Life since 1865* (2003)
Charles W. Calhoun, ed., *The Human Tradition in America: 1865 to the Present* (2003)
David L. Anderson, ed., *The Human Tradition in America since 1945* (2003)
Eric Arnesen, ed., *The Human Tradition in American Labor History* (2003)
James C. Klotter, ed., *The Human Tradition in the New South* (2005)

The Human Tradition in the New South

Edited by
James C. Klotter

ROWMAN & LITTLEFIELD PUBLISHERS, INC.
Lanham • Boulder • New York • Toronto • Oxford

ROWMAN & LITTLEFIELD PUBLISHERS, INC.

Published in the United States of America
by Rowman & Littlefield Publishers, Inc.
A wholly owned subsidiary of The Rowman & Littlefield Publishing Group, Inc.
4501 Forbes Boulevard, Suite 200, Lanham, Maryland 20706
www.rowmanlittlefield.com

PO Box 317
Oxford
OX2 9RU, UK

Copyright © 2005 by Rowman & Littlefield Publishers, Inc.

All rights reserved. No part of this publication may be reproduced, stored in a retrieval system, or transmitted in any form or by any means, electronic, mechanical, photocopying, recording, or otherwise, without the prior permission of the publisher.

British Library Cataloguing in Publication Information Available

Library of Congress Cataloging-in-Publication Data

The human tradition in the New South / edited by James C. Klotter.
    p. cm.
Includes bibliographical references and index.
ISBN 0-7425-4475-3 (cloth : alk. paper) — ISBN 0-7425-4476-1 (pbk. : alk. paper)
    1. Southern States—Biography. 2. Southern States—History—Anecdotes.
I. Klotter, James C.
F208.H86 2005
975--dc22   2005011096

Printed in the United States of America

$\otimes^{TM}$The paper used in this publication meets the minimum requirements of American National Standard for Information Sciences—Permanence of Paper for Printed Library Materials, ANSI/NISO Z39.48-1992.

Contents

Acknowledgments   vii

Introduction: The American South   ix
James C. Klotter

1   The Lost Cause Legend about Winnie Davis, "the Daughter
    of the Confederacy"   1
    Cita Cook

2   Black Zack and Uncle Amon   19
    Paul K. Conkin

3   Asa Candler: Old Southerner in the New South   31
    Kathryn W. Kemp

4   Alfred Holt Stone: Conservative Racial Thought in the
    New South   47
    John David Smith

5   Hester Calvert: Farm Wife   67
    Rebecca Sharpless

6   Ma Rainey: Mother of the Blues   79
    S. Spencer Davis

7   Dizzy Dean: Baseball's Quintessential Southerner   91
    William J. Marshall

8 Eleanor Copenhaver Anderson and the Industrial Department of the National Board YWCA: Toward a New Social Order in Dixie 111
   Margaret Ripley Wolfe

9 Harland Sanders: The Man Who Would Be Colonel 129
   John Ed Pearce

10 Blanche Terry and the White Knights of the Ku Klux Klan 157
   Christopher Waldrep

11 Ralph David Abernathy and the Civil Rights Movement 173
   Gerald L. Smith

12 Bill Henry Terry Jr.: An African American's Journey from Alabama to Vietnam and Back 193
   David L. Anderson

Index 209

About the Editor 215

Acknowledgments

The following chapters were previously published and are reprinted with permission:

Chapter 5, "Hester Calvert: Farm Wife," by Rebecca Sharpless, from *The Human Tradition in Texas*, edited by Ty Cashion and Jesus F. de la Teja. Wilmington, DE: Scholarly Resources Books, 2001.

Chapter 6, "Ma Rainey: Mother of the Blues," by S. Spencer Davis, from *The Human Tradition in America between the Wars, 1920-1945*, edited by Donald W. Whisenhunt. Wilmington, DE: Scholarly Resources Books, 2002.

Chapter 12, "Bill Henry Terry Jr.: An African American's Journey from Alabama to Vietnam and Back," by David L. Anderson, from *The Human Tradition in Vietnam*, edited by David L. Anderson. Wilmington, DE: Scholarly Resources Books, 2000.

Introduction:
The American South

James C. Klotter

For those who study the South, questions abound. Why examine this region? What, in fact, is the South? Is there one South or several? What is its history, and how does it influence the present and the future? And, most of all, what stories can the people of this region tell to help explain the South and those who call it home? How can those human traditions help us understand this distinct place, this South?

If many questions exist, so too do many answers, some of them contradictory. But on the matter of why the South deserves special study, the explanations generally agree. W. J. Cash, in his controversial, entertaining, and still influential *Mind of the South* (1941), wrote that people of all regions of American had "a profound conviction that the South is another land." With justification, said Cash, the South should be viewed as "not quite a nation within a nation, but the next thing to it." Historian Carl Degler remembered that when he grew up in the North, he considered the South "not only a different but an exotic place . . . almost a foreign country." Another student of the region's history, Charles P. Roland, similarly noted that more than any other part of the United States, the South gave expression to its sectional consciousness. The region "bore the mark of a different past reinforced by a widespread awareness and interpretation of it." Settlement patterns, culture and folkways, slavery and segregation, defeat and the Lost Cause—these and more contributed to the shaping of the particular history that created a different region, this almost foreign place to some, this almost-nation to others.[1]

While all those observers described a distinctive South in the twentieth century, the idea of the South as a separate entity had been well developed much, much earlier, even before Charles Pinckney declared in 1787, "When I say Southern, I mean Maryland and the states to the southward of her."[2] Debates over slavery already had created divisions during the revolutionary era; sectional voting emerged more clearly by the time of the Missouri Compromise and had grown by the Compromise of 1850; discord developed into secession, full-scale war, and a separate nation by the Civil War. After what the South called the War Between the States and what some northerners termed the War of the Rebellion, the ex-Confederacy generally became occupied territory, subject to Reconstruction, and with an emerging story not found anywhere else in America. Other chapters added to that account over the years, so that Dixie became recognized as a region different from any other in the nation. History shaped and formed a southern identity.

THE REGION

If there is an identifiable South, with a past worthy of study, what exactly constitutes the region? Definitions vary. Most include the eleven states that formed the Confederacy as the core of the South—Virginia, North Carolina, South Carolina, Florida, Georgia, Tennessee, Alabama, Mississippi, Louisiana, Arkansas, and Texas. Most also place Kentucky in that mix; although it was a slave state that did not leave the union, its actions before and after the war tied it closely to the South. Beyond those states, various places have and have not been included—infrequently Delaware, occasionally Missouri or Maryland or West Virginia, more often Oklahoma. Sociologists generally define a region as "an area of which the inhabitants feel themselves a part." In asking people a series of questions, they seek to find whether the individuals consider themselves southern. As Cash said, the South might be, most of all, a state of mind. If so, the degree of "southern-ness" determines placement in the region. Using that method of preference, for example, indicates that Kentuckians consider themselves more southern than Floridians, with their large number of out-of-state retirees, or Texans, with their western traditions. Yet those and the other ex-Confederate states all rank high on the scale of "southern-ness." Combining, then, history and preference, the South, as defined in this work, consists of the eleven original Confederate states that left the Union, plus Kentucky and Oklahoma—the definition also used by national polling organizations. Still, as John Shelton Reed notes, "some are born southern, some achieve it, and some have it thrust upon them."[3]

THE ENDURING SOUTH

What has created that South, however defined? What has formed this region, this enduring South? First of all, as others have noted, many Souths exist in memory and mind, not just one. Various images make up the national—and the southern—view of the area. For example, there is the Romantic South of "moonlight, magnolias, and mint juleps," where Rhett Butler—or Colonel Sanders—and Scarlett O'Hara sit on the porches of their white-columned mansions, sipping drinks—perhaps sweetened iced tea—watching thoroughbreds romp or cotton grow, while dutiful black servants in white coats stand nearby. On the other hand, another image focuses on the Defensive South, one that supports an indefensible slave system and then segregation; a South under attack from without, which resulted in what Jim Cobb terms "the siege mentality that prevailed among white southerners." Similarly, another stereotype addresses the Fundamentalist South. Baltimore satirist H. L. Mencken in the 1920s contemptuously snarled about the "degraded nonsense which country preachers are ramming into yokel skulls" and the "Baptist and Methodist barbarism" of a region 90 percent Protestant. That portrayal of wild-eyed, religiously intolerant evangelist preachers has not disappeared over the years. Conversely, however, a newer image of the Sunbelt South has pictured it as a place of promise, more so than that so-called Rustbelt North. As the nation has faced its own identity crisis and self-doubt over Vietnam and Watergate and has had to deal with poverty and racism, the South has not seemed so subject to criticism and has been viewed more favorably. Balancing that, however, the Bubba South continues strong as a portrayal of the region, one featuring "hillbillies" and "rednecks," with Klan sheets in the back of their pickups and whiskey on the seat. And there remains the Tragic South, where every battlefield and every grave reminds of the deaths and defeats of long ago, still alive in the memories, the statues, the symbols. Such different images have formed—and do form—various aspects of the region's view of itself, and the nation's. Some might explain the past and the people of the present; others may simply cloud and confuse with their exaggerations. Like an early morning fog, the various myths and realities of the region make it difficult to see clearly the heart and soul of the South.[4]

Moreover, any look at the region should remember to ask, as Paul Conkin does, "But which South?"[5] For many heartbeats run through the land, and it has many faces, many souls. In Conkin's youth, the majority of the South stood Confederate in sympathy and Democratic in politics, with African Americans all around. Yet his Tennessee mountain area was a white, Republican, Union, non-grits South. When we speak of the South, then, are we talking about the plantation South, or the South of textile mill workers, mountain miners, and poverty-stricken sharecroppers, or the New South of skyscrapers and steel? Is it the region of poor education and one-room schools, or the literary South that produced writers such as Thomas Wolfe, William Faulkner, Robert Penn Warren, Eudora Welty, and Richard Wright, among others? Is this the South of slavery, segregation, white supremacy, lynchings, church burnings, fire hoses, and police dogs, or the place that produces courageous leaders on race, such as a Judge Frank M. Johnson Jr., a President Lyndon B. Johnson, a Reverend Martin Luther King Jr., or a Fannie Lou Hamer?

When the South is discussed, is it the black and white Protestant place, or the Cajun, Catholic South, or the Native American one, or the Hispanic South? Is it the lowland, coastal region, or the Piedmont, or the Appalachian, or the Western Plains South? Does it have an urban or suburban locus or a rural, agricultural one? Is it the deeply moral and religious South that supports Prohibition, or the cavalier, hedonistic South that can reconcile religion, horseracing, and red-eye whiskey? Is it a region of Bluegrass and country music, or of jazz and the blues, or of Elvis Presley and rock and roll, or of big city symphonies? Is it a political place of demagogic speakers making racial and class appeals, or the place of presidents and New South leaders? Is this a South of farms or of factories, of furrows or of fax machines, of forests or of forges?

Obviously the South is all these things and even more. Just as there are many Souths, so too does each of them have various faces, all part of the region's overall makeup. Yet, at the same time, such differences should not obscure the underlying truth of a section that goes beyond the differences and divisions and considers itself different and special. As one author concluded, "If it can be said that there are many Souths, the fact remains that there is also one South," a place with "a fairly definite mental pattern, associated with a fairly definite social pattern."[6] And all of that has emerged through the region's history.

HISTORY AND THE SOUTH

Historian C. Vann Woodward stressed that a central theme of the region may be southern history itself. Another author has suggested that the two sections did differ historically, but turns the argument around and asks if the South with its rural and traditional society was not more the norm: "Perhaps it was the North that was 'different,' the North that departed from the mainstream of historical development, and perhaps therefore we should speak not of southern exceptionalism but of northern exceptionalism." In any case, then, understanding sectional distinctiveness must begin—not end—with studying the area's heritage and history. Doing that makes it plain, also, that the buildings, the battlefields, the oral traditions, the stored memories, all combine to form a special past, a "history with a southern accent." As one author concisely noted about the differences in the history of the South versus the history of the United States overall: "The South retained slavery while the rest of the nation abandoned it; the South ruptured the national union; the South stayed agricultural while the nation industrialized; the South expanded legal segregation as the nation relinquished it; the South remained rural as the nation became urban; the South remained poor while the nation grew rich; in a nation of immigrants, southerners were overwhelmingly natives."[7]

Yet the South has more recently gone beyond that history. Slavery and segregation have died and race relations have changed. The region has industrialized as well; by 1980 only a little more than 3 percent of southerners farmed. Currently the area's per capita income nears national averages and, given the lower cost of living, may exceed it in reality, though poverty remains a problem. Finally, people from outside the region—migrants or immigrants—dot the landscape. But in change, the ghosts of the past still ride, still influencing the present, still shaping the future of the region.

To understand the South since 1865 means understanding the long influence the Civil War had on southerners, in fact and memory. If the fighting ended with Appomattox, the struggle continued. A conquered people found the blue coats—hated by most whites and welcomed by most blacks—occupying their land. With former slaves in positions that suggested an equality that most white southerners still found difficult to accept, some whites soon struck out again and again in an almost guerrilla-style violence directed toward African Americans. The Civil War and its aftermath solidified white racial unity, and, as one historian wrote, "peace became war carried on by other means." Not just during Reconstruction, but for decade after decade, the black population of the South—a quarter of the population as late as 1940—found itself struggling not just for equality but for basic rights, and even for their lives. Riots, lynchings, and individual acts of terrorism left the dead behind; by century's end, increasing segregation was followed by subterfuges such as grandfather clauses or literacy tests that took away social and political rights. As David Blight has noted, "As the sections reconciled . . . the races divided," in a form of American apartheid. African American liberties became sacrifices on the altar of reunion. Another historian has stressed how, at the same time, white southerners seemed to ignore the fact that slavery had anything to do with the Civil War, and wrote it out of their historical record and memory. Blacks, in the resulting new southern stage, played only marginal roles.[8]

Such actions coupled with better economic opportunities in the North to spur an increasing out-migration of African Americans, with some half million departing during World War I alone, and more in the next conflict. Only when the *Brown* decision sparked the so-called Second Reconstruction of the 1950s and after, and then a civil rights revolution, did the walls of segregation begin to crumble. Boycotts, sit-ins, and marches brought change, despite the efforts of names of shame, such as Faubus, Wallace, and others, to fight those actions. Only after much pain—and more deaths—did the new order win out, perhaps appropriately led by a southern president, Lyndon B. Johnson, and a southern black leader, Martin Luther King Jr. Yet those still solid walls of racial inequality proved harder to tear down, in a struggle that goes on yet.

The long fight for civil rights, begun at the end of the Civil War, was only one thing that continued to separate the South from the rest of the nation. As historian Dewey Grantham notes, "At the end of Reconstruction, the South stood out as the nation's poorest, most isolated, most distinctive section. It was less industrialized, less diversified, and less literate than other parts of the country. Its per capita income was barely half that of the national average." Nor would that, for the most part, change over the next half century. Despite the efforts of late-nineteenth-century New South spokesman Henry Grady, who called for more industry, on the eve of the Great Depression in 1929, only 9 percent of national industrial output came from the South. Soon after, new president Franklin D. Roosevelt, who spent some of his time at Hot Springs, Georgia, would call the region "the nation's No. 1 economic problem." Earlier, farmers tied to crop liens and sharecropping, or to a one-crop economy and its fluctuations in prices, had sought a greater political voice in their plight and had been part of an agrarian revolt of sizable force. By the 1930s those same economic factors still operated, still miring them in poverty.[9]

That soon changed. The New Deal, then World War II, proved to be tremendous forces that remade the South. Agricultural controls helped stabilize farm prices; the demand for the products in wartime brought more prosperity. At the same time, farm laborers existing on starvation wages soon saw more opportunity and much higher salaries in factories and cities. Appalachian miners then, and entering into the 1950s, followed a similar pattern and massive migrations depopulated the countryside. Now southerners went to town, and jobs brought new lifestyles. At the same time the military presence grew, and with it jobs and income. Of one hundred new army camps in wartime, sixty were built in the South; near war's end, some 25 percent of the region's wages came from government payrolls. Shipbuilding, ordinance plants, chemical production—all added to the growth. With gender and racial lines more fluid, with unions expanding, with income rising faster than the national average, it is little wonder that one historian told his class that "World War II probably had a greater impact on the South than the Civil War."[10]

Changes took place in politics as well, particularly after the conflict ended. Not long following the conclusion of that other war, the one between the states in 1865, those who had waved the Confederate flag attacked Republicans until they had regained political dominance and made the Democratic Party the party of the Solid South. Whether unreconstructed rebels or later "Dixie demagogues," whether aristocratic former generals or hill-country yeomen, like Huey Long in the twentieth century, all ruled through that party. They thus helped fellow Democrats Woodrow Wilson and Franklin D. Roosevelt initiate their national reform programs, which often went beyond the conservatism of southern political leaders. But as race reared its head as an issue following World War II, as the party took more liberal stands on various social issues, as northern Republicans moved to southern suburbs, the once solid South splintered, fragmented, and then faded. If at one time, as a southerner noted, the holding of office by a Republican in the South was enough to cause questions about the wisdom of the Almighty, then such feelings soon ceased as the party of Lincoln challenged for supremacy across the region.

In addition to the changes wrought by wars, civil and worldwide, besides the political and civil rights revolutions going on, national attention focused on the region in other, often contradictory, ways as well. The 1920s would see antievolution sentiment emerge full blown in the Scopes Monkey Trial in Tennessee, and while in that same decade the reborn KKK would become more a national phenomenon than a regional one, its presence in the South still brought up long-past memories. Yet, at almost the same instance, the flowering of the southern literary Renaissance brought the region practically to a place of dominance in American writing.

Such negative and positive trends continued into the twenty-first-century South, but, by then, they operated under new conditions. Aided by another revolution—air-conditioning—the South could now provide a more hospitable physical setting in the heat of summer; now medical science controlled diseases once the scourge of the South, including cholera, hookworm, and malaria; now relative racial stability removed many of the reasons others had fled the region or hesitated to go there; now Sunbelt job prospects made it a growth area rather than the nation's chief economic problem. And now southerners worried not about their isolation from the American success story, but about their incorporation into it. Would these changes bring about, as John Egerton entitled his book, *The Americanization of Dixie* (1974), bringing in the worst of the North and losing the best of the South, or would it be more as his subtitle stated—*The Southernization of America*? As another historian pointed out, perhaps what had been viewed as American traits "are nothing more than watered-down southern characteristics."[11] Was this, as another book suggested, *An Epitaph for Dixie* (1958)? Had it finally symbolically rejoined the Union, with the death of the South as a result?

The region certainly had moved closer than ever before to national norms on matters of gender and race, its economy, and more. But that did not mean that the South would soon vanish as a distinct place. As a president of the Southern Historical Association observed, "Outsiders continued to say that southerners lived in the past. Not so, replied the poet Miller Williams: the past lived in southerners."[12] Its history cannot be cast aside so easily, nor can the cultural ways and the many memories of generations past be discarded overnight. Its writers continue to stress how people there hold fast to traditional aspects of the region—its heritage, devotion to family, large church membership, sense of place, violent tendencies, racial interactions, and cultural patterns, among others. Across all the years, the South will not go away. It lives on.

SOUTHERN STORIES

To tell the full, representative story of the New South in the pages of this book would take many more chapters and a much longer work. But people's lives help us see through the mists of history and aid us in understanding the many Souths, the different individuals, the varied stories. Often looking at the human condition at an elemental level reveals larger truths and greater insights. After all, history is often presented as a story of individuals, and this book thus seeks to tell some of those same stories, and by so doing, to explain the region. The chapters tell of people from the Upper South to the Deep South to the Southwest; they tell of men and women from varied backgrounds and different eras. Since the New South was not some monolithic place, some of these accounts portray those who sought to tear down the walls of orthodoxy—in race relations, for instance. Others portray the more traditional South. Many stories, many places, many themes remain untold in all this. But in their totality, the lives here recounted tell us of various worlds of the past, while speaking to us still about our own world and about our future.

NOTES

I wish to acknowledge the aid of John David Smith and Harold Tallant in connection with this introduction.

1. W. J. Cash, *The Mind of the South* (New York: Vintage, 1941), vii–viii; Carl N. Degler, "Thesis, Antithesis, Synthesis: The South, The North, and The Nation,"

Journal of Southern History (hereafter *JSH*) 53 (1987): 3; Charles P. Roland, *The Improbable Era: The South since World War II* (Lexington: University Press of Kentucky, 1975), 1.
   2. Quoted in Monroe Lee Billington, *The American South* (New York: Scribner's, 1971), 35.
   3. John Shelton Reed, *The Enduring South* (Chapel Hill: University of North Carolina Press, 1986), 12–13.
   4. Roland, *Improbable Era*, 2, 189, 191–92; James C. Cobb, "An Epitaph for the North: Reflections on the Politics of Regional and National Identity at the Millennium," *JSH* 66 (2000): 4, 6–7, 8, 16; Dewey W. Grantham, *The South in Modern America* (New York: HarperCollins, 1994), 112.
   5. Paul K. Conkin, "Hot, Humid, and Sad," *JSH* 64 (1998): 3.
   6. Cash, *Mind of the South*, viii.
   7. C. Vann Woodward, *The Burden of Southern History* (Baton Rouge: Louisiana State University Press, 1960); James McPherson, "Antebellum Southern Exceptionalism: A New Look at an Old Question," *Civil War History* 29 (1983): 242; Roland, *Improbable Era*, 192; Degler, "Thesis," 5.
   8. George C. Rable, *But There Was No Peace: The Role of Violence in the Politics of Reconstruction* (Athens: University of Georgia Press, 1984), 15; David W. Blight, *Race and Reunion: The Civil War in American Memory* (Cambridge, MA: Harvard University Press, 2001), 4, 9, 139; Kirk Savage, *Standing Soldiers, Kneeling Slaves: Race, War, and Monument in Nineteenth-Century America* (Princeton, NJ: Princeton University Press, 1997), 18, 129.
   9. Grantham, *South in Modern America*, xv; Numan V. Bartley, *The New South, 1945–1980* (Baton Rouge: Louisiana State University Press, 1995), xi.
   10. Morton Sosna, "More Important Than the Civil War? The Impact of World War II on the South," in *Perspectives on the American South: An Annual Review of Society, Politics and Culture*, ed. James C. Cobb and Charles R. Wilson (New York: Gordon & Breach, 1987), 4:145.
   11. Quoted in Degler, "Thesis," 5.
   12. Roland, *Improbable Era*, 193. See also Numan V. Bartley, "Social Change and Sectional Identity," *JSH* 61 (1995): 3–4, 6, 10, 13; and Grantham, *South in Modern America*, 153.

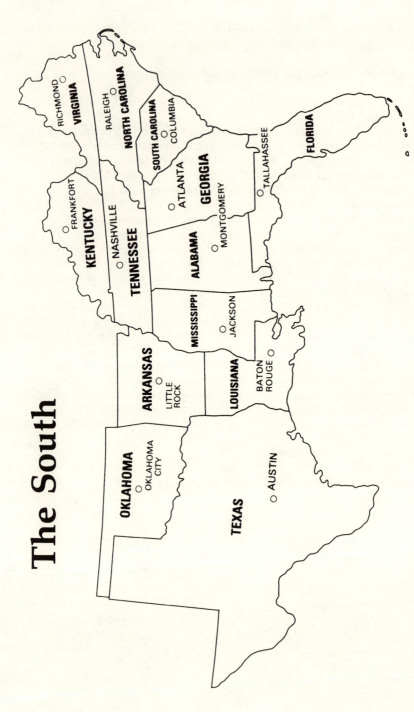

From Dewey W. Grantham, *The Life and Death of the Solid South* (Lexington: The University Press of Kentucky, 1992), 30, *Courtesy of the University Press of Kentucky*

1

The Lost Cause Legend about Winnie Davis, "the Daughter of the Confederacy"

Cita Cook

The defeat of the Confederacy brought many results—thousands of deaths, the loss of leaders, economic disruption, the end of slavery, occupation by Federal armies in Reconstruction, and more. But perhaps one of the most significant effects of defeat was on the mind of the white South. Psychological wounds remained long after physical ones healed or were forgotten. Historians have noted that many white people of the region attempted to deal with those wounds by creating a southern civil religion, one tied with the idea of a glorious "Lost Cause." They honored the dead soldiers, rewarded the living ones, and worshiped at the shrine of heroes such as Robert E. Lee, Stonewall Jackson, and Jefferson Davis. Myth mixed with reality until the two could not easily be separated.

Yet one group seemed little changed by the war. Although black males achieved at least some equality before the law, southern women did not. For decades after the conflict's end, married women in various states could not own property, make wills without their husbands' consent, keep any wages they earned, or sign contracts. For many, their lives of daily toil and common want differed little from centuries before. At almost the same time, however, faint stirrings of what would become a movement toward equal rights started to emerge. Still, few took up that cause at first. Instead, more became creators and supporters of the Lost Cause myth and joined groups such as the United Daughters of the Confederacy (UDC).

Cita Cook looks at the daughter of a Confederate icon and examines how her own myth emerged, along with the ironies and contradictions in it. She also shows the depth of feelings toward the North in the late-nineteenth-century South, and how these feelings had an impact on a young woman's life and legend.

Cita Cook is associate professor in the history department of the University of West Georgia in Carrollton. In addition to writing a book chapter, "The Challenges of Daughterhood for Winnie Davis," in Mississippi Women *(2003), she is completing a manuscript entitled "Growing Up White, Genteel, and Female in a Changing South: Natchez Young Ladies, 1830–1910."*

In the spring of 1886, Jefferson Davis, the former president of the Confederate States of America, traveled through Alabama and Georgia for a series of events honoring the Civil War veterans who had fought under his leadership. Since the end of Reconstruction a decade earlier, commemorators of the Confederacy had begun to move from mourning the dead in cemeteries to celebrating the living supporters of their "Lost Cause" in more public places. An appearance by Davis, one of the best-known Confederate leaders still alive, drew white admirers of all ages and classes. By 1886 he was too aged and feeble to travel alone so he asked his twenty-one-year-old daughter, Winnie, to accompany him. When he was too ill to appear at some of the whistle-stops their train made, she came out in his place and waved to the crowd. At West Point, Georgia, General John B. Gordon, the Democratic candidate for the governorship of Georgia, introduced her as "*the* Daughter of the Confederacy," alluding to her birth in the Confederate White House in the last year of the Civil War. The cheers this title evoked inspired the politician and the press to repeat it at every opportunity. For the remaining twelve years of her life, Winnie Davis, in the persona of the Daughter of the Confederacy, was one of the most popular honorees at meetings of believers in the Lost Cause.

The sudden celebrity status of this young woman arose at a critical time in southern history. While some families were enjoying the fruits of new economic developments, more were losing their land to the falling price of cotton and the rising cost of ginning and transporting it. Both white and black farmers were channeling their frustrations into activist farmers alliances, creating a transracial populist movement with space for both male and female leaders. White and black workers in mills, mines, ports, and sugar fields were joining the Knights of Labor. Young men and women were socializing on streetcars and trains without adult supervision. A few white women had become intrigued enough by political issues to seek the right to vote. Together, these developments seemed to threaten the newly redeemed political and social authority of Democratic party leaders, leading them to seek ways to recreate unity among all white southerners. Focusing on their fears of the economic and political potential of black southerners, they first legalized racial segregation. Politicians and newspapers then created a panic about an imaginary epidemic of southern black men raping young white women, which led to an

Varina "Winnie" Davis. *Courtesy of the Virginia Historical Society, Richmond, Virginia*

actual epidemic of lynchings of black men and antiblack race riots. These terrorist actions warned both black people and white women not to stray from their traditional social roles as deferential dependents of white men.

Within this historical context the Lost Cause movement proclaimed the honorable nobility of the antebellum slave society and all who had tried to protect the Confederate nation. Believers in this civic religion granted Winnie Davis public acclaim not because of what she had done but because of who she was—or who many white southerners wanted to believe she was—simply because her father had been the only president of the Confederate States of America. Her admirers developed a stubborn faith in an invented history of the life and character of the Daughter of the Confederacy that often departed markedly from her actual experiences. All they asked was that she appear regularly (and silently) as a living monument upon whom they could project their most cherished dreams and values.

As the saintly model of the most awe-inspiring qualities of elite white southern womanhood, Davis became a personification of Confederate patriotism similar to the feminized symbol of Liberty. At the same time, many men thought of her as a central figure in an Arthurian legend in which she made every Confederate veteran her champion. Some seemed to think of her more as the Virgin in a Confederate passion play.[1] White southern men could regain a sense of brotherhood when each of them envisioned her as his loving daughter. Men's adulation of the Daughter of the Confederacy then inspired their wives and daughters to emulate her rather than New Women who relished their ability to be independent of the protective arms of white men. As white southerners united to create a mythology about their symbolic daughter, they found it easier to set aside divisions between them based in assumptions about class, age, and gender. Feeling a closeness that most had not experienced since the Civil War, they likewise found it easier to strengthen and heighten the barriers they were erecting between themselves and those they demeaned as racial inferiors.

Varina Anne Davis, usually known as "Winnie," was born in the Confederate White House in Richmond, Virginia, on June 27, 1864, less than a year before the defeat of the Confederacy. According to her admirers she had been, from her first arrival on earth, an angel sent "to brighten the dark path which her father's people were destined to tread."[2] During the two-year imprisonment of Jefferson Davis after the war, Winnie and her mother, Varina Howell Davis, visited him in his cell. One eulogy envisioned a heavenly tableau in which "her little hands lifted up the weary head of our noble chief, who had beaten against his prison walls like a caged eagle, and her tender touch smoothed away the prints of the cruel chains which had shamefully fettered his proud limbs."[3]

Winnie's childish ways probably did bring joy to her captive father, but her mother's appeals to authorities and new northern supporters such as Horace Greeley did much more to alleviate the conditions he faced, a fact the veterans did not acclaim so loudly.[4] They were apparently more attracted to the power of magical children than to the influence of determined adult females.

Once Jefferson Davis was free, the troubles of the Davis family were not over, both because of the political tensions of Reconstruction and because he never managed to become a successful businessman. Winnie lived with her parents and siblings in Canada, England, Baltimore, and Memphis until, at the age of twelve, she left for a Protestant girls' school in Karlsruhe, Germany. During her five years there, she became accomplished in German, French, art, music, and the proper ways to honor European royalty. Later biographical sketches praised her linguistic and artistic abilities without discussing how her experiences abroad and her slight German accent distinguished her from most southern young women. In 1892, Davis herself published an article in the *Ladies Home Journal* in which she indicated that she had returned to America and the South feeling somewhat alienated from the culture that awaited her.[5]

Although Davis had never been free from public recognition of her blood relationship to the head of the Confederacy, she did not receive much special attention until General Gordon anointed her "the Daughter of the Confederacy" in 1886. From then on, whenever honored at Lost Cause events, she projected the perfect blend of feminine modesty, genteel graciousness, and regal distance. When the Lee Camp of Confederate Veterans in Richmond made her an honorary member, she indicated her opposition to women speaking in public by asking Dr. J. William Jones to read for her a statement assuring the veterans that their fight had been an honorable one for a just cause.[6]

Whatever her inner thoughts, Davis never directly challenged the basic tenets of her admirers. She reacted to a stranger's comment about how young she had been during "the rebellion" by saying, "I know of no rebellion, but I know all about the war between sovereign states."[7] With her close friends, however, she revealed a sharp wit and sometimes expressed more independent political opinions. Her mother complained in late 1886 that whenever she tried to urge her daughter "to rearrange some half worn dress," Winnie would change the subject to "the woes of the Irish, the labor question, or some system of philosophy which she has been studying with intense interest."[8]

Henry Grady of the *Atlanta Constitution* and other newspaper editors supporting New South boosterism were more than ready to establish links with the Daughter of the Confederacy as a popular symbol of a romanticized southern past. Grady assured her father in late 1886 that her "manner was so perfect, so modest, and unaffected, and yet so earnest and appreciative, that we all fell in love with her."[9] Even some papers in New York City treated her as southern royalty, in part because the wife of Joseph Pulitzer, publisher of the *New York World*, claimed to be a cousin of Jefferson Davis and served as a surrogate big sister for Winnie whenever she was in the Northeast. In addition, the launching in 1893 of the *Confederate Veteran* as a journal for Lost Cause organizations created a perfect vehicle for proclaiming the gospel of the noble femininity of the Daughter of the Confederacy.

The more journalists and speakers praised the charm and modesty of the Daughter of the Confederacy, the more her fame spread to all ages. In 1893, for example, a four-year-old girl exclaimed at the first sight of her baby sister, "Oh, Mama, can we name her Winnie Davis?"[10] Over the years many parents did just that and wrote Davis about her new namesakes. When her admirers, like any fans, wanted to possess a perpetual reminder of her awe-inspiring qualities, numerous people readily obliged them. Six months after her public debut, Henry Grady asked her father for permission to distribute a picture of her to the hundreds of *Atlanta Constitution* subscribers who had been requesting one.[11] Two years later, Jefferson Davis discovered that a patent medicine company had handed out 100,000 free pictures of his daughter. When Davis protested, the manager of the company asked if he could distribute the remaining 75,000 as long as he promised not to print any more.[12]

The purity and loyalty of Winnie Davis as a symbolic daughter became so important to some that they claimed the paternalistic authority to determine whom she could and could not marry. A letter to Jefferson Davis from a semiliterate veteran in 1887 implied that a marriage of the Blue and Gray would not be acceptable for such a significant figure of southern royalty. He fantasized the coming of a southern savior through the birth of a child to Winnie Davis and a man with a heritage as honorable as hers.

> I have often prayed that your only child living [a statement that would have frustrated Margaret Davis Hayes, the oldest child of Jefferson Davis and the only one to marry and give him grandchildren] might marry a near descendant of R. E. Lee or Stonewall Jackson, A. Sidney Johnston, or John C. Breckenridge that something pure might be handed to generations to come after us for there preservation and protection. it would be a thousand times more Precious and valuable to them than all the Host of Lincons Grants Clevelands Vanderbuilts or Jay Golds or of any King or Zar.[13]

In a region where beliefs about "blood" determined who could vote or walk freely on the sidewalks, it was not much of an extension to believe that only the untainted blood of Confederate heroes could bring forth a new generation of knightly leaders for the white South. Unknown to the veteran who wrote that letter, however, Winnie Davis was already in love with Alfred Wilkinson, a patent lawyer from Syracuse, New York. They had met at a party in Syracuse when she was visiting friends of her parents. She kept the relationship a secret for almost two years not only because Wilkinson was a northerner but also because he was the grandson of Samuel May, one of the antebellum leaders of the abolitionist movement.

In September 1888, Alfred Wilkinson went to Mississippi to ask for permission to marry Winnie. Her mother first told him they could never allow a "union with a yankee." Winnie declared that although she would honor her parents' wishes, she would never love anyone else. Varina eventually decided that since Fred was a "refined well born yankee, full of energy, spirit, and love" for Winnie, they should not sacrifice their daughter to the memory of the Confederacy. But when she suggested this to her husband, he answered, "Death would be preferable. I will never consent." In spite of this refusal, however, he warmed up to Fred and allowed Winnie to hope that they might marry someday.[14] After agreeing to keep the engagement secret, Winnie returned to Syracuse for another visit.

Just enough news of the betrothal leaked out to inspire a few negative responses. Winnie's chronic physical and emotional ailments increased so markedly under the strain of her divided loyalties that the Pulitzers took her to Europe in 1889 to try to calm her nerves. In December 1889, two months after her departure, Jefferson Davis died without having notified Winnie that he was ill. When she heard of his death, she suffered a total nervous collapse. Varina asked Fred to go to Europe to try to restore her daughter's spirits. At first she refused to consider restoring their relationship, but in the end she agreed to marry him.[15] Her mother began notifying friends of the engagement in March 1890, stressing that her husband had approved of the match because Alfred Wilkinson, only a little boy during the Civil War, had always been a states' rights Democrat.[16] Formal announcements followed in April in newspapers across the country.[17]

Some Confederate veterans immediately began to register their protest. One letter from a man claiming to have been a colonel under Robert E. Lee warned Wilkinson:

> The very sleeping dead Southern soldiers would rise from their graves, and hustle you back to Yankeedom ere they would see the daughter of Jefferson Davis ruined, and shame-covered forever, by marrying one whose desire in marrying her is to get a Southern woman—preferring such an one with warm feelings to the Salamander-like girl of Yankeedom. No, Sir, a thousand balls would be shot into your Negro-loving heart ere we would permit such an humiliating outrage consummated in our own Southland—and even should Miss Winnie whom we so deeply love as infinitely purer than any Yankee woman on

earth, consent to go North, then we will bind ourselves together to lay you in the dust.[18]

Alfred Wilkinson's true personality and ideals were no more relevant to how some people saw him than were those of Winnie Davis to how they saw her. To the extent that the veterans considered Davis special because she carried the blood of her father, they would not be able to forgive Wilkinson for being the descendant of a "black Republican." They concluded that he, like the "black beast rapist" figure of the imaginations of lynchers, wanted to possess and "outrage" the model of white southern femininity. A symbol could only marry another symbol and, in this case, many felt she had chosen the wrong one. Some might not have been much more welcoming to a southern fiancé, preferring to think of Davis as a sacrificial Confederate nun, a public version of the daughter who rejects marriage so that she might stay home and take care of an aging father.

Such letters must have been disturbing to the couple, but an article announcing their wedding date came out two months after the threatening letter and they also heard from supporters of the marriage.[19] The engagement ended after Varina Davis, for various reasons, began to suspect that Wilkinson had not been totally truthful with the Davises, especially concerning his financial condition. Lost Cause emotions had certainly put a strain on the relationship, but there is no reason to believe that Winnie Davis and Alfred Wilkinson would not have married if they had had enough money and mutual trust. Whether the veterans would have forgiven them is less certain.

Neither Winnie nor Fred ever married, but she led an active social life after she and her mother moved to New York City. Both women received retainers from the *New York World* for their occasional articles. Winnie also published two novels: *The Veiled Doctor* (1895), about the failed marriage of a doctor and a self-centered beauty, and, posthumously, *A Romance of Summer Seas* (1898), about the tensions caused by gossips on a cruise to Asia. Her primary hope was to earn enough money from her writing to buy a house at Bar Harbor, Maine.[20] Most of her socializing was in the Northeast, but she sometimes answered the call of the veterans and went south to appear at a Lost Cause event.

At the Confederate reunion in Houston in 1895, for example, Davis was the main focus of almost every event, many of which were held in the new Winnie Davis Auditorium.[21] So many thousands tried to attend one reception for her that she came out on a balcony and waved to them in classic regal form. The previously impatient crowd cheered and then showed their satisfaction and respect by dispersing quickly and quietly.[22] Those lucky enough to make it into the reception wanted nothing more than to shake the hand of the daughter of their old commander in chief. Her mother described her returning home with "her hands sore and swollen with greetings to 'all sorts and conditions of men.'" She then added that in spite of the physical tedium, her daughter had been very sensitive to the veterans' "kind and unselfish motives."[23]

The reference to "all sorts and conditions of men" is one of the few reminders that although the Lost Cause did encourage a form of white herrenvolk democracy, it did not erase the expectation that people of the "lower orders" would show the proper deference to their so-called "betters." While Winnie Davis attended teas and balls with genteel officers and their bourgeois allies, "all sorts" of men wandered about the temporary tent cities erected for the reunions. The poorer veterans were thrilled to serve, from time to time, as a Greek chorus of admiring masses for their Confederate Daughter, but they also had a class culture with its own version of conviviality. The opportunity of some to gain access to alcohol and possibly gambling and women never appeared in the pages of the *Confederate Veteran*. Several memoirs published in the mid-twentieth century, however, indicate that at least some girls from more established families did not like being kissed by old men who reeked of whiskey and tobacco.[24] In the carnival atmosphere of Confederate reunions, men who could never have approached Winnie Davis as a social equal could ask officers to kiss her for them or openly call out their love for her as the Daughter of the Confederacy, protected by both the father–daughter incest taboo and the myth of Lost Cause egalitarianism.

While men were the official directors of these commemorative festivals, women from the middle and upper classes feminized the events in various ways. Confederate reunions gave white women of all ages various opportunities to appear as ladies-in-waiting to their Confederate princess or to stand in for her. When on display in their finest clothes, they counterbalanced the more masculine military culture. There were two major categories of white females at these functions: teenage "sponsors" of local units of the United Confederate Veterans (UCV) and adult "ladies" serving as hostesses for elite teas and receptions. The closer their association with Winnie Davis, the greater the recognition they received. A number of society matrons at one reception for Davis became so determined to be next to her that she had to beg them to "preserve order and decorum."[25]

The older "ladies" were so entranced by Winnie Davis, in part, because she was willing to share her celebrity status by being a guest of honor at the private parties for which they were hostesses. The souvenir album for the Houston reunion praised Davis not only for her grace when allowing ragged veterans to greet her with a rebel yell but also for her "remarkable talent for entertaining" displayed at a buffet luncheon.[26] When the wives and daughters of leading businessmen and Confederate officers determined who was and was not invited to such events, they were helping redraw the boundaries of the New South social hierarchy. While cementing new alliances between descendants of the old planter elite and the nouveau riche bourgeoisie, they reminded the excluded people that their society recognized a class hierarchy to supplement that based on assumptions about race. "Common" people were not allowed to eat finger sandwiches while standing near the Daughter of the Confederacy.

In spite of the willingness of southern ladies to appear in public as ornamental symbols of passive elite white femininity, behind the scenes some females took on more active roles. After the Civil War, women had been the primary organizers of the first memorial associations and celebrations to honor the Confederate dead. In 1890, four years after Winnie Davis had first become "the Daughter of the Confederacy," the founder of a Missouri women's association to build and furnish a home for disabled Confederate veterans named her organization "Daughters of the Confederacy" as "a compliment to the Daughter of the Confederacy par excellence—Miss Winnie Davis."[27] Over the next few years, similar organizations in other southern states sought permission from the Missouri group to use the same name. In 1894 they came together in a national organization, eventually calling themselves the United Daughters of the Confederacy (UDC). Their enthusiasm when greeting "the Daughter of the Confederacy par excellence" was second only to that of the veterans.

In the summer of 1898, just after celebrating her thirty-fourth birthday, Winnie Davis traveled to Europe and Egypt with the Pulitzers, returning in time to participate in a Confederate reunion in Atlanta. While riding in a carriage in a summer storm, she began to feel ill. She returned to her mother in Narragansett Pier, Rhode Island, where, on September 18, 1898, she died at the age of thirty-four from malarial gastritis. Changing contingents of first Union and then Confederate veterans stood guard by her body on the train trip to Richmond, Virginia, where her father's body lay. At several points along the way, more flowers were put in the combination Pullman and parlor car made available by the New York, New Haven, and Hartford Railroad. After a crowded service in St. Paul's Episcopal Church in Richmond, the body traveled to that city's Hollywood Cemetery in a hearse drawn by four white horses, each attended by a black groomsman. The procession of mourners that followed them was a mile long, even with the carriages moving two abreast, and thousands of people lined the streets. As the sun set on September 23, 1898, the Daughter of the Confederacy was buried next to her father with full military honors.[28] This may have been the largest public funeral for any American female up to that time.

In the days and weeks following the death of Winnie Davis, mourners across the nation expressed their sorrow through various actions. Chapters of the UCV and the UDC organized memorial services and wore mourning badges for a month. The national and state flags flew at half-mast over the Mississippi capitol and at many other locations. Most of the permanent memorials to Winnie Davis were the result of the work of the UDC, including a tablet in St. Paul's Church in Richmond and a seven-foot marble statue entitled *The Angel of Grief* unveiled over her grave on November 10, 1899.[29] The Royal Art Gallery in Bucharest then gained permission to put on exhibit a plaster-of-paris copy of the statue.[30] Stained-glass windows honoring Davis were installed in the churches she had attended in Biloxi, Mississippi, and Narragansett Pier, Rhode Island. A Kentucky seed company proudly offered for sale in 1900 the Winnie Davis Rose, an apricot pink "cross between the Empress Augusta Victoria and Mme. Caroline Testont."[31] One Winnie Davis Memorial Hall was erected at a teacher training (normal) school for "young women of Confederate descent" in Athens, Georgia.[32] Another, at Limestone College in Gaffney, South Carolina, served as a Civil War museum.[33]

Some veterans groups commissioned portraits of Davis as permanent sources of inspiration. One was unveiled in a Mississippi courthouse before being sent "on a tour of the South."[34] The Nathan Bedford Forrest Camp of the UCV in Chattanooga expected the large painting of her in their hall to "incite her father's veterans to better deeds and purer lives." A camp in Monticello, Virginia, resolved at what they labeled their "Bivouac of Sorrow" that "in the death of our Winnie, a chair in the Bivouac and the banquet hall is vacant to remain so forever."[35]

The bereaved mother of the Daughter of the Confederacy received hundreds of telegrams, letters, and resolutions expressing admiration for her daughter, from a combination of private individuals and formal organizations.[36] The vocabulary of sentimental hyperbole was similar to that found in ordinary eulogies throughout the nineteenth century, but these documents used the romanticized images to establish more than ever that "their" Confederate Daughter was truly unique. As one New Orleans woman claimed, "no parallel can be found in history for the position this charming young woman held in the hearts of a people."[37] For many, Winnie Davis represented a quasi-religious figure whom they "worshiped" and "idolized."[38] Some offered Varina Davis the standard evangelical promise that her daughter was with God, but others depicted her, in the purported words of Stonewall Jackson, as having crossed "over the river" to "rest under the shade of the trees" in a Confederate Valhalla where she could continue to thrill her father and his troops as a part of "the peaceful unending reunion of the Confederate hosts beyond the tomb."[39]

The fact that many of the descriptions of the life and virtues of Winnie Davis were in direct conflict with her actual experiences probably seems more paradoxical to us than it would have to the authors. Most were remembering an iconic Daughter of the Confederacy who existed only in their minds rather than a private Winnie Davis who had preferred life in the Northeast to a Mississippi society she had considered "dull." Instead of trying to paint a realistic picture of a complex individual woman, mourners praised Davis as a representation of all that they wished to emulate. Although Winnie, as a little girl, had been too young to understand what her father and Confederate citizens were experiencing at the end of the war, many spoke of her as "the golden," "tenderest," "loving link with the heroic past of the South."[40] It was almost as if she had been a spiritual medium capable of connecting them to her father and the other dead heroes.

All mourners depicted the loss as in some way "creating a void in southern womanhood."[41] Winnie Davis was never, for them, a genderless "southerner." They remembered her as "the type of a gentle womanhood which inspired men to deeds of valor and poets to sweetest minstrelsy."[42] In the words of the members of one group of Confederate veterans, "She was the embodiment of all that is great and noble in Southern womanhood and her life made her an exemplar for the women of all nations, and the uncrowned queen in the hearts of her own people."[43] A Nashville minister used her as a countermodel for young ladies tempted by the opportunities claimed by the New Woman. "It is well . . . that the chief figure on our escutcheon should be a woman—not clad in armor nor robed in learning's garb, but clothed upon with the tender grace of pure womanliness." He reminded the mourners that the chivalry of Confederate men committed them to protecting women "not only against violence and oppression, but also from the sharp competitions of business and the eager rivalries of politics."[44]

One of the more intriguing images of Winnie Davis involved assertions by some women of her great courage and heroism, possibly a rebuff to the growing trend to portray men in battle as the only true model of brave sacrifice.[45] Plaques on the statue by her grave speak of the "blameless and heroic career" of this "brave and steadfast" woman.[46] "Perfected through suffering," she had supposedly put forth a "brave endeavor in the struggle of life."[47] Some women, such as the South Carolinians who described her as "the virgin martyr of the South," may have been thinking of her alleged willingness to sacrifice the love of one man, her fiancé, so as to be true to the love of many men, the Confederate veterans.[48] Others depicted her as a heroine for following the expectations of a proper female even while "she met duties never before thrown upon young womanhood."[49] By pledging to teach "the youth of this and future generations . . . the story of her heroic life as fulfilling the Southern ideal of true womanhood," they were announcing that for a woman to be a proper female and daughter, she sometimes had to resort to heroic measures.[50]

Not long after the death of the Daughter of the Confederacy, a few people suggested passing her title on to some other woman. But most were convinced that she had filled a "place in the hearts of the [southern] people, which no other [could] claim."[51] Although Winnie Davis limited her public performances to smiling and handshaking, she nevertheless paved the way for female speakers who praised the traditional southern gender values while contradicting them with their oratorical ease and fervor.[52] In 1902, in a speech to the UCV of Missouri that was so popular that it was reprinted two years in a row in the *Confederate Veteran*, Edmonda Nickerson announced that "all the women of the South" had hailed the Daughter of the Confederacy as "their queen," gathering "in knightly array around their enthroned idol" and attesting "by the wildest acclaim that the love they bore the father had descended in full measure to his child." To this female knight, the "angelic figure" over Winnie's grave portrayed "the beauty of her spotless life and her virgin hope of a glorious immortality."[53]

Just as the legends created about Winnie Davis diverged in many ways from her actual life, the unambiguous values her admirers projected onto the Daughter of the Confederacy did not necessarily indicate how they lived their own lives. Individuals who did not always behave as perfect southern ladies and gentlemen could feel protected from public condemnation or discomfiting self-awareness when they joined others in praising ideals that they could not follow themselves. Edmonda Nickerson was less apt to receive criticism for speaking in public and portraying herself as a knight if she did so in order to honor an icon of southern femininity whose "spotless" life would never have included public speaking. In a similar fashion other women and men at Lost Cause ceremonies set aside the contradictions of their lives, including the political and social divisions among those cheering next to each other.

When the Confederate veterans made Winnie Davis the center of attention, they turned both the public spotlight and their own eyes away from the economic sacrifices their families were facing and away from the black bodies swinging from too many trees. A particularly revealing resolution about Davis proclaimed that "like the creeping ivy from the disjointed stones of our ruined temple, she climbed about us and clung to the veteran until the end of her sinless life."[54] As long as they could imagine that their virginal Confederate Daughter was clinging to them instead of the reverse, they could ignore some of the wounds history had bestowed on their masculine pride. Her existence and her manner helped them and the women who loved them believe that their lives and the sacrifices they had made for the Confederacy had meaning. If the perfect southern lady was their proverbial daughter, they could think of themselves as chivalrous fathers who might dream about serving her memory again some day, possibly by cheering on younger men to protect their granddaughters from more modern enemies.

NOTES

1. I would like to thank Ken Noe for suggesting this point.
2. Robert E. Lee Camp, United Confederate Veterans, Eleanor S. Brockenbrough Library, Museum of the Confederacy, Richmond, Virginia (henceforth referred to as Museum of the Confederacy).
3. Judge H. W. Lightfoot, quoted in "Memorial Services," unnamed newspaper, n.d., Museum of the Confederacy.
4. For information on the efforts of Varina Davis to secure her husband's release, see Hudson Strode, ed., *Jefferson Davis: Private Letters, 1823–1889* (New York: Harcourt, Brace & World, 1966), 251–54, 266–68; and Varina Davis, *Jefferson Davis, Ex-President of the Confederate States of America: A Memoir*, 2 vols. (1890; Freeport, NY: Books for Libraries Press, 1971), 2:767–95.
5. Varina Anne Davis, "The American Girl Who Studies Abroad," *Ladies Home Journal* 99 (1892): 6.
6. Gaines M. Foster, *Ghosts of the Confederacy: Defeat, the Lost Cause, and the Emergence of the New South, 1865 to 1913* (New York: Oxford University Press, 1987), 97.
7. "The Daughter of the Confederacy," *Macon Telegraph*, November 188[6], scrapbook of an anonymous Georgia woman, 1885–1896, Duke University, Durham, North Carolina.
8. Varina Davis to Connie [Constance Cary Harrison], December 20, 1886, Harrison Family Papers, Alderman Library, University of Virginia, Charlottesville.
9. Henry W. Grady to Jefferson Davis, November 15, 1886, Museum of the Confederacy.
10. Otis S. Tarver to the *Confederate Veteran* 1 (1893): 74.
11. Henry W. Grady to Jefferson Davis, November 15, 1886, Museum of the Confederacy.
12. F. M. Sterrett, secretary and manager, the Dr. Harter Medicine Co., to Jefferson Davis, July 15, 1888, Jefferson Davis Papers, Rice University, Houston, Texas.
13. Theodore Nunn to Jefferson Davis, April 1, 1887, Museum of the Confederacy.
14. Varina Davis to Major Morgan, September 1888, Jefferson Davis Papers, Library of Congress, Washington, DC.
15. Varina Davis to Margaret Davis Hayes, November 8, 1889, Jefferson Davis Papers, University of Alabama, Tuscaloosa; Fred Wilkinson to Varina Davis, February 25 and March 1, 1890; Fred Wilkinson to Major Morgan, March 1, 1890; and Varina Davis to Major Morgan, March 9, 1890, Jefferson Davis Papers, Library of Congress.
16. Varina Davis to Major Morgan, 1890, Jefferson Davis Papers, Library of Congress; Varina Davis to Jubal Early, April 20 and April 27, 1890, Jubal A. Early Papers, Virginia Historical Society, Richmond.
17. *New York Times*, April 27, August 10, 1890; *Fort Worth Daily Gazette*, April 24, 1890; *Richmond Times*, May 8, 1890, in an anonymous scrapbook, Museum of the Confederacy.

18. Unknown writer to Alfred Wilkinson, June 10, 1890, from Americus, Georgia; reprinted in Mary Craig Sinclair, *Southern Belle: The Personal Story of a Crusader's Wife* (Phoenix, AZ: Sinclair, 1957). As far as can be determined, all or most of these letters were eventually destroyed, but Varina Davis did pass some to a family friend in Mississippi whose daughter, the wife of the socialist author Upton Sinclair, later published this particular one in her autobiography.

19. See, for example, Mrs. M. Hoover to Winnie Davis, May 20, 1890, Museum of the Confederacy.

20. Winnie Davis to Marquis de Ruvigny, March 21, 1893, Museum of the Confederacy.

21. William Bledsoe Philpott, ed., *The Sponsor Souvenir Album and History of the United Confederate Veterans' Reunion, 1895* (Houston: Sponsor Souvenir Company, 1895), passim.

22. Philpott, *Sponsor Souvenir Album*, 54.

23. V[arina Howell] Jefferson Davis to Constance Cary Harrison, May 28, 1895, Burton Harrison Collection, Library of Congress.

24. Virginia Foster, "The Emancipation of Southern, Pure, White Womanhood," *New South*, Winter 1971, 51; Marietta Minnegerode Andrews, *Memoirs of a Poor Relation* (New York: E. P. Dutton, 1927), 190–91, 197; Evelyn Scott, *Background in Tennessee* (Knoxville: University of Tennessee Press, 1980), 135–36.

25. Philpott, *Sponsor Souvenir Album*, 25.

26. Philpott, *Sponsor Souvenir Album*, 26.

27. Poppenheim, *The History of the United Daughters of the Confederacy, 1894–1929* (n.p., 1923), 2–3.

28. *Richmond Dispatch*, September 24, 1898, transcribed in Tommie Phillips LaCavera, *Varina Anne "Winnie" Davis* (Athens, GA: Southern Trace, 1994), 34–48.

29. Poppenheim, *History of the United Daughters of the Confederacy*, 42–43, 45.

30. LaCavera, *Varina Anne "Winnie" Davis*, 73–75.

31. "Miss Winnie Davis," unidentified article in the Jefferson Davis Papers, Museum of the Confederacy.

32. LaCavera, *Varina Anne "Winnie" Davis*, 78.

33. *Southprint*, 1990, 7.

34. Program for "An Evening in Dixie," n.d.

35. Unidentified newspaper report of a meeting of a UCV camp on October 7, 1898, Museum of the Confederacy.

36. Many of the telegrams, letters, and resolutions concerning the death of Winnie Davis are available at the Museum of the Confederacy.

37. Mrs. J. Pinckney Smith, UDC, New Orleans, Louisiana, October 1898, Museum of the Confederacy.

38. See, for example, the resolutions from the United Sons of Confederate Veterans in Jacksonville, Florida, and from the UCV in Victoria, Texas, Museum of the Confederacy.

39. Resolution of James Longstreet Camp, UCV, Ennis, Texas, September 25, 1898; Resolution of R. E. Lee Camp, Monroe, Georgia, November 1, 1898, Museum of the Confederacy.

40. Lucy Jordan Blount, UDC, Waynesboro, Georgia, November 10, 1898; UDC, Chattanooga, postmarked September 24, 1898; Mrs. Joseph Hutcheson,

UDC, Houston, Texas, November 5, 1898; all at the Museum of the Confederacy.

41. Mollie E. Moore Davis Chapter, UDC, Resolutions, September 1898, Museum of the Confederacy.

42. I. M. Porter Ockenden to Varina Davis, Ladies Memorial Association, Montgomery, Alabama, September 23, 1898, Museum of the Confederacy.

43. Pat Cleburne Camp, no. 22, October 7, 1898, Museum of the Confederacy.

44. "Tributes to Miss Winnie Davis," *Confederate Veteran*, 1898, 467.

45. For information on this trend, see especially Alice Fahs, "The Feminized Civil War: Gender, Northern Popular Literature, and the Memory of the War, 1861–1900," *Journal of American History* 85 (1999): 1461–94.

46. LaCavera, *Varina Anne "Winnie" Davis*, 75.

47. UDC, Selma, Alabama [1898], Museum of the Confederacy; UDC, Birmingham, Alabama [1898], Museum of the Confederacy.

48. UDC, Columbia, South Carolina [1898], Museum of the Confederacy.

49. Mrs. Robert H. Pearson et al., UDC, Birmingham, Alabama, October 12, 1898, Museum of the Confederacy.

50. Hollywood Memorial Association, Resolutions, in *Confederate Veteran* (1898), 460.

51. UDC, Lake City, Florida, Resolutions, October 27, 1898, Museum of the Confederacy. See also Mrs. V. C. Tarrh, Daughters of the Confederacy, Florence, South Carolina, October 10, 1898, Museum of the Confederacy.

52. Jacquelyn Dowd Hall, "'You Must Remember This': Autobiography as a Social Critique," *Journal of American History* 85 (1998): 439–65.

53. Edmonda Augusta Nickerson, "Women as Patriots," *Confederate Veteran* (1903), 500.

54. Resolution, Camp Bill Slemons, UCV, Museum of the Confederacy.

SUGGESTED READINGS

For studies of Winnie Davis both as a member of her family and as the Daughter of the Confederacy, see Cita Cook, "The Challenges of Daughterhood for Winnie Davis," in *Mississippi Women: Portraits of Achievement* (Athens: University of Georgia Press, 2003), ed. Elizabeth A. Payne, Marjorie Spruill, and Martha H. Swain; as well as two articles by Suzanne T. Dolensky in *The Journal of Mississippi History*: "Varina Howell Davis, 1889 to 1906: the Years Alone" (May 1985) and "The Daughters of Jefferson Davis: A Study of Contrast" (November 1989). More on Davis's parents can be found in Joan Cashin's biography of Varina Howell Davis (forthcoming from Houghton Mifflin) and William C. Davis, *Jefferson Davis: The Man and His Hour, a Biography* (New York: HarperCollins, 1992).

Ghosts of the Confederacy: Defeat, the Lost Cause, and the Emergence of the New South, 1865–1913 (New York: Oxford University Press, 1987) by Gaines Foster is a particularly valuable overview of the history of Lost Cause concerns, activities, and organizations. Also useful are David Blight, "Quarrel Forgotten or a Revolution Remembered? Reunion and Race in the Memory of the Civil War, 1875–1913," in *Union and Emancipation: Essays on Politics and Race in the Civil War Era*, ed. David W. Blight and Brooks D. Simpson (Kent, OH: Kent State University Press, 1997), 151–79; William C. Davis, *The Cause Lost: Myths and Realities of the Confederacy* (Lawrence: University Press of Kansas, 1996); Rollin G. Osterweis, *The Myth of the Lost Cause, 1865–1900* (Hamden, CT: Archon, 1973); and Charles Reagan Wilson, *Baptized in Blood: The Religion of the Lost Cause, 1865–1920* (Athens: University of Georgia Press, 1980).

Donald Sutherland covers supporters of the Lost Cause living in New York City in *The Confederate Carpetbaggers* (Baton Rouge: Louisiana State University Press, 1988). Stuart Charles McConnell, *Glorious Contentment: The Grand Army of the Republic, 1865–1900* (Chapel Hill: University of North Carolina Press, 1992), and Nina Silber, *The Romance of Reunion: Northerners and the South, 1865–1900* (Chapel Hill: University of North Carolina Press, 1993), discuss related activities by U.S. military veterans and their supporters.

Works about women's role in creating and reacting to the Lost Cause culture include: "White Women and the Politics of Historical Memory in the New South, 1880–1920" by W. Fitzhugh Brundage in *Jumpin' Jim Crow: Southern Politics from Civil War to Civil Rights*, ed. Jane Dailey, Glenda Elizabeth Gilmore, and Bryant Simon (Princeton, NJ: Princeton University Press, 2000), 115–39; Antoinette G. van Zelm, "Virginia Women as Public Citizens: Emancipation Day Celebrations and Lost Cause Commemoration, 1863–1890," and Rebecca Montgomery, "Lost Cause Mythology in New South Reform: Gender, Class, Race, and the Politics of Patriotic Citizenship in Georgia, 1890–1925," both in *Negotiating Boundaries of Southern Womanhood: Dealing with the Powers That Be*, ed. Janet L. Coryell et al. (Columbia: University of Missouri Press, 2000), 71–88, 174–98; and Angie Parrott, "'Love Makes Memory Eternal': The United Daughters of the Confederacy in Richmond, Virginia, 1897–1920," in *The Edge of the South: Life in Nineteenth-Century Virginia*, ed. Edward L. Ayers and John C. Willis (Charlottesville: University Press of Virginia, 1991), 219–38.

For the historical context of the New South, see especially C. Vann Woodward, *Origins of the New South, 1877–1913* (Baton Rouge: Louisiana State University Press, 1951), and Edward L. Ayers, *The Promise of the New South: Life after Reconstruction* (New York: Oxford University Press, 1992). Two books that compare Lost Cause commemorative activities to similar activities and concerns at various times are *Where These Memories Grow: History, Memory, and Southern Identity*, ed. W. Fitzhugh Brundage (Chapel Hill: University of North Carolina Press, 2000), and Grace Elizabeth Hale, *Making Whiteness: The Culture of Segregation in the South, 1890–1940* (New York: Random House, 1998). Leon F. Litwack reveals the difficulties African American southerners were facing at the time of the Lost Cause in *Trouble in Mind: Black Southerners in the Age of Jim Crow* (New York: Vintage, 1998).

2

๖

Black Zack and Uncle Amon

Paul K. Conkin

After the end of the Civil War, former slaves began to fashion a new order, a new world built on the ruins of the old and on different foundations as well. But such attempts did not come easily. Violence, segregation, and peonage represented attempts to control change and create a society that other groups sought. The struggle between such forces continued for decades after the war ended. However, not all areas of the South had sizable black populations. The Appalachian mountain region had long been stereotyped as a place where few blacks lived, an image that had much to support it. Yet in some places in the highlands, particularly the coal camps of the twentieth century, fairly sizable African American populations existed. Like many stereotypes of Appalachia, the totally white Appalachia represents both truth and fiction.

This region has borne the burden of such stereotypes for many years. After the Civil War, when most of this story takes place, writers from outside the region suddenly "discovered" it once more. Though never as isolated as many of the accounts stressed, the area now came under endless scrutiny. Was it violent, as feuds suggested, or were its people mostly hospitable? Did they represent the best parts of an earlier time, hidden away in mountain coves, or did they show old ways that were best forgotten? Were they the hope of America's future or the remnant of an outdated society? Were these places of pristine beauty to be preserved, or immense mineral wealth to be mined? Was the real Appalachia rural or almost urban, as were the coal camps? In truth, just as there are many Souths, there are various Appalachias, although many of them seemed ignored and forgotten by those who tried to tell the stories.

Historian Paul Conkin tells a very personal narrative about one Appalachian community. He talks to the reader in a conversational tone as he tells what he discovered about two people who held special memories for him. While the nicknames suggested the racial mores of that time, the careers of Zachariah Bennett and Amon Hays show, once more, how difficult it is to stereotype a region and those who live there.

Paul K. Conkin has published widely on a variety of topics, including New Deal *(1967),* Big Daddy from the Pedernales: Lyndon Baines Johnson *(1987),* The Southern Agrarians *(1988),* Cane Ridge: America's Pentecost *(1991), and* When All the Gods Trembled: Darwinism, Scopes, and American Intellectuals *(1998). A former president of the Southern Historical Association, he currently is Distinguished Professor of History, Emeritus, at Vanderbilt University in Nashville, Tennessee.*

I have two stories to tell. They are as truthful as scanty sources and my own memories from childhood and youth allow. I have tried to minimize any historical interpretations. I have avoided analysis like the plague. The stories involve two black men—Zachariah Bennett and Amon Hays. For much of their lives they represented the only two black families in my home village or anywhere else in a radius of at least five miles. They were thus blacks in an all-white world, and their stories are fascinating.

A small farm community in northern Greene County in upper East Tennessee is the setting for the first story. It was located between the county seat, Greeneville, and Kingsport, in Sullivan County, both seventeen miles away and both with small black populations. But the closest town, at fourteen miles, was tiny Jonesborough, the state's oldest town and the county seat of Washington County, and also the home of a small black community. My village has three names. A walk-in post office in the late nineteenth century was called Cedar Lane, a name still on some maps. The one church, Cumberland Presbyterian, adopted the biblical name Bethesda at its 1834 founding. Later the county school was named Bethesda (the name I will use). But almost no one locally refers to the village as Bethesda but as Green Shed, or just the Shed. This name derives from the preaching stand at a well-developed antebellum camp meeting site. In the early twentieth century, the village had the church, a two-room school, a blacksmith shop, a water-powered grist mill and sawmill, and usually at least one all-purpose store.

Otherwise quite similar to other communities in a rather prosperous farming county, after 1900 Bethesda had one clear distinction. It had, as residents, the only black families still remaining anywhere in this northern part of Greene County. After 1910 it also had a visible landmark—Zack's Monument, as we all called it. It was on a hill behind the church, visible for over a mile from the highway that leads into the valley and by the church. In the 1930s it was surrounded by a hay field or an occasional tobacco patch. The road to my grandparents' home passed within thirty feet of this obelisk, which is over twenty feet high. I read the inscription and often asked questions about the well-to-do black man buried beneath it. Only much later, when the monument gained widespread attention and newspaper coverage, did we learn that it was the second-largest monument in Greene County, exceeded in size, not necessarily height, only by the tomb of President Andrew Johnson in Greeneville.

How did such a monument get to this unlikely site? Zachariah Bennett was born a slave about 1847 on a large farm, or the nearest approach to a plantation anywhere close to our home, about twelve miles north of Bethesda. This was in western Sullivan County, in the midst of the only large pocket of Confederate supporters in upper East Tennessee. This valley farm bordered what is now called Horse Creek, which probably gained its name from the farm. It was noted for the horses it bred. All the legends about Zachariah Bennett, or Black Zack as he was called locally, note that as a slave youth he became an expert horse trainer. I cannot confirm this. Note that he was only eighteen at emancipation. But his later life did involve horses, and he was obviously skilled in training the best riding stock.

I know nothing about his immediate postemancipation years. Possibly he remained on this farm and continued to work with horses. He first appeared in the Bethesda community records in the census of 1880. By then he was a hired hand on a local farm. As far as anyone knows, he never married. He had no children, at death no known relatives. From 1880 to 1892 he must have worked hard and saved his money. In that year he bought a farm, the second downstream from what later became our family farm. The recorded deed makes clear that he paid $1,000 cash for 100 acres, an average to above average farm in our area (my father later owned only 51 acres). One thousand dollars cash in 1892, albeit a year before the crash of 1893, was a lot of money, comparable to a small fortune today. The land he bought for $10 an acre now sells for $2,000; my first cousin owns it. At a multiple of only 100, Zack's $1,000 in 1892 would be worth $100,000 today. I doubt that any other landowner in our community had ever bought such a large farm without a mortgage or promissory note. I do not know how Zack, working as a hired hand, accumulated so much money. I suspect he bought, trained, possibly bred, and sold horses.

Little is known of Bennett's life in Bethesda. Did he join the Bethesda Church? (No records survive, but he would have been welcome as a member.) He clearly identified with the church and later became a benefactor of it. My father was ten when Bennett died and retained hazy memories of him. The image that remains is of an ambitious man driven by a desire to make money. He was a cagey horse trader, frugal and stingy, and was reputed to lend money to his white neighbors at the highest interest the market would bear. This moneylending image is borne out by the probate of his will, when his assets included three outstanding loans. Two of the notes bore the name of a next-door neighbor of our family and my distant cousin. The trustees collected not only the $455 of principal but also $178 in interest due. Around 1900, Bennett built a very nice farmhouse and apparently lived in it alone. He died in 1910, leaving behind an estate valued at $4,950, again a lot of money for the time. His unusual deathbed will is signed with an X, but I suspect he was literate. He obviously knew his numbers, since in effect he ran a local lending bank.

In his will, Bennett requested that his three named trustees, all prosperous local white farmers, distribute his assets as follows: First, they were to erect at his grave a nice monument, costing no less than $1,000. Then they were to place the remainder of his estate in a perpetual trust, with the principal never to be spent, but 25 percent of its annual earnings going to the Bethesda Church and 75 percent to be used by the trustees and their successors to maintain his monument and the grounds around it. He also specified that he be buried in the cemetery of the Bethesda Church and that all his property be sold at public auction. Clearly he was very concerned about his tomb, and at the end of the will made careful provisions for the succession of trustees in order "to have my grave cared for as long as time lasts."

The trustees did much of what Zack wanted. For reasons unclear, they did not set up a continuing trust. After costs of his tomb and other expenses, they had $3,318 left. Instead of giving the church one-fourth of the earnings of a trust, they simply gave it one-fourth of the remaining estate, or $830 after taxes, surely the largest gift the congregation had ever received up until that time. The average collection on Sunday was often less than a dollar. Children brought a penny, adults nickels or dimes. I am sure the indebted congregation preferred the instant cash to future interest payments and did not protest the failure to set up a trust. It may even have conspired to block the trust.

Within the next three years the trustees finished their work and turned over an unspent $1,786, in escheat, to the state, leaving no money to care for Zack's monument or the cemetery. This failure to follow Zack's will had to be approved, or possibly mandated, by the probate judge. A few years ago, I made these facts available to the church session, and some elders were shocked that the state took the money. They even talked, unrealistically, about legal action to recover their stolen cemetery fund, which, with interest of 6 percent compounded annually, would be now worth over $500,000.

During the three years the trustees managed the estate, apparently with full knowledge that the state would get any remainder, they sought every opportunity to spend money, including ample fees for themselves. Everyone who contributed any labor to the monument received full pay. In the final settlement the trustees also charged the estate $500 for their services. They worked hard and I suspect no impropriety, but they pushed the limits, getting as much as legal out of Zack's estate. Did his race influence the disposition of his estate? I have no way of knowing, but I doubt it. There is no mention of Bennett's race in the probate proceedings or on the deeds.

The trustees' great achievement was Zack's monument. He would have been pleased. They mounted it on land owned by the church but not really in the cemetery, which was then grown up in weeds and full of graves. Instead they placed it on the opposite side of the church, at the highest point on the church lot. The old cemetery, almost hidden down in the valley, was not a good place for Zack's monument. Burials had practically ceased at this old cemetery. We think some of the illegible tombs were those of former slaves. But it is possible that some local families did not want a black man buried among their relatives, and that they influenced the choice of the site. In retrospect the trustees made the best possible choice.

The trustees had to travel to Morristown, forty miles away toward Knoxville, to find anyone who could order a tombstone costing as much as $1,000 (a very good gravestone cost no more than $30 or $40). They paid $1,085 to the Morristown Marble Company and hauled the heavy monument on wagons to the site. They must have dug a deep foundation, on top of which they poured an 18- by 24-foot concrete platform. Into this concrete they embedded an encircling steel fence. The concrete work and the fence cost around $150. After ninety years the concrete platform is as solid as ever, with only one small, almost invisible crack. Despite its weight the tomb shows no signs of settling in any direction. And the fine granite obelisk shows no water damage and no moss, unlike the other older tombs in the cemetery. About thirteen local men did all the work. Only one of them was black—the Amon Hays of my next story. He collected over $12, probably as payment for about twelve days of labor. In total, hundreds of hours of work were involved. The total cost of the mounted monument was about $1,400, or just over half the sale price of Zack's 100-acre farm, house, and barn.

The farm auction revealed a great deal about Bennett. All his personal property, save the outstanding notes, sold for just under $1,600. Household and kitchen items sold at what would seem a giveaway price today, with few items from the house selling for even a dollar. (His silverware sold for twenty-five cents, his dinner plates for the same amount, chairs for ten cents, the best table for $1.55, a cast-iron outdoor kettle for $1.75, and only a shotgun for as much as $3.50.) Farm tools did not do much better, with a farm wagon leading at $8.50, a corn planter at $5.10, plows for around $2.00. In total, over 150 household and farm items sold for less than $150. Two of my paternal uncles and my grandfather bid on different items. Zack left a representative inventory of a well-stocked, turn-of-the-century farm.

What sold well in Zack's auction was the farm inventory and livestock. The corn, wheat, hay, and straw sold for $235, all more than for the household goods and farm implements combined. The livestock sold for $1,236, or over three-fourths of the value of the total sale, excluding the farm itself. Local farmers paid $381 for thirteen cows and steers, $61 for six hogs, and $23 for 199 chickens (a larger than average inventory for a local farm). But the big items were five horses. One, a male draft horse, sold for only $61, or the going price for draft horses. But one breeding mare, named Mary, sold for a then astonishing $230; a second, named Nina, for $160. They went to the two wealthiest farmers in the area. Two yearling mares sold for $177 and $130. These prices give a clue as to how Zack made his money. He had continued to breed the best of riding stock, perhaps what he learned to do well as a slave. He was getting as much at $300 a year from the sale of his colts, more than the total gross income of most local farmers. He improved on his income by the sale of steers, pork, and eggs, and by interest earned from the money lent to other farmers. By all measurements, the tomb inscription is correct—he was well-to-do, I suspect the most affluent black man in the county. He must have relished being able to lend money to less prudent white farmers and have gained enormous satisfaction from his dream of a great monument that would be ten times more expensive, and thus more imposing, than that of any white man in any rural cemetery that he had ever seen.

The subsequent story of Zack's monument is checkered. An indebted congregation sold the land containing Zack's monument in 1917, an act of betrayal to one who had been so generous to the church. The new owner respected the monument, but plowing and erosion lowered the surrounding ground level. The local farm economy almost came to an end after 1945. Bethesda became a bedroom community for people who worked in Kingsport. The church became more prosperous, repurchased the land surrounding Zack's monument in the fifties, and by 1980 had incorporated it into an expanding cemetery. As one elder said, they reintegrated Black Zack. The civil rights movement changed racial views. Some church members, including my mother, welcomed the Civil Rights Acts and admired Martin Luther King. Suddenly, local people recognized that Zack's monument was a village asset. Young ministers, some just out of seminary who came to presbytery when it met at Bethesda, were fascinated with the monument and tried to find information about old Zack. Newspapers ran articles. A man and wife, now deceased, former friends of mine, worked for weeks clearing the honeysuckle from the monument and sanding and repainting the rusted steel fence. As the cemetery committee plotted new grave sites, they left plenty of room around Zack's monument and built a paved street up the hill by it. Finally, as Zack tried to ensure by his will, his tomb is now well-cared for, although I cannot assure it will be so as long as time lasts.

I turn now to Amon Hays and a less dramatic story, but a story of a much more complex and less conventional man than a focused Zachariah Bennett. I have one advantage: Hays lived on until after World War II. I knew him reasonably well. His background is also clearer. His father, Jackson Hays, was born in 1837, at the end of the popular Jackson administration. He was a slave on the farm of a Captain George Hays, who may have gained his military title in Jackson's Florida campaign. The Scotch-Irish Hays family had been one of the first to settle in our part of Greene County, moving down from the Shenandoah Valley of Virginia in the 1790s. George Hays was probably the only slave owner in the village or, at the very least, the only one to own several slaves. Hays had a very large farm, possibly 400 acres. But it scarcely qualified as a plantation.

When George Hays died (circumstantial evidence suggests this was in 1877 or 1878), he apparently willed a part of his farm to Jackson Hays. This is what everyone locally believed when I was a boy, and I have no reason to doubt it. Jackson took the Hays name at emancipation and remained a worker on the George Hays farm. The gift of a farm, when land prices were very low, was a type of belated pay for his loyalty and work. One might suspect, in a case like this, that Captain George was the father of Jackson Hays. But the very dark complexion of Amon Hayes (I have no description of Jackson Hays), although not conclusive, makes this blood relationship less likely. In any case, the black and white Hays families remained intimate friends. They would join at one home or another for Sunday dinners. The relationship must have been paternalistic on one side, deferential on the other, but by the time I knew both families, it seemed to be a relationship of social equals.

Jackson Hays married a Peggy Swinney, and they had at least four children. Two of the four, a twin boy and girl, died young. Amon Hayes, born in 1868, was the oldest child and the only surviving male when Jackson Hays died in 1892, leaving only Amon and his younger sister, Esther, locally always pronounced Easter. For the rest of his long life, Amon operated his father's farm. Esther lived with him until her death, five years before Amon. Amon delayed marriage until he must have been over forty. Before his marriage, according to well-substantiated local gossip, he briefly kept company with a white widow in the community, a liaison that sullied her already tarnished reputation. When he finally married, he traveled to Jonesborough to get his bride. I suspect some of Jackson Hays's family had also moved there, creating a link back to the farm. I know almost nothing about Oliveve, the wife. She died when I was young. At her death, Amon buried her back in Jonesborough, but he did not join her there at his death. They had no children. My first cousin, who now owns the Zack Bennett farm, often worked on Amon's farm as a youth and tells me that she was a superb cook. He enjoyed the dinners she prepared for the field hands.

The Amon Hayes farm was about the size of our own, around 50 acres. Eventually Amon built a modest new home, a much better home than I lived in during the first ten years of my life. The only black man in an all-white community, he seemed to blend in well. I doubt that most whites, whatever the stereotypes they had of blacks in general, ever applied them to Amon. My father noted that a nearly middle-aged Amon was still very strong and loved to wrestle (a game in which each wrestler tried to get the other off his feet and to the ground). When wild young country boys challenged Amon, he almost always threw them. He somehow had the personality to do this without offense, or without exciting racial resentment. In his dealing with neighbors, he always seemed to me to be direct, businesslike, without any special deference or clear role-playing.

Amon was, by the verdict of my mother and the most pious church members, anything but a role model for youth. He joined with a white neighbor to run a still in the 1920s and made money. He loved music and led in the formation of a local hillbilly band. He played the instrument whose proper English name was "fiddle," although ignorant people sometimes refer to it by a foreign, Italian name. Throughout the 1920s he hosted periodic Saturday evening square dances, using his large living room for the dancing. Although most young men and women, and this includes my father, attended these dances, a few families kept their daughters home. My mother was not allowed to attend and had perhaps exaggerated images of the sinfulness that prevailed. My father attests that nothing untoward happened. Most of the band members were older men, one a church elder. Most who came were church members. And, of course, Oliveve and Esther were there, the only black folk save Amon. It is possible that young men moved outside the house to drink moonshine whiskey. Some hot "sparking" probably took place as couples walked home, but this also happened after church every Sunday night.

Amon was a good but in no way exceptional farmer. He grew burley tobacco and later sold grade B milk. He exchanged labor with white neighbors. When too old to farm, he rented his farm to white sharecroppers. He did well economically but had none of the driving ambition of Zachariah Bennett, a near neighbor until Zack's death in 1910. Amon was genial and had a wide array of friends. He enjoyed the reputation of growing excellent watermelons. My father recounted how a group of white boys stole many of his melons on a summer night, probably around

1925. Stealing watermelons was a near rite of passage for young men. It is not clear that they picked on Amon, at least not because he was black. Boys stole everyone's melons. But Daddy swore Amon usually had the best. Amon, like most farmers, had to smile and profess his willingness to share his melons with anyone who asked. But getting them that way would have spoiled all the fun. I often wondered if his race, his visible minority status, forced him to be more careful in reacting to this thievery, and if to some extent he had to assume carefully outfitted roles.

I knew Amon when he was old. I can remember visiting his home only once, with Daddy, and this to buy sweet potato plants. Although unschooled, he was quite literate and well informed. When the man who held the mortgage on our farm seemed, unintentionally, to overcharge on interest, my mother turned to Amon Hayes to mediate. He was the local expert on figuring interest. Unfortunately, as he aged his eyesight weakened. In his last five years, after Esther died, he was totally blind. Even my mother forgave his earlier transgressions. One day, feeling the side of the pavement with a cane, Amon walked by our house on the way to the store, probably to buy groceries. Usually someone gave him a ride before he walked the half mile to our house, but not this day. Always, at the store, he could depend on someone to drive him home. Daddy went out to greet him and invited him to the house to rest and to talk. They loved to visit and tell stories. My mother probably served him a piece of cake. On this day, as Daddy guided Amon through the yard, my mother turned to me and said I should always respect this elderly man, and that out of respect I should always address him as Uncle Amon. I was in high school and did not need such instruction. By then everyone called him Uncle Amon.

Amon Hays was never a member of Bethesda Church or of the almost equally close Pleasant Hill Church, where he was buried. In fact, many considered him a lost sinner. I remember seeing him in church only once. It was during a summer revival. The minister went to get a nearly blind Amon, and he came. He was the center of attention, as everyone almost fawned over him. Now very old, he loved the singing and seemed affected by the hotter than usual preaching. I now suspect he knew another religious style from visiting his relatives in Jonesborough and did not feel comfortable with our Presbyterian services. This experience may have revealed an unknown side of Amon. Some Sundays his yard would fill with cars of visiting relatives from Jonesborough. Even at a distance one could hear the laughter and singing. In these interludes white neighbors sensed an alien culture, one that excluded them. But Amon's main life was among whites. When he died in 1952, black relatives attended his funeral, but all the pallbearers were white neighbors, and he was buried in the Jackson Hays plot, amid white people in a white cemetery. His cousins in Jonesborough inherited and promptly sold his farm.

Amon had kept his ties to the white Hays family. Childless, he knew that he would be the last black in Bethesda. Marion Hays, the grandson of Captain George, and the last owner of the old Hays home place, also had no children. Amon and Marion died within a year of each other. Thus this branch of the Hays family, black and white, is now gone from Bethesda. After Amon died, a close friend of my family, and for years my Sunday school teacher, Haven Middleton, bought his farm. Like Zachariah Bennett, he paid cash. He had lived for thirty years on a farm that adjoined Amon's. I did not realize it as a child, but Marion Hays owned this land, and Haven was a sharecropper—a sharecropper with tenure. Haven owned his own horses and tools; owned cows and sold milk in town. In fact, he probably had more money in the bank than any of his immediate neighbors, including my father. He was a very close friend of the owner, in every way a social equal in the perspective of the church and community. Most people thought Marion Hays, when he died in 1951, would will the farm to Haven. He did not but did give him a small bequest. My cousin bought some of the land and added it to the old Zack Bennett farm. Haven had only a year to evacuate his long-term house, and he bought Amon's old house and moved next door, still on the ancestral lands of the Hays family. His wife died in five years of breast cancer, and Haven lived on, alone, for eighteen years. He was found dead in the Amon Hays house in 1979. His heirs split up the farm and sold Amon's house to outsiders that no one locally ever knew. The vacant house eventually burned, with the empty shell only removed recently. Old-timers still refer to the Amon Hays place. But soon no one will remember the last black person to live in Bethesda. No blacks live anywhere near the community today. Zack's monument remains the only tangible but still impressive symbol of what was once an unusual biracial community.

My two stories are complete. I do not know what they mean. I have many unanswered questions. I know that Black Zack and Uncle Amon were exceptional men, black or white. In no wise were they saints. Against great odds, they made a good life for themselves. I can only wonder how, in private moments, they saw the world around them, what they really thought of their white neighbors. I have always wondered if they were active politically, if they voted (the county automatically collected the poll tax with land taxes, so they were eligible, and undoubtedly would have followed over 90 percent of the local whites in voting Republican). I have also wondered what would have happened had they had children. Where would they have gone to school? I suspect—I cannot prove—that in no other southern village were local black farmers as successful, or as respected by white neighbors, as Black Zack and Uncle Amon. I am all but sure that no rural black farmer, anywhere in the South, left funds for a monument as large or impressive as Zack's.

SUGGESTED READINGS

For general studies of the region in this time frame, see Richard B. Drake, *A History of Appalachia* (Lexington: University Press of Kentucky, 2001); John Alexander Williams, *Appalachia: A History* (Chapel Hill: University of North Carolina Press, 2002); Ronald D Eller, *Miners, Millhands, and Mountaineers: Industrialization of the Appalachian South, 1880–1930* (Knoxville: University of Tennessee Press, 1982); and Mary Beth Pudup, Dwight B. Billings, and Altina Waller, eds., *Appalachia in the Making: The Mountain South in the Nineteenth Century* (Chapel Hill: University of North Carolina Press, 1995). Dealing with the idea of the image of the area and race are Henry Shapiro, *Appalachia on Our Mind: The Southern Mountaineers in the American Consciousness* (Chapel Hill: University of North Carolina Press, 1978); and James C. Klotter, "The Black South and White Appalachia," *Journal of American History* 66 (1980): 832–49. Dealing even more specifically with race in the region are William H. Turner and Edward J. Cabell, eds., *Blacks in Appalachia* (Lexington: University Press of Kentucky, 1985); and John C. Inscoe, ed., *Appalachians and Race: The Mountain South from Slavery to Segregation* (Lexington: University Press of Kentucky, 2001).

3

Asa Candler: Old Southerner in the New South

Kathryn W. Kemp

Southerners, black and white, faced a post–Civil War South that had been devastated by the conflict. Livestock had been taken by rampaging troops; crops had been destroyed; homes had been burned or abandoned; lives had been lost. On top of all that, citizens sought to adjust to new racial patterns, while both sexes continued to struggle over gender issues.

As individuals sought to rebuild their societies and to forge new ones, debates sprang up almost immediately about the directions the South should take. Should it basically continue prewar agrarian patterns of life, with as little change as possible? Should it attempt to create a new mind-set focused more on industry and business? Would older patterns of life on matters of race, gender, religion, and the like, live on in this postwar South, or should changes occur? Should the region and its people simply reflect an Old South reborn or be reborn into a New South? Answers would prove elusive then, and remain difficult to find, even now.

Kathryn W. Kemp tells about one of those southerners and his response to that world. Born before the Civil War, Asa Candler came to represent, for some, a model for entrepreneurial leaders of the region after the conflict. Yet, as Professor Kemp shows, his heart and soul mostly reflected his prewar youth. His product—Coca-Cola—lives on. The question is, Do his ideas continue as well?

Kathryn W. Kemp received her Ph.D. from Georgia State University and is assistant professor of history at Clayton College and State University in Morrow, Georgia. She is author of God's Capitalist: Asa Candler of Coca-Cola *(2002).*

From the late nineteenth century to the present, Atlanta's business elite has usually supported the concept of an innovative, commercially vigorous "New South," as articulated by *Atlanta Constitution* editor Henry Grady. Coca-Cola Company founder Asa Candler, as a leading figure in early-twentieth-century Atlanta, publicly honored Grady's memory in 1909. He reminded an audience of Grady's "eloquence . . . gentleness of heart, and warmth of love." But Candler, unlike most Atlantans, declined to praise Grady's tireless promotion of the idea of the New South:

> For myself, I do not like the phraseology. I believe [that] the best that is in us to-day has been handed down to us from our fathers. . . . Not "A New South"—god forbid—but the dear old South, aroused to a realization of her God Given Opportunities, this . . . is the South of today.[1]

In spite of Candler's rejection, not to mention the fact that the concept of the New South was never sharply defined, it is here to stay. The term "New South" remains a hardy perennial, offered by chambers of commerce and journalists to signal yet another great new day soon to come to the states of the old Confederacy. Scholars have argued about the usefulness of the idea of the New South, and some even condemn the whole notion as a myth or a mask for hypocrisy. At the very least, the concept of the New South may be used to demonstrate those basic themes of historical analyses, continuity, and change. On that basis, the life and ideas of Asa Candler and his vision of the New South reveal much.

Candler rose to success in his "South of today" as a patent medicine manufacturer who founded The Coca-Cola Company. With the profits from Coca-Cola, he diversified to become a banker and real estate entrepreneur, as well as an advocate of social reform and a philanthropist. Because of this success, and the era in which he achieved it, Candler can easily be assigned the identity of New Southerner. However, closer examination will show that Candler's Georgia roots penetrated deep into the red clay soil of old Georgia. The values of the "new" represented a veneer on a very traditional individual.

Born in December 1851, Asa Candler spent his childhood and youth in the waning days of the Old South. During Georgia's gold rush of the 1830s and 1840s, his parents, Samuel and Martha, settled in Carroll County, about thirty miles west of Atlanta. His father, who had been a mining engineer, helped found the town of Villa Rica, where the elder Candler traded with local residents in his general store. Samuel Candler did business with miners who exchanged goose quills packed with gold dust for merchandise. The family, which grew to include eleven children, lived on a farm in the nearby countryside. As the third youngest of the family, Asa experienced pre–Civil War years typical of rural southern children who were comfortably well-off, although not wealthy. Books and a piano graced the Candler home, but the children were required to help with farm chores. Asa followed his father's entrepreneurial example, sending mink skins to Atlanta to sell for fifty cents each and peddling pins to neighborhood housewives. His older brothers (with the exception of one, who suffered from a developmental disorder) were all business or professional men. His father planned a career in medicine for young Asa, but the Civil War disrupted his education.

The family endured the wartime difficulties common to most Georgians of their time and social situation. Mrs. Candler concealed the family's supply of hard money in her clothing, in the event of raids by Federal forces. They boiled the dirt from the smokehouse floor to recover valuable salt, and they celebrated Christmas with gingerbread but no gifts. However, after the war ended, Samuel Candler came out of retirement and recovered most of the family fortune.

At this late point in his life, the elder Candler joined the Methodist Church, a decision that was to have momentous consequences for the denomination. Although his wife, Martha, had always worshiped with a Primitive Baptist congregation, Samuel declined to be baptized by immersion. After attending a revival meeting led by a one-armed Confederate veteran, he received the dignified sprinkling of the Methodist rite. Mother and children followed him to join the Methodist Church in Villa Rica. The younger sons—already firm in the Christian faith that their mother had taught them—now attended a Sunday school class led by their father. As a result of this association, Asa's younger brother Warren went on to study for the Methodist ministry and eventually rose to the rank of bishop. Asa would become one of the most important Southern Methodist laymen of his time, giving millions in support of its causes.

Young Candler's path to wealth began at the end of the war, when he spent several months living with his married sister while catching up on some of his missed schooling. He then was apprenticed in an apothecary shop operated by a pair of physicians in Cartersville. There he made the crucial decision that, in spite of his father's wishes, the doctor's life was not for him. He wrote a letter declaring that "there is more to be made as a druggist than a physician . . . with a great deal less trouble." Having learned to mix medicines, he went to Atlanta in search of a place "where I can get sufficient compensation for my services."[2]

In the city, Candler's first "prescriptionist" job was with a druggist named George Howard, in his store at 47 Peachtree Street. When Howard relocated his drugstore a short distance away to Marietta Street, Candler and a fellow employee resigned and went into competition with their former boss, taking over "Howard's Old Stand" (as they called it in their advertisement) and luring away most of his former clientele. For

Howard, the final blow came soon after, when his daughter Lucy eloped with the audacious young entrepreneur. Howard refused to speak to the couple, until his daughter gave birth to the first of five children. He then wrote a terse note to Candler: "Sir—I am disposed to 'bury the hatchet' and to be friendly in the future—if this should meet with your approval you can let me know."[3] The young couple accepted the offer and did their part to repair the damage by naming their firstborn son Howard.

Candler's drug business, wholesale and retail, thrived. In addition to filling prescriptions, he manufactured patent medicines and related items, such as Delectalave, a tooth cleanser. He also dealt in products as varied as vanilla extract, paint, baking powder, and perfume. The business expanded to serve not only Atlanta but customers across the state of Georgia.

As a dealer in patent medicines, Candler bought and sold control of recipes for many of the products he manufactured. This activity, plus a bad headache, introduced him to a "brain tonic" and pain reliever called Coca-Cola, the invention of another prescriptionist, Dr. S. J. Pemberton. Coca-Cola helped Candler's chronic headaches so he began to buy up shares of the product, which were owned by a number of individuals. He gained total ownership of the formula in 1892, at which point he incorporated The Coca-Cola Company in Georgia.

Some Atlantans had already begun to mix the Coca-Cola syrup base with soda water and use it as a soft drink. Candler followed this lead to produce and sell the syrup base to fountains and restaurants. A determined teetotaler, he began marketing the product as a temperance beverage rather than a tonic and achieved an immediate success. As he entered his forties, the father of five children abandoned his other business interests to concentrate on Coca-Cola.

Candler was at his most modern in merchandising his famous soft drink. His development of Coca-Cola would have been impossible in the South of his youth. However, because of advances in printing and transportation technology that appeared in the late nineteenth century, a new type of product rose to importance. Small items such as chewing gum and cigarettes—and soft drinks—earned profits on a high volume of sales at low individual prices. Efficient distribution made these products readily available. At the same time, the newly emerging mass print media carried energetic advertising that induced the public to make the multitude of purchases necessary for the success of the new products. A newsboy on a hot, crowded city street could sell a freshly printed daily paper to a pedestrian who not only read the latest headlines from Cuba but also was reminded that Coca-Cola is "Delicious—refreshing!" The buyer of the paper might step into the nearby drug store, take a seat at the fountain, and buy a cold Coke made from syrup delivered frequently to the store. Enjoying his Coca-Cola, he would read the story of Teddy

Roosevelt's exploits, hardly conscious of his place in an ever-growing global web of commercial relationships.

From The Coca-Cola Company's beginnings in the 1890s, Candler recognized the market value of a trademarked brand name. He invested heavily in magazine and newspaper advertising that displayed lush illustrations of handsome and successful people enjoying his product. Sports figures such as Cleveland baseball star Napoleon Lajoie endorsed its good qualities. The famous circular red-and-white Coca-Cola sign could be seen in grocery and drug stores and on billboards all over the country. Candler fought vigorously to defend the product from scores of imitators. His lawyers relentlessly pursued the makers of drinks with names like Koke, Coca-Ola, Cold Cola, Ko-Kola, and Taka-Kola, forcing them to drop their dubious product names. The Coca-Cola brand name also suffered from the persistent rumor that the drink contained cocaine. The "Coca" portion of its name did derive from a nonnarcotic flavoring extract of the coca leaf. To combat the narcotics slander, advertisements presented the results of university laboratory studies that declared the beverage to be free of narcotics of any sort. A youthful customer, up on the latest slang, made the mistake of ordering a glass of "Dope" within Candler's hearing and received a stiff lecture from the company's teetotaling president.

In 1909, the senior enforcers of the new federal food and drug regulations rejected Coke's claims of purity. Dr. Harvey Wylie, head of the Bureau of Chemistry of the Department of Agriculture, turned his considerable fury on Coca-Cola, in part because he opposed caffeine, found in generous quantities in Candler's beverage. Inspectors arrived unannounced to peek into vats of syrup and carry away samples for analysis, engaging in hostile confrontations with Candler and his son as they did their work. The government seized a syrup shipment, and the result was a case styled United States v. Forty Barrels and Twenty Kegs of Coca-Cola. Dueling experts swore that the product was either healthful or a menace, and appeals dragged on until 1918. By then Wylie had left government service. A negotiated settlement ended the matter, resulting in very minor changes in Coca-Cola.

If Coca-Cola presented a public face as modern as the fashionable young people who populated its advertising images, the core of the company reflected the nineteenth-century origins of its founder. In the progressive era, when professional management increasingly dominated large firms, Asa Candler owned and managed The Coca-Cola Company personally. Family and a few friends held only a handful of shares, although several relatives served as company executives, all under the firm hand of the founder. Even Candler's right-hand man, Frank Robinson, who had designed the Coca-Cola logo in the Pemberton days and whose taste buds were a significant factor in the product's quality control, owned only a limited number of shares.

Candler's youth in Carroll County shaped his traditionalist worldview, and specifically his opinion of urban life. Although he would say "I love Atlanta," Candler held an extremely pessimistic view of cities: the only thing that saved a city like Atlanta from an inevitable decline into decadence was the regular infusion of "the sweet and wholesome influences of rural Christianity" brought in by immigrants from neighboring regions.[4] To protect his family from the malignant influences of the city, he made his first home east of the city, in the suburban village of Kirkwood. Life there, on what his son later described as a "miniature farm," replicated Candler's own Carroll County boyhood. The family kept horses—Candler was a skillful rider—and slaughtered a hog, country style, in the first cold spell of the fall. Mrs. Candler canned and sewed and baked. The boys helped with chores around the place and with other tasks, such as chopping quantities of vanilla beans for their father's use in the manufacture of vanilla extract.

As a founding member of the local Methodist congregation, Candler actively supported its activities, both financially and as a Sunday school teacher. He loved to lead hymns, although according to his son, his high tenor voice at times set the pitch to a level that left him making a solo performance. Methodists change the assignments of their clergymen on a regular basis, and each new pastor in Candler's church arrived to find his pantry had been well stocked by Candler. The Candler family began each meal with a prayer, but Candler liked this grace to be brief and to the point—long-winded demonstrations of piety annoyed him.

Candler's devotion to his church, which began during boyhood in Villa Rica, remained strong all of his life. He was no Sunday morning Christian; his principles operated seven days a week. This raised a challenging moral question: how can an aggressive capitalist live by the principles of a religion that seems to reject materialism? His answer (and perhaps his hope of salvation) came in the doctrine of Christian stewardship. As his affluence increased, Asa turned to his clergyman brother for advice. The bishop responded that "the ability to make money is a gift of God (Deuteronomy viii: 10) just as any other sort of talent and it must be consecrated in the service of God." The bishop's reply then outlined the duties of a Christian steward in managing his money: First, he should care for the needs of his family; second, he should attend to the "maintenance of the business which God has given one to the end that he may serve Him by making money"; and finally, he should apply his wealth "for the promotion of benevolent causes for the up-building of the Kingdom of God."

As the parable of the talents taught, God gave wealth for a reason, and the wealthy Christian had a duty to manage it properly. Candler lived comfortably but avoided the ostentatious extravagance indulged in by many wealthy individuals of his era. He managed his funds so closely that he charged his sons interest on money he advanced for their college tuition. Nor did dispensing charity satisfy the obligations of the steward. Rather, the money should be carefully put to work in God's behalf. Because of this conviction, Candler tended to work through institutions. In particular, he gave both money and service to causes, such as hospitals, schools, and orphanages that were associated with the Southern Methodist denomination.

In 1907 Atlanta's Methodists held a "gathering in" (fund-raising campaign) for Wesley Memorial Enterprises, a collection of Methodist projects that included a hospital and an urban mission church that provided services similar to those offered by settlement houses in other cities. Clergy all over the city preached special sermons, and then supporters of the project met at the Wesley Tabernacle to count up the results. Candler had promised a matching gift of as much as $12,500 if Atlanta's Methodists could find an equal sum. Although a good deal of money was collected during the morning, more was needed to reach the goal. As the afternoon wore on, enthusiastic onlookers added pledges to raise the total, but it soon was evident that the target was still far out of reach. Then Bishop Charles B. Galloway electrified the audience by announcing Asa Candler's additional pledge of $7,500. Someone called out, "Do you mean it?" and when he answered positively, the cheering audience began to sing "Praise God from Whom All Blessings Flow" as Candler wept and sang with them. This was only one of many gifts he made to Southern Methodist causes over his lifetime.

In the 1870s, "Commodore" Cornelius Vanderbilt occasionally accompanied his wife to services in the Church of the Strangers, a Southern Methodist congregation in New York City. Impressed by its pastor, and probably encouraged by his wife, he endowed the Nashville university that still bears his name. There Southern Methodist clergy could receive professional preparation along lines acceptable to the denomination. Methodist bishops served on its board of trustees. However, over the ensuing decades, the close relation between university and denomination became increasingly strained, as the trustees disagreed over hiring policies. The bishops on the board of trustees (Warren Candler was an ex officio participant in the dispute) wished to give preference to Methodists in filling faculty vacancies. They eventually resorted to a lawsuit in an attempt to gain control of Vanderbilt's administration. The issue reached a crisis in 1913, when the philanthropist Andrew Carnegie offered a million-dollar gift for the creation of a medical school at Vanderbilt, with the proviso that the school's administration be strictly secular and that hiring and promotion be based solely on academic merit. The bishops would have declined Carnegie's gift, but they lacked the power to impose their view on the rest of the board. Frustrated, the General Conference of the Southern Methodists officially severed ties to Vanderbilt and set out to create two schools of higher learning—one on each side of the Mississippi—to preserve their principles and educate future clergy. Southern Methodist University, established in Dallas, Texas, satisfied half of the plan, while the Candlers steered the conference to choose Atlanta as the site of the eastern university. With some other prominent Atlanta Methodists as allies, they carried on a campaign to bring Emory College from Oxford, Georgia, to a new campus in Atlanta, situated on land donated from Candler's new Druid Hills development in the eastern part of Atlanta. The Candler family had long-standing connections to Emory. Several family members studied there, including Warren. He also taught at the Oxford school and had served as its president at one point in his career. One of its trustees and a major financial supporter, Asa Candler wrote a personal check for $1 million to seal the proposition, in July 1914. A letter, written for public consumption, accompanied the donation and explained his motivation as "a deep sense of duty to God and an earnest desire to do good to my fellow men." Implicitly criticizing Vanderbilt University and Carnegie, he condemned secular education as "creating dangerous ambitions and arousing selfish passions faster than it supplies restraints on these lawless tendencies."[5] Additional cash gifts completed the process that enabled the creation of Emory in Atlanta, an institution that dominated Candler's philanthropic interests for the rest of his life.

Candler also demonstrated stewardship in action in the business world in his response to the disastrous slump in the cotton market that attended the outbreak of World War I. Just as Europe plunged into war at the end of the summer of 1914, American farmers harvested a record cotton crop. The large crop alone would have tended to glut the market and lower the price of cotton, but the outbreak of war also cut the cotton farmers off from a large segment of their potential buyers. The fact that many small farmers lived from season to season, depending on earnings from this year's crop to pay last year's loan, placed the cotton growers in great peril. A number of plans to ease the situation appeared. The Buy-a-Bale campaign urged individuals or groups to buy a single bale of cotton, but that thinly disguised charity proved impractical. Financial institutions developed other, sounder programs. For example, a group of St. Louis banks planned to lend sums based on the depressed market value of the cotton, hold the crop as collateral, and return a portion of the profit to the farmers when increased wartime demand drove the cotton price back up. However, before the other banks could put their plans into action, Candler moved swiftly to capture many of these borrowers. He presented a well-publicized plan: farmers could place their cotton in the hands of

Candler's Central Bank & Trust Company and immediately receive its currently low market value in the form of a loan. When the market recovered, the bank would sell the cotton and the farmer would be paid the proceeds of the sale, minus the principal and interest of the earlier loan. Candler put up $30 million for the project and built a gigantic warehouse to store the cotton. This system was not original with Candler, but he was the first to put it into action. The vice president of his bank stated, "We are not out with a charity proposition." Although the program entailed little risk over the long term, people perceived it as a great philanthropy. They rightly hailed Candler for having saved the small Georgia farmer from bankruptcy. His actions preserved his God-given wealth and served the needs of the community. Thus it was a great feat of stewardship.

Religion obviously had a great influence on Asa Candler's personal conduct. His particular opinions on religion or theology also may be inferred from statements made by his two brothers—Warren, a Methodist bishop, and the youngest brother, John, a jurist—who often provided Asa with legal advice. All three Candler brothers are found in the ranks of southern traditionalists, but the Candlers of Asa's day were specifically *Southern* Methodists. Disputes over slavery had split the denomination in 1845 and the Methodists did not reunite until 1938, a change that Bishop Candler opposed vigorously. John and Warren disparaged the Methodist churches of the North because they stooped to ordain African American clergy. Warren also condemned higher criticism, the theological practice that applied the tools of modern scholarship, such as linguistics and archaeology, to biblical study. Warren served variously as chancellor and president of Emory University, while Asa chaired the trustees; under their influence, Emory's religious scholarship did not innovate. Indeed, the school also rejected student theater and intercollegiate athletics as improper or distracting.

The family once confronted modernism within its own ranks when Bishop Candler's son-in-law Andrew Sledd, an Emory classics professor, wrote a rather mild call for the fair treatment of blacks. He also condemned lynching. The article, published in the July 1902 issue of *Atlantic Monthly*, outraged southerners in general and Emory supporters in particular. The president of the university wrote to Sledd, stating that even Bishop Candler and two of his brothers (doubtlessly Asa and John) deplored his views. Within two weeks, the controversy drove Sledd to resign. According to a letter from Sledd to Warren Candler, "Uncle Asa" helped him out financially. However upset he may have been with young Sledd's opinions, the good steward loaned $2,400 to the professor at 6 percent.

Beyond his desire to conform his own conduct to his religious standards, Candler held ideas about public morality, labor, African Americans, and women that also reveal his traditional, paternalist viewpoint.

Although he was to serve as mayor of the city of Atlanta for one term, Candler was only occasionally outspoken in matters of public interest. In particular, issues of public morality seized his interest. He supported efforts to promote prohibition, such as those carried out by the Young Men and Religion Forward organization. During the early 1910s, this group placed advertisements in the local newspaper, denouncing by name the owners of disorderly boarding houses and users of "locker clubs," which evaded the antisaloon laws by storing bottles of whiskey privately owned by their members. This campaign to rid the city of prostitutes and liquor found a ready ally in chief of police James L. Beavers, who delighted in raiding illegal "blind tigers," where Atlantans could buy liquor by the drink. Diligently rounding up working girls and shipping them out of town, he had seemingly limitless puritanical energies. Even sweethearts who stole a kiss in a public place might find themselves under arrest.

The morality crusade soon attracted national attention, much to the chagrin of local commercial interests, which did not care to have their city widely publicized as a sinkhole of drunkenness and vice. Taking a slightly different perspective, some of Beavers's opponents also groused that his activities had made Atlanta "a damn unpleasant town." In the case of the chief, although Candler was a former president of the chamber of commerce, he stood up for Beavers against the mainstream opinion of the city's business leaders, defending him in advertisements and public meetings. When the opposition began a campaign to force Chief Beavers from office, Candler declared that this action would "penalize virtue and eulogize vice."[6] Although Beavers did temporarily lose his position, Candler was elected mayor the following year and put his influence behind a successful move to restore a somewhat chastened Beavers to his former office. For Candler, the values of old-time morality entirely outweighed the importance of Atlanta's national image as a hub of commerce.

In articulating the concept of the New South to northern audiences, Henry Grady reassured them that the large African American population of the South would present no obstacle to progress. While asserting that the South had greatly changed, he also claimed that managing "the Negro" should be left to the southerners. Liberty and enfranchisement having been provided, "The rest . . . should be left to those among whom his lot is cast, with whom he is indissolubly connected and whose prosperity depends upon their possessing his intelligent sympathy and confidence."[7] In the end, although he argued their mutual interests, Grady made a claim for the traditional authority of whites over blacks, based on long-standing indissoluble connections. It was an argument that could have come from an antebellum planter.

Grady's view differed little from that of other Atlantans, including Asa Candler, in its traditional paternalism. Neither Grady nor Candler seems to have been entirely in touch with the real situation. In fact, by Candler's era, a large community of middle-class African Americans, including professionals, scholars, and even a self-made millionaire, called Atlanta home. In spite of this, when Asa Candler looked at Atlanta, this affluent, educated population seemed to vanish. He might support Paine College, which at that time promoted a modest program of industrial education for African Americans, but he had little to offer the more ambitious, traditionally black institutions that now make up the Atlanta University Center. This becomes more understandable, given Candler's personal history.

He was about to enter his teens when the first of the Confederate states seceded from the union. On his Carroll County boyhood home, slaves had carried out the greater part of the labor. Although control of fewer than twenty persons (seventeen in 1860) put Samuel Candler at the upper edge of the "small" category of southern slaveholders, this farm was not in the region of large plantations, and in his neighborhood the elder Candler ranked among the most prominent employers of chattel labor. As a boy, Asa had worked in the fields beside those bondsmen. Such a childhood impression must have been very strong. The Civil War began when Asa was entering his teens, and only a few years later slave labor ended forever. By this time, however, Candler was old enough to have the foundations of his racial views set in the paternalistic traditions of the landowning classes of the Old South. Life in Reconstruction Georgia probably had little effect on these views.

Candler did not exhibit racist hatred of blacks, but rather showed the complacent attitude of one who assumed himself to be their natural superior. In matters of race (as well as others) he demonstrated the paternalism of the traditional southern gentleman. He could be magnanimous, making a cash gift to Morris Brown College, for example. In 1906, when Atlanta was torn by a race riot, the newspaper reported that he addressed a mass meeting to condemn the violence. According to the account, he declared that too many people were talking too much and were carrying too many pistols. He went on to say that all the blame for crime should not be placed on "the members of a weak race," adding that "We are trustees of a great nation [and] we should conduct ourselves with Christian righteousness."[8] As was the case in other areas of his life, he viewed his position as one of a responsible steward—a trustee appointed to oversee the doings of the "weak race" and protect them if need be.

Issues of race came to the fore again, entangled with a labor controversy, when the business and political elite of Atlanta drafted Candler to run for mayor in the Democratic primary of 1916. This was the era of the white primary. The general election, with candidates from competing parties, had devolved to become a mere formality. With only a handful of Republicans to back the opposition, Democrats effectively elected the officeholders for the coming term by voting in their primary—a private event that excluded blacks from participation.

Candler's most serious opposition came from a representative of the laboring segment of the city's electorate, but Candler prevailed in the primary. Newspapers began to refer to him as the "mayor elect." However, in the interval between the primary and the general election, Atlanta's streetcar operators went out on strike. They sought recognition of their union and complained of low pay and unreasonable work schedules. Candler opposed them. He was not only a leading figure in the business community but also a director of the Georgia Railway and Electrical Company, which operated the trolley system. In public meetings, he condemned the actions of the strikers. Although mostly law-abiding, a few union men did resort to violence. Small quantities of dynamite bounced cars off the tracks, and from time to time bullets flew out of the darkness. On occasion they wounded a passenger. On the other hand, a union organizer charged that the company had influenced the police to take improper actions against the strikers and that the police "know that Mr. Candler is soon to [be] in power in Atlanta and a lot of people would lose their jobs," if they failed to comply with the company's wishes.[9]

As a result of Candler's opposition to the strike, the union element of the city's electorate found a candidate willing to challenge him in the general election. Although reasonably certain of victory, the Candler campaign responded by resorting to a racial appeal. Candler's campaign managers publicized a claim that a vote for Candler would preserve the white primary. As a result, they secured a second victory for their candidate in the December vote. The strike failed, although a transit workers union did receive recognition a few years later. As for the new mayor, Candler devoted himself to straightening out the city's tangled finance problems and shepherding his city through the challenges of World War I, which the United States entered after his election.

As far as his own employees were concerned, he seems to have felt a certain duty toward them, without ever entertaining the idea that they should do much thinking for themselves. In family letters, Candler warmly remembered certain faithful employees. His traditional, paternalistic approach to management allowed him to shepherd employees to church and lead them in hymns, not to mention dosing them with medicines when they were ill. As mayor, however, he economized by cutting the number of city employees, without a hint of remorse.

Like his ideas about African Americans and labor, Candler's attitudes toward women reflect long-held perceptions of society as a hierarchy with well-to-do white males at the apex. Nor did anything in his immediate personal experience challenge this viewpoint. His mother, who helped pioneer the family lands in Villa Rica, Georgia, and hid family assets from the encroaching Yankee military, powerfully influenced his character, but did so as a traditional woman who devoted herself entirely to the service of her family. When she was widowed, she soon came under his protection. He managed her affairs and provided her with a home until she died. He honored her memory in a letter written some seventeen years after her death, "I do not believe a good mother can ever die. Mine has not, though absent from the flesh since 1897."[10]

His wife resembled his mother in her devotion to domestic life. She kept his dinner warm when he worked late and poured cool water over his aching head. She mended, sewed, cooked, and cared for their children. However, the closest thing to a known opinion on anything outside of family concerns is her reaction to a Confederate Memorial Day parade, when she wept at the sight of the old Confederate vets. Candler clearly expected that this quiet domesticity would govern his daughter's life as well. When all of the children had become adults and some serious matter arose, their father would consult with the four sons, but would inform his daughter. In a speech naively titled "Pegs and Holes," Candler told students at the Martha Berry School for Girls that they should not attempt roles for which they were unsuited. Another talk, called "Home!" made it clear that the ideal woman should make the home "holy and happy," thus fulfilling "the highest duty of Christian womanhood."[11]

Mrs. Candler's life presented no challenge to her husband's ideas about women, but her importance to him is clear from the anguished inscription he entered in the family Bible at the time of her death in 1919: "Why so soon!!!" In the last decade of his life, he sought unsuccessfully to find another life partner who resembled her. One woman attracted him, and they came close to marriage. Onezima deBouchel, a New Orleans "socialite," was mildly feminist, and he teased her in a letter for being "one of those things." She replied with a sprightly defense but then dropped the issue. Flirtation, not persuasion, marked the tone of her letters to her elderly suitor. The relationship remained private until a story in a New Orleans newspaper told the world of their engagement. Friends and total strangers offered unsolicited advice to the effect that marriage to a divorced, Catholic, non-Anglo-Saxon woman would be a great mistake on Candler's part. Many argued that his position carried unusual responsibilities that denied him the freedom of action enjoyed by ordinary folk. He held his ground for a while, but slanderous stories eventually moved him to bow to the opinions of his family and break the engagement. The outraged deBouchel sued him for breach of promise but lost on a legal technicality.

By the time the lawsuit concluded, Candler had already found a new wife, Mae Little Ragin, who operated a public stenography business in Candler's office building. They married secretly and then informed his family and the public. The new Mrs. Candler proved a disappointment to her elderly spouse. Suspicious of her behavior, he had her followed, and subsequently she was arrested while drinking whiskey in an apartment with two male acquaintances. They separated and Candler briefly entertained a divorce suit. During this interval Mrs. Candler's automobile hit and killed a young girl who was playing with friends at the edge of a suburban street. Although the death was ruled accidental, her parents filed suit against Candler, under the principle that a husband was legally answerable for his wife's conduct. After an out-of-court settlement, some sort of reconciliation brought Mae back into his household and no further scandals are recorded.

When he became mayor, Candler had largely retired from commercial activity. He passed control of Coca-Cola to his children, who shortly sold control of the company without consulting their father. In spite of the personal frustrations of his last decade, in 1926 Candler carried out his final responsibilities as a steward of God by arranging to transfer his remaining assets to Emory University. Three years later, he died. In his last will and testament, he bequeathed to his children "my good name as it has come to me from an honorable and honest ancestor."

Candler's life is a story of tradition more than innovation. Although a prominent figure in the New South, Candler held traditionalist values that clearly drew on those he developed in the culture of the Old. His most obviously modern characteristic was his briskly competitive, innovative business life. Yet even this energetic pursuit of commerce was not entirely new. Although Candler's father raised crops with slave labor, he also pursued commercial profits by doing business with gold miners. Like his son, he took swift advantage of any opportunity that came his way. Hard-driving commerce appears in the Candler family both before and after the war.

Clearly Candler looked to traditional religion to structure his social beliefs and personal behavior. Perhaps as a part of this, the old value of paternalism emerges as a dominant theme. He believed in the innate superiority of the Anglo-Saxon "race," and this belief led to the conclusion that the superior group owed a duty of supervision to those of a lesser sort. Similarly, he had no enthusiasm for women's independence but saw women as a species of being assigned a special but narrowly limited sphere of action. The traditionalism of the women close to him reinforced his views. Candler's attitude toward labor was likewise paternalistic, and again, the circumstances of his life did little to challenge his old-fashioned opinions. If he opposed the streetcar operators' attempt to unionize, he did not differ from other business leaders at the turn of the century. However, his interest in taking his employees to church demonstrates his sense of authority over lesser beings. There was nothing new—or uniquely southern—in the notion that upper-class white males should run things. This continuity had prevailed for millennia.

To what extent did he resemble his fellow New Southerners? The fact that they respected him and looked to his leadership suggests little distance between them. In spite of the claims of some that the South had undergone a great change, old social values clearly persisted into the postwar period, and even up to the present in some cases. This Old South was not a moonlight-and-magnolias fantasy but was capable of producing one of the most effective, energetic entrepreneurs of the New South era. Economic relations clearly had changed, but otherwise Asa Candler's life argues that the New South and his "dear old one" had more to unite them than to distinguish them from one other.

NOTES

1. Introduction of Speakers at Taft Banquet 1/15/1909, folder 38, box 2, Asa Griggs Candler Papers, Woodruff Library Special Collections, Emory University (hereafter cited as AGC papers).
2. Asa G. Candler to Dr. A. W. Griggs, both excerpts from a letter quoted in Candler, *Asa Griggs Candler* (Atlanta: Emory University, 1950), 55.
3. Candler, *Asa Griggs Candler*, 76. The original letter is in Candler's papers at Emory.
4. "Rural Sunday School Celebration," typescript of speech, n.d., folder 28, box 2, AGC papers.
5. The complete text of this letter may be read at www.emory.edu/history/candler.million.html.
6. *Journal of Labor*, November–December 1915, passim. Several stories refer to this comment.
7. Henry W. Grady, "The New South" (speech before the New England Society of New York), December 22, 1886, http://www.ucc.uconn.edu/~PBALDWIN/grady.html.
8. "Closing of Low Dives Urged by Citizens," *Atlanta Journal*, September 25, 1906, 1.
9. "Few Arrests Made of Pedestrians Who Refuse to Move On," *Atlanta Journal*, October 2, 1916, 1.
10. Asa G. Candler to Dr. W. H. Galloway, September 30, 1914, AGC Papers and Biography, The Archive, The Coca-Cola Company.
11. Typescripts of Candler speeches are found in Box 2, AGC papers.

SUGGESTED READINGS

Allen, Frederick. *Secret Formula How Brilliant Marketing and Relentless Salesmanship Made Coca-Cola the Best-Known Product in the World*. New York: HarperBusiness, 1994.
Candler, Charles Howard. *Asa Candler*. Atlanta: Emory University, 1950.

Davis, Harold E. *Henry Grady's New South: Atlanta, a Brave and Beautiful City.* Tuscaloosa: University of Alabama Press, 1990.
Kahn, E. J. *The Big Drink: The Story of Coca-Cola.* New York: Random House, 1960.
Kemp, Kathryn W. *God's Capitalist: Asa Candler of Coca-Cola.* Macon, GA: Mercer University Press, 2002.
Russell, James M. *Atlanta, 1847–1890: City Building in the Old South and the New.* Baton Rouge: Louisiana State University Press, 1988.

4

Alfred Holt Stone: Conservative Racial Thought in the New South

John David Smith

Alfred Holt Stone of Mississippi was a racist. He was not some unthinking, uneducated, uninformed advocate of white supremacy and a segregated society. Instead, in some ways he was more dangerous, for he cast his racism in a scholarly cloak and sought to justify it through learned discourse. His example shows how some individuals write history through their prejudices and how, if that history is not challenged, it can influence the uncritical reader.

Born during Reconstruction, Stone lived into the so-called Second Reconstruction of the 1950s. During his life, he represented the conservative racial mind-set of the South. By the time he was a young man, the region had begun to restrict already limited black rights. The writings of Stone and others justified such actions, and their words would be used by political demagogues to support greater segregation and continued racial violence.

African American leaders such as Booker T. Washington and W. E. B. Du Bois called on Stone to write fairly and carefully about black life in the South, but he generally ignored their pleas and went on presenting a story shaped by his own moral and intellectual blinders. Stone wanted the South of the future to be one where his white planter class would always be in control; a docile black lower class would nod dutifully and follow the dictates of its superiors. He simply did not display what should be one of the greatest tools of a historian—empathy.

Stone presented the views of many people of the late nineteenth and early to middle twentieth centuries. Such views would long dominate and would make change difficult and, in the end, divisive.

John David Smith, Charles H. Stone Distinguished Professor of American History at the University of North Carolina at Charlotte, has written or edited eighteen books on race relations, slavery, the Civil War, and the Old South. His Black Judas: William Hannibal Thomas and "The American Negro" *received the Mayflower Society Award for Nonfiction.*

In July 1903 the Mississippi planter and amateur scholar Alfred Holt Stone was disturbed, he said, because the *Washington Post* had misquoted him on the "race question." "It is, and has always been, my opinion," Stone informed Booker T. Washington, "that a man should hold his peace, rather than, in attempting to discuss any phase of our 'race question,' give utterance to any expression in the least calculated to mar kindly relations, or beget feelings of harsh[n]ess or distrust between men who have the good of both races at heart. I have faithfully tried to live up to this idea," Stone assured Washington. Thirty years later, Stone recalled that during his life he had spoken and published much on race relations in the South. "But not one word has ever come in harshness from my lips or pen. I have set down naught in uncharity or malice." Stone had lived and labored with African Americans for more than forty years "in the intimate contacts of plantation life." He insisted that his conscience was "void of offense toward them, individually and as a race. I have never abused one of them nor taken advantage of one in any transaction. It was not in the blood which I inherited to act otherwise."[1]

Though he may have had "the good of both races at heart," Stone nevertheless typified what historian Joel Williamson termed the "conservative" mentality of race relations during the Jim Crow era. Conservatives on the race question believed unequivocally in black inferiority and agreed that whites should define the place and status of Negroes in American society. One of the most vocal and influential racial paternalists of the early twentieth century, Stone used his personal connections and an unrelenting focus on the economics of southern black agricultural labor to establish himself as a leading "scientific" authority on the "Negro problem." On the surface, Stone was friendly to African Americans, but his pessimistic economic and social analyses (he pronounced blacks economically less productive than whites and predicted their competitive extinction) documented his deeply embedded white racism, his belief that emancipation was a mistake for both races, and his unwillingness to treat blacks as free men and women. Historian David Levering Lewis characterizes Stone as "brilliant, charming, gregarious, and intellectually duplicitous"—the "standard bearer of the South's planter oligarchy."[2]

Stone is best known for his collection of essays *Studies in the American Race Problem* (1908), a work racial conservatives embraced warmly. For example, the influential New Englander Charles Francis Adams considered it "the most illuminating book in relation to the [race] problem I have come across." "The extent of his [Stone's] knowledge and the variety and thoroughness of his research are most remarkable," wrote the lawyer-historian Theodore D. Jervey of Charleston, South Carolina. J. Franklin Jameson, a dean of American historiography and editor of the *American Historical Review*, lauded Stone as "a high authority on the economic history of the negro in the South since the war," and "also a person who has read and thought much of all Southern history." According to Thomas Pearce Bailey of the University of Mississippi, Stone's book "represents the high-grade Southerner's attitude toward the negro question . . . that the negroes should be treated as a 'peasant class.'" Smith College historian and racial liberal John Spencer Bassett complimented Stone's work as "probably, the most considerate and reasonable statement of the negro question ever made by a Southerner who holds the view usually held by his people."[3]

Other critics, however, did not share Bassett's qualified praise for Stone's writings on African Americans. Thomas Jesse Jones, a professor at Hampton Institute, judged Stone "probably the most able living apologist for many of the Southern policies which relate to the Negro." Reform journalist Oswald Garrison Villard admitted that Stone had published much about blacks but, he added, "always from the prejudiced point of view." Booker T. Washington agreed. "I think I have read with some care almost everything that Mr. Stone has printed" on blacks, Washington said, "and without exception there has been but one conclusion to his investigations . . . to damn the Negro." W. E. B. Du Bois had little patience with Stone's repeated attacks on blacks as innately lazy, careless, thriftless, and unproductive workers and with his predictions that they would be replaced by white workers. Writing in 1906, Du Bois informed Stone, "I hope you will have the moral courage, which is so fearfully lacking in the white South, to tell the truth & not to distort it against a helpless people." A decade later Du Bois mocked Stone publicly as a deluded and failed prophet in *The Crisis*, the journal of the National Association for the Advancement of Colored People. For his part, Stone considered Du Bois too pessimistic, too bitter, too prone to moralize. They held mirror images of each other.[4]

Stone is an intriguing historical subject because he wove his determination to maintain racial control over African Americans into his considerable body of serious scholarship on African American history, economics, and sociology. Stone studied race relations in the early-twentieth-century South determined to provide a solution to the contemporary "Negro problem," but also to understand his region's past and to predict its future. "It seems almost as impossible," Stone wrote in 1904, "for men to agree upon the purely historical aspects of the negro's life as it is to reach a common ground upon the more speculative question of his future status as an American citizen." Priding himself as one of "those who know the South of the present as well as the South of the past," Stone looked for clues to past and present racial problems by conducting experiments with the organization and management of black labor at Dunleith—his family's Mississippi Delta cotton plantation near Greenville. Adept at analyzing population and demographic statistics and economic productivity data, Stone also claimed to "have read everything [Booker T.] Washington has yet written on the negro" and concluded that "he has yet a very great deal to learn, not only about the so-called negro problem, but about the actual condition of his own people." Stone is important because, in the name of "scientific" inquiry, he defended southern traditions, espoused conservative ideas on race, and ultimately drew direful conclusions about the future of blacks in southern agriculture and in American life. This chapter addresses these three components of Stone's racial thought.[5]

Stone is also interesting because though untrained in history, economics, or the social sciences, he became an influential member of the leading professional associations of American historians, economists, and sociologists. Stone did so at a time when the lines were blurred between amateur and professional scholars—before the "professionalization" of academe became complete and when lay scholars competed head-to-head with professors for notoriety. Taking note of this in 1916, Du Bois joked, perhaps jealously, that Stone had "quite captured the American Economic Association and other organizations of the kind." Du Bois deeply resented the fact that in 1906 the Carnegie Institution of Washington entrusted Stone, a white racist from the Mississippi Delta, and not him, with funds to support a major research project on African American history.[6]

Stone obviously was well connected in the North while Du Bois stood marginalized, laboring under the veil of racism in Atlanta. The project that so chagrined Du Bois was Stone's proposed documentary history, "The Negro in Slavery and Freedom," for which the Mississippian scoured the country searching for archival materials "which will throw the least light upon the economic side of the institution of slavery." While Du Bois struggled to secure funding for his research and conferences at debt-ridden Atlanta University, Stone engaged professionally and socially with such influential scholars as historian Ulrich Bonnell Phillips, economist Walter Willcox, and German anthropologist Felix von Luschan. Lacking academic credentials, Stone nevertheless lectured at various universities and presented papers at professional conferences. According to historian Merton L. Dillon, Stone "wrote on southern topics with authority virtually as great as Phillips himself."[7]

Stone lived a long and successful life. Born in New Orleans in 1870, the grandson of a delegate to Mississippi's secession convention and the son of a Confederate officer, Stone recalled that for the first sixteen years of his life he "lived on a plantation," where he "began early in life to take a deep interest in the study of the Negro race." He grew to manhood surrounded by former Confederates who condemned the alleged injustices of carpetbaggers and scalawags during Reconstruction, worshiped southern white women, feared armed blacks, and savored the South's "redemption" after 1876. Yet Stone refused to blame African Americans for the alleged excesses of "bayonet rule." "In the main," he wrote, "the negro was simply the hopeless dupe and tool of both the Carpetbagger and the Scalawag." Stone, for example, fondly recalled "Uncle Jim Weaver," "old, but erect, and of superb dignity and commanding presence. He was jet black. His hair and beard were full and snow white. Like hundreds of his kind throughout the South, he was more, much more, than a faithful servant. He was our companion and friend."[8]

Stone earned a law degree in 1891 from the University of Mississippi, practiced law briefly, and then began planting cotton in the Delta. His duties as a planter, Stone wrote, "brought him into close practical relations with the Negro race." These experiences convinced him to write "a history of that race upon an exhaustive scale." From 1900 to 1901 he edited the *Greenville (Mississippi) Times*. In order to conduct research on African Americans, from 1903 to 1910, Stone relocated to Washington, DC, where, he remembered, "I was constantly associated with the activities of the various American learned societies, in the field of history, economics, political science and sociology." A founder in 1921 of the Staple Cotton Cooperative Association, he served for thirty-four years as the organization's vice president and edited its journal, the *Staple Cotton Review*. In 1912 the Mississippi Historical Society selected Stone as its president, and from 1916 to 1923 he represented Washington County in the Mississippi legislature. In 1932, Mississippians elected Stone tax commissioner and chairman of their State Tax Commission, a position he held until his death in 1955.[9]

Though a son of the New South, Stone looked back to the Old South nostalgically and affectionately. Like his friend Ulrich Bonnell Phillips, he remained an unabashed apologist for slavery. Stone never addressed the morality of slavery, stating merely that the "peculiar institution" was, at its core, simply an economic system. For example, he asserted that "both biblical and secular history are replete with testimony to the magnificent achievements of nations whose glorious epochs were those during which slavery flourished." His first scholarly article, published in 1899, dealt with Mississippi's slave laws. According to Stone, the existence of such benevolent laws proved that slavery was a humane system. Slave owners provided blacks with food, shelter, clothing, and medical care. They converted their African slaves to Christianity. Slavery was, in fact, beneficial for African Americans. It "transformed the savage negro into a civilized man; it taught him to work, and showed him what could be accomplished by the labor of his hands." Slavery in the American South, Stone wrote, was an inefficient economic system, but only because the slaves were naturally idle and intellectually inferior to white laborers.[10]

Stone disagreed with arguments that slavery had lingering negative effects on African Americans and on poor whites. The "peculiar institution" actually benefited race relations in the New South, he said, because it simplified contact between the races and minimized the inevitable "race friction" that resulted when two dissimilar groups interacted. Writing in 1908 in the *American Journal of Sociology*, Stone explained that "the simpler the relations between diverse races, the less friction there will be; the more complex the relations, the greater the friction. . . . The accepted relation of superior and inferior may exist not only without bitterness on one side, or harsh feelings upon the other, but it may be characterized by a sentiment and affection wholly impossible between the same groups under conditions demanding a recognition of so-called equality." Addressing the Mississippi Historical Society in 1914, Stone asserted that "the most fallacious assertion ever made concerning the influence of slavery and the presence of the Negro is that they engendered in white people a feeling of contempt for manual labor. The truth is that the effect has been to develop a racial solidarity which makes every white man feel absolutely sure of a certain status and a certain recognition simply because he is white."[11]

Good race relations in the South, to Stone's eye, resulted from the rigid hierarchal system established under slavery. Outbreaks of racial antipathy, he said, "will be fewer and milder when one race accepts the position of inferiority outwardly, or really feels the superiority of the other." Areas such as Stone's native Yazoo-Mississippi Delta, in which the inflexible racial hierarchy of slavery times still reigned, exhibited the best race relations. "Nowhere else is the line marking the social separation of the two races more rigidly drawn, nowhere are the relations between the two more kindly." Stone acknowledged slavery's role in laying the foundation for harmonious race relations in the New South, circumstances he feared would deteriorate if slavery's memory faded.[12]

In 1903, for example, Stone tried to convince Du Bois of the virtues of his paternalistic relationship with the 300 African Americans who lived and worked at Dunleith. "I feel that I have their confidence," Stone explained, "and I never abuse it. They come to me with their domestic troubles, and I am called upon to prevent divorces, to make peace. . . . There is no particle of abuse there, either in field or office, and every man is free to go as he comes, and this they do, often to their injury and mine." Stone was proud that, much as in slavery times, he maintained elderly black "pensioners"—"our worthy friends"—on the plantation after they had completed their years of productive labor. Much like Old South planters,

Stone felt a sense of noblesse oblige to his black workers. "I would not drive the Negro out, nor molest him, nor interfere with him in the slightest degree," he wrote in 1914. "On the contrary, he needs and is entitled to the white man's encouragement and protection, for the white man brought him here against his will."[13]

Stone both identified with and defended the master class of slavery times. Contrary to postbellum stereotypes, he said, most Old South planters were harried businessmen, not aristocrats who reveled in idle luxuries. "As a class, they were the pioneer captains of industry in America, and, in the main, they worked hard, lived on credit and died in debt." Stone justified the right of the southern planter class to secede in 1861, arguing that the North's insistence that the South accept moral responsibility for the Civil War was shortsighted at best. "There could have been nothing more unhealthy or dangerous to the future of the country than to have had in the Southern states a mass of people servilely willing to regard the outcome of the war as a demonstration of the inherent unrighteousness of their conduct, glad to fawn upon their successful opponents, and willing to accept and wear without a protest the degrading brand of treason."[14]

Stone dismissed the Reconstruction years, 1865–1877, as "a travesty which forms the most forbidding chapter in American history"—"one of the greatest and most criminal legislative tragedies in the history of the English speaking world." He held a special animus for the Freedmen's Bureau. According to Stone, it destroyed "the whole course of former relations" between blacks and whites. When, for example, searching for sources on the economic history of black southerners, Stone solicited evidence to support his assumption that the modus operandi of the Freedmen's Bureau was to "swindle negroes and blackmail or 'hold up' planters."[15]

According to Stone, during Reconstruction, ignorant African Americans fell prey to unscrupulous Yankees and mulattoes who exploited their votes. The ballot was "forced . . . into the ex-slave's hand." Stone found it significant that blacks tended to vote en masse against their former masters—a point he considered indicative that carpetbaggers manipulated newly enfranchised and easily deceived black men. "He [the former slave] was made to believe that his only enemy was his former master, his only friend the conqueror. . . . He was made the spoiled pet of misdirected philanthropy—the ignorant tool of political hate." Such exploitation of the freedmen, Stone wrote, forced white southerners to bury their political differences and band together against black voters who represented "the disease which was eating at the very vitals of their [whites'] domestic life." When Reconstruction ended, Stone insisted, African Americans generally lost interest in politics and never regained it. He dismissed the "fanciful notion that tens of thousands of qualified Negroes are illegally kept from the polls." Most black southerners simply had no desire to vote.[16]

Though Stone considered himself an unbiased, dispassionate student of race relations, even by the standards of his day he was a racist, a paternalist, and a white supremacist. In his writings Stone repeated almost verbatim the litany of antiblack racial stereotypes of the Reconstruction Era, convinced that the race was culturally and genetically inferior to Caucasians. In 1903 he remarked that though "the Negro is one of the oldest races of which we have any knowledge, . . . its very failure to develop itself in its own habitat, while the Caucasian, Mongolian, and others have gone forward, is in itself sufficient proof of inferiority."[17]

He judged persons of African descent to be inherently lazy, unreliable, and thriftless, crediting them with an instinctive love of finery and disrespect for authority. In 1904 he wrote candidly "that the negro is a negro, and not a black-skinned white man; that as such he possesses certain racial traits and tendencies, as much deserving of study, as if he is to be wisely helped." Average blacks, according to Stone, were less likely to adopt businesslike farming practices because they were less intelligent than whites. The African American possessed little concept of political or personal integrity, Stone said, and would "sell himself body and soul to any political charlatan who will stoop low enough to fill his ears with false promises and to inspire him with racial hate." Blacks even lacked personal integrity in their relations with each other, Stone argued. "The marriage contract possesses for them little, if any, sanctity." Stone also dismissed blacks' mental capabilities, asserting that "the Negro in the mass is still a child, and for some generations to come may so remain." African Americans, Stone averred, were a burden on any society. "No country, no state, no community on the civilized globe has ever realized the full measure of its advance toward real peace, prosperity, and happiness in the face of a preponderating or even relatively heavy Negro element in its population."[18]

Though prone to write about "the Negro in the mass," as early as 1903, Stone differentiated between what he termed mulattoes and "real Negroes"—a distinction that Booker T. Washington and Du Bois, both light skinned, considered to be insidious. According to Stone, their Anglo-Saxon "blood" rendered mulattoes more intelligent, capable, and ambitious, but also more devious and likely to commit violent acts, than "real Negroes." Despite contemporary usage, Stone asserted, "the mulatto is not a Negro, and neither written nor social law can make him one." "Real Negroes"—whom he judged to be docile, carefree, and intellectually inferior to mulattoes—descended primarily from West Africans. They, however, were not to be confused with descendants of North Africans, especially the Hausa and Fulah of Sudan, and people from Madagascar, "who were not docile or cheerful, who were not blessed with short memories for wrongs, who were not happy even when well-fed." Stone worried that northerners would generalize about African Americans, confusing the accomplishments of some mixed-race individuals with those of African Americans en masse.[19]

Stone, however, confident that his plantation background and management experiences rendered him an expert on racial issues, generalized freely on African Americans. He considered them naturally childlike but not without redeeming qualities. They were capable of great physical activity. They were naturally happy. And, as a result of their alleged undeveloped mental state, they were highly adaptable. Although blacks often were unfaithful to one another, they were capable of great devotion to whites. Stone agreed with other postbellum proslavery authors who theorized that the racial traits of blacks made them ideal slaves. Writing in *The South in the Building of the Nation* (1909), for example, he argued that blacks were "a mass of people possessing racial characteristics which enabled it to submit to slavery with a maximum degree of cheerfulness, and without the chafing of other races under restraint." The African American, he explained, was "docile, tractable, and obedient to command," but also "abundantly able, physically, to provide from the soil a return for his own labor and upon the investment of its owner."[20]

In "The Negro in the Mississippi Yazoo Delta" (1902), Stone praised postwar blacks' capacity for manual labor and sought to entice more African American workers to the Delta, promising conscientious blacks independence and advancement. According to Stone, African Americans had a clearly defined, if subservient, role in society that they could play and play well. "It is inevitable," Stone wrote, "that there must always be a large class of Negro tillers of other men's soil." But Stone acknowledged that many African Americans also filled "places of responsibility and trust" in the southern rural economy—as foremen, engineers, and submanagers of cotton gins. Others plied as constables, mailmen, telephone linemen, and merchants. In 1914 he was careful to note that free blacks in the antebellum South, far from being uniformly lazy and idle, "were engaged in all forms of occupation and business, from manual labor up to bridge and shipbuilding, contracting, merchandising, and planting." Stone complained that the major problem with black workers, however, was getting enough of them to labor consistently, efficiently, and reliably.[21]

In 1899, determined to maximize the productivity of his black workers, Stone began a plantation experiment at Dunleith designed to establish a permanent, nontransient black labor force. Stone asserted that most planters were too lenient with their black workers and failed to operate their plantations according to proper business procedures. Consequently planters faced high annual turnover rates among their workers. In contrast, Stone attempted to run Dunleith on a strictly business basis. He hoped to turn a profit by banking on "ties of self-interest" between himself and his black work force.[22]

Organizing his laborers as farm tenants, not sharecroppers, Stone rented them acreage at a fixed fee and offered them what he considered comfortable housing, ample opportunities to acquire livestock, and fair terms when it came to selling crops. He refused to advance loans for travel and other frivolous expenses or to grant tenants the "Christmas money" that planters traditionally gave to their hands. In lieu of cash for incidentals, he provided his tenants with coupons that could only be exchanged for necessary foodstuffs. The contracts signed by Stone and his tenants gave Stone total control over plantation affairs. Stone's managers supervised the planting, cultivating, harvesting, and sale of the crop. "The problem before us," Stone wrote, "was to place in the hands of these people the means of acquiring something for themselves, and then, in every instance of deficient individual initiative, by proper supervision make them acquire it."[23]

By 1905, Stone deemed his plantation experiment an utter failure. The amount of cotton produced at Dunleith decreased during the six-year period. Moreover, his renters did not repay Stone's "generous" terms with the loyalty that he had hoped would develop. Though many of the black families profited financially from the labor arrangement, between 22 and 44 percent of them nonetheless left at the close of each season. Stone attributed his tenants' departure not to rational decision making but to their resistance to supervision by whites, to their disloyalty, and to what he considered their seemingly instinctive urge to "migrate." "We demonstrated our ability to make independent, property-owning families out of poverty-stricken material," Stone wrote bitterly. "These families in turn demonstrated . . . their independence by severing relations with us almost as promptly as we put them on their feet."[24] Stone concluded that sharecroppers made better, less independent workers than farm tenants, who placed their profits and freedom over loyalty to their employer. Accordingly, Stone replaced his tenants with sharecroppers, increased their supervision by white overseers, reduced the size of their plots, and discouraged them from buying their own tools and livestock. He reasoned that workers who remained dependent on landlords for supplies would be less mobile and hence more valuable as producers of the South's cash crops.

Discouraged by his failed plantation experiment at Dunleith and disappointed in blacks as workers, in 1905 Stone promoted another scheme—the substitution of black southerners with Italian laborers—that he hoped would reduce his region's dependence on African American agricultural workers. Italian immigrants, Stone assumed, would be more docile and tractable than American blacks. They also would be thrifty, loyal, ambitious, and hardworking—qualities that Stone found wanting in African Americans. Italians would save for the future, Stone predicted, and would remain on one plantation for years, unlike the mobile black tenants of the Mississippi Delta.[25]

Further, Stone noted approvingly, Italian men would remove their wives and daughters from fieldwork as soon as it was financially feasible. "No large class of our population," he explained, "can make substantial social progress as long as its women and children are compelled to play the role of breadwinners in the field of manual labour." Though Stone reiterated his faith in Italian cotton growers for several years, by 1909 he had abandoned this campaign. Years later Du Bois quipped that Stone "tried to substitute Italians on his own plantations, until they became too handy with the knife." Disappointed with both African Americans and Italians, by 1910 Stone reluctantly accepted the inevitability of black labor. "In so far as the Negro's part in the future of southern agriculture is concerned," he wrote, "whatever it is destined to be, it is linked with the future of cotton."[26]

Stone's negative experiences renting to blacks at Dunleith supported the findings of his "scientific" research on African Americans. Repeatedly he concluded that African Americans could not compete equally with white laborers in a free market economy. In 1906, for example, in the *Publications of the American Economic Association*, Stone asserted that blacks as a race had lost economic ground since 1865 and that any perceived gains resulted from the benevolence of whites and the natural increase of the black population. "It is inconceivable," he explained, "that any people who could increase in numbers from four and one half millions in 1860 to nine millions in 1900 could fail to also increase their property during that period." Blacks were losing jobs to European immigrants in northern and southern cities. White immigrants, with their habits of thrift and industry, increasingly displaced African Americans from their traditional jobs as skilled laborers and personal servants. Stone attributed this to black incompetence rather than to white prejudice. "I can hardly believe that any considerable body of labouring men, regardless of colour or race, anywhere have ever been successfully and permanently deprived of their opportunities by any other body of men, unless the latter proved themselves the more competent to do the work desired by the two."[27]

Like Booker T. Washington, Stone believed that the blacks' best hope to improve themselves economically was by staying in the South, not migrating to the North. Stone argued that working-class white southerners, unlike their northern counterparts, did not feel threatened by competition from black laborers. This, Stone said, was a legacy of slavery. Not only had whites become accustomed to black labor, under slavery they also had established a strict, inviolable racial hierarchy. Economic equality was possible in the South, Stone explained, precisely because the possibility of social equality was not. "The white mason and carpenter work side by side with the negro because they know that that [color] line exists for them just exactly as it does for the lawyer or doctor. The negro recognizes that the white man is not lowered one particle in the estimation of the community because of his occupation. Each knows that the status of the other remains unchanged—the negro is still a negro, the white man still a white man." Despite the economic niche that white paternalism created for blacks in the Jim Crow era, Stone warned that unless blacks changed their ways and became industrious, reliable, and frugal, European immigrants would replace them as laborers. "In its last analysis, it will be his own, not the white man's hand, that closes in the negro's face the door of economic hope."[28]

Stone had no problem, however, with whites slamming the door shut on African Americans' social and political rights. In the first place, he doubted that most black southerners sought social or political equality with whites. The "real Negro," Stone assured readers, was not genuinely interested in social equality. "He infinitely prefers the freedom and privileges of a [railroad] car of his own to the restraint of one in which he would be compelled to mingle with white people."[29] Stone suspected that demands for black civil rights came not from the "real" African American community, but rather were concocted by white northerners and mulattoes.

Southerners also were justified, Stone said, to pass Jim Crow laws and employ poll taxes and other devices to keep blacks segregated and disfranchised. Black men unable or unwilling to save enough money to pay the poll tax, Stone argued, obviously were too shiftless and too irresponsible to deserve the vote. Free blacks, both before and after emancipation, he said, "drifted" from place to place. Further, Stone explained, no nation in world history had enfranchised blacks without incurring troubling consequences. He cited South Africa, Cuba, and Jamaica as examples of nations that mistakenly had allowed blacks to participate in politics. Stone dismissed those Caribbean republics where blacks served in government, declaring that "the artificial travesties erected upon the bloodstained ruins of white civilization in Haiti and Santo Domingo . . . will sometime disappear in a night, when the American white man wants another island for some real or fancied use."[30]

Though Stone published fewer articles on race relations after he entered Mississippi state politics in the World War I years, he nonetheless remained totally committed to paternalism as a means of maintaining white racial control. In 1915, for example, in "The Responsibility of the Southern White Man to the Negro," Stone remarked that southern whites had a responsibility to blacks, "a primitive people, taken from a state of lowest barbarism and suddenly transplanted to an environment possibly some thousands of years normally in advance of their own." He underscored the importance of whites serving as role models for African Americans. Too often, Stone alleged, lower-class whites encouraged blacks' negative behavior. "There is not a negro dive, a crap joint or a 'blind tiger' in any county in the South which does not exist through either the connivance or indifference of the white man."[31]

Stone's concern for African Americans, however, always stemmed from his ingrained fear of social and economic change, not from altruism toward blacks. Sober, law-abiding industrious black workers should be encouraged, Stone maintained, because white southerners lived surrounded by blacks and depended upon them for their livelihoods. As a result, Stone explained, "it is for us [southern whites] to say whether we shall drop the burden, let the Negro drift with his own current, increase in criminality, grow in idleness, and finally develop into an incubus too heavy to carry." Stone thus implored whites to establish relationships with leaders in the black community, to promote industrial education for blacks, and to lead by moral example. The latter was particularly important, he said, because "the negro is an imitative creature, or we may say that his race is in its imitative stage. It is human nature for the negro to seek justification for his own shortcomings in the conduct of some member of the race which he is taught to regard as his superior example."[32]

Stone's brand of racial paternalism dominated southern folkways and state ways into the 1940s and beyond, but following World War II it increasingly came under intense fire. Looking back in southern history, he nonetheless continued to defend segregation and disfranchisement both on the principles of states' rights and black inferiority. "The negroes have not asked for the privilege of voting," Stone asserted in 1948, and "the vast majority of them have no idea what it means." He defended the poll tax because "it [the Fifteenth Amendment] does not say that a negro must be allowed to vote because he is a negro. It simply says that he cannot be prevented from voting on that account." Though literacy tests and poll taxes had the practical effect of disfranchising blacks, Stone insisted that these devices did not explicitly deny blacks the vote on account of race. His 1944 article, "The Basis of White Political Control in Mississippi," states that "the negro can ultimately meet any qualifications which the white man is willing to erect and accept for himself."[33]

For Stone, post–World War II federal civil rights legislation was as nightmarish as the federal amendments and civil rights acts of the Reconstruction era had been for his ancestors. He considered the recommendations of President Harry S. Truman's Committee on Civil Rights "more drastic in substance and more potentially dangerous in consequences than anything attempted in this country since the Reconstruction period of our history." Stone also looked with disdain on "the generally understood New Deal objective of wiping out all color line differences and distinctions." He predicted that just as white southerners circumvented the laws imposed by northern carpetbaggers and former slaves during Reconstruction, they would prevail once again against the federal government's trampling upon their rights. "There is no instance in history," Stone wrote, "in which any considerable group of English speaking people has ever been successfully compelled to submit to the imposition upon them, of any action, purpose, custom or law which ran counter to their own beliefs, convictions and will." History, he prophesied, would repeat itself.[34] White southerners did resist integration, and in this respect at least, Stone was right. But ultimately southern segregationists succumbed to federal authority. History *did* repeat itself.

Like his slaveholding Confederate forebears, Stone never lived to see the fruits of de jure racial integration—what they would have considered to be a blight on the southern racial landscape. Stone's day-to-day management of an isolated Mississippi cotton plantation, on which he was surrounded by blacks, and his avocation as a "scientific" economic historian and sociologist, reinforced his deeply embedded white supremacist ideology premised on paternalism. "Certainly," Stone wrote in *Studies in the American Race Problem*, "the relation of master and slave no longer exists here, but out of it has been evolved that of patron and retainer. I so designate it because I know of no other to which it more nearly approaches. It is not at all one purely of business, the ordinary relation of landlord and tenant, or of employer and employee." A decade later Ulrich Bonnell Phillips, when analyzing plantation paternalism, concluded similarly that "it was less a business than a life; it made fewer fortunes than it made men."[35] Phillips, however, was romanticizing about chattel slavery. Stone longed for the simpler racial dynamic of servitude on Dunleith in the twentieth century.

The human dimension, the relationship between "patron" and "retainer" that Stone analyzed, celebrated, and yearned for, was the most insidious element of the conservatives' racial thought. Stone and his fellow southern white elites believed that they understood what blacks wanted and what they needed. Defining African Americans partly as children, partly as prisoners, whites considered it their natural right to control ("guide") and exploit blacks. "In many respects," Stone admitted, "the Negro is a model prisoner—the best in this country. He accepts the situation—generally speaking—bears no malice, cherishes no ill will or resentment, and is cheerful under conditions to which the white man refuses to reconcile himself."[36] Just how well did Stone know "Uncle Jim Weaver"? And how many masks did "Uncle Jim" wear?

Racial conservatives like Stone, as Du Bois and other critics complained repeatedly, generally were clueless about the lives and labors, the hopes and dreams, of African Americans. Some blacks were criminals, to be sure, but most African Americans led honest and decent lives. Blacks were efficient laborers, they were not dying off, they saved money, and they wanted to own land—not to rent from or sharecrop for the likes of Alfred Holt Stone. African Americans craved equality—social and political equality, equal opportunity, and equal protection before the law. Blacks of Stone's day sought to be treated as freed men and women in word as well as in deed.

Camouflaging his racism under the guise of plantation paternalism and "scientific" historical, economic, and sociological analysis, Stone, like other racial conservatives, worked to control blacks socially and to exploit them economically. Seemingly oblivious to the racial violence that stained the turn-of-the-century South, Stone virtually ignored the various forms of physical and psychological intimidation whites employed to keep blacks a landless, impoverished "retainer" class. In his writings, Stone also omitted the roles of class, environment, and history in shaping black behavior and circumstance. And finally, as a planter-capitalist, it is impossible to omit from consideration Stone's economic self-interest—a factor that unquestionably shaped his historical and sociological analyses of African American rural laborers.

Always perceptive, Du Bois appreciated Stone's candor but grasped the venom of his regressive pessimism regarding American blacks. Stone's work, he wrote in 1908, was of negligible value, "except when it encourages those Philistines who really believe that Anglo-Saxons owe their preeminence in some lines to lynching, lying, and slavery, and the studied insult of their helpless neighbors. God save us from such social philosophy!"[37]

NOTES

Two of my former graduate students at North Carolina State University, Sharon Baggett and Stephen A. Ross, provided invaluable research assistance with the preparation of this essay. Jeffrey J. Crow generously critiqued a draft of the article.

1. Alfred Holt Stone to Booker T. Washington, July 2, 1903, in Louis R. Harlan, ed., *The Booker T. Washington Papers* (Urbana: University of Illinois Press, 1972–1989), 7:192; Alfred Holt Stone, "Some Recollections of a Southern Planter," chap. 1, p. 6, unpublished manuscript, c. 1938, Mississippi Department of Archives and History, Jackson (hereafter cited as MDAH).

2. Joel Williamson, *The Crucible of Race: Black–White Relations in the American South Since Emancipation* (New York: Oxford University Press, 1984), 6; David Levering Lewis, *W. E. B. Du Bois: Biography of a Race* (New York: Henry Holt, 1993), 367.

3. Charles Francis Adams to W. E. B. Du Bois, November 28, 1908, in Herbert Aptheker, ed., *The Correspondence of W. E. B. Du Bois* (Amherst: University of Massachusetts Press, 1973–1978), 1:143; Theodore D. Jervey to Ulrich Bonnell Phillips, February 13, 1909, Theodore D. Jervey Papers, South Carolina Historical Society, Charleston; J. Franklin Jameson to Edward B. Krehbiel, January 14, 1913, in Elizabeth Donnan and Leo F. Stock, eds., *An Historian's World: Selections from the Correspondence of John Franklin Jameson* (Philadelphia: American Philosophical Society, 1956), 154; Thomas Pearce Bailey, *Race Orthodoxy in the South and Other Aspects of the Negro Question* (New York: Neale, 1914), 29–30; John Spencer Bassett, review of Alfred Holt Stone, *Studies in the American Race Problem*, in *American Historical Review* 14 (1909): 837.

4. T. J. Jones, review of Alfred Holt Stone, *Studies in the American Race Problem*, in *Southern Workman* 38 (1909): 52; Oswald Garrison Villard to Robert S. Woodward, March 20, 1907, Carnegie Institution of Washington Archives, Washington, DC; Booker T. Washington to Carroll D. Wright, March 26, 1907, Oswald Garrison Villard Papers, Harvard University; W. E. B. Du Bois response to Alfred Holt Stone, n.d., inscribed on reverse of Stone to Du Bois, June 23, 1906, W. E. B. Du Bois Papers, microfilm, University of Massachusetts, Amherst (hereafter cited as Du Bois Papers); [W. E. B. Du Bois], "Stone," *The Crisis* 11 (1916): 243; Alfred Holt Stone, review of W. E. B. Du Bois, *The Souls of Black Folk*, in *Publications of the Southern History Association* 7 (1903): 395–96.

5. Alfred Holt Stone, "Some Recent Race Problem Literature," *Publications of the Southern History Association* 8 (1904): 458; Alfred Holt Stone, review of Ulrich Bonnell Phillips, ed., *Plantation and Frontier*, in *American Historical Review* 16 (1910): 139; Alfred Holt Stone to Walter F. Willcox, October 26, 1901, Walter F. Willcox Papers, Manuscript Division, Library of Congress, Washington, DC.

6. [Du Bois], "Stone," 243; W. E. B. Du Bois, *The Autobiography of W. E .B. Du Bois* (New York: International, 1968), 225.

7. Alfred Holt Stone to William E. Dodd, July 10, 1907, William E. Dodd Papers, Manuscript Division, Library of Congress; Carroll D. Wright, "Report of the Director of the Department," *Carnegie Institution of Washington Year Book no. 5, 1906* (Washington, DC: Carnegie Institution, 1907), 158; Merton L. Dillon, *Ulrich Bonnell Phillips: Historian of the Old South* (Baton Rouge: Louisiana State University Press, 1985), 62–74; Mark Aldrich, "Progressive Economists and Scientific Racism: Walter Willcox and Black Americans, 1895–1910," *Phylon* 40 (1979): 9; William Darity Jr., "Many Roads to Extinction: Early AEA Economists and the Black Disappearance Hypothesis," *History of Economics Review* 21 (1994): 47, 55; Felix von Luschan to Charles B. Davenport, April 5, 1915, Charles B. Davenport Papers, American Philosophical Society, Philadelphia; Merton L. Dillon, "Ulrich B. Phillips: An Assessment of an Historian's Debts" (paper presented at the Annual Meeting of the Southern Historical Association, 1982), 8 (copy in possession of the author).

8. James B. Lloyd, ed., *Lives of Mississippi Authors, 1817–1967* (Jackson: University Press of Mississippi, 1981), 422–23; "Alfred Stone, Veteran Tax Official, Dies,"

State Times, May 12, 1955, unidentified clipping, MDAH; Frank E. Smith, "Alfred Holt Stone," *Journal of Mississippi History* 17 (1955): 289–92; [Alfred Holt Stone], "Alfred Holt Stone," typescript autobiographical sketch, n.d., p. 1, Works Progress Administration biographies, MDAH; Stone, "Some Recollections of a Southern Planter," chap. 2, p. 9; chap. 1, pp. 5–6.

9. [Stone], "Alfred Holt Stone," 1; Stone, "Some Recollections of a Southern Planter," chap. 1, p. 8.

10. Alfred Holt Stone, "The Early Slave Laws of Mississippi," *Publications of the Mississippi Historical Society* 2 (1899): 133; Alfred Holt Stone, "The Negro in the South," in Julian A. C. Chandler et al., eds., *The South in the Building of the Nation* (Richmond: Southern Historical Publication Society, 1909), 10:177–78; Alfred Holt Stone, "Some Problems of Southern Economic History," *American Historical Review* 13 (1908): 779–97.

11. Alfred Holt Stone, "Is Race Friction between Blacks and Whites in the United States Growing and Inevitable?" *American Journal of Sociology* 13 (1908): 684; Alfred Holt Stone, "Fact and Tradition in Southern History," 4, unpublished paper, January 9, 1914, John Lipscomb Johnson Papers, Southern Historical Collection, University of North Carolina at Chapel Hill.

12. Stone, "Is Race Friction between Blacks and Whites in the United States Growing and Inevitable?" 681; Alfred Holt Stone, "The Negro in the Yazoo-Mississippi Delta," *Publications of the American Economic Association*, 3d ser., 3 (1902): 239.

13. Stone to Du Bois, July 18, 1903, Du Bois Papers, microfilm; Stone, "Fact and Tradition in Southern History," *Journal of Mississippi History* 17 (1955): 15–16 (hereafter cited as "Fact and Tradition in Southern History," *Journal of Mississippi History*).

14. Alfred Holt Stone, "The Negro and Agricultural Development," *Annals of the American Academy of Political and Social Science* 35 (1910): 12; Alfred Holt Stone, "The South in National Politics, 1865–1909," in *The South in the Building of the Nation*, 4:555.

15. Alfred Holt Stone, "The Responsibility of the Southern White Man to the Negro," in *Lectures and Addresses on the Negro in the South* (Charlottesville: Michie Company, 1915), 5; Alfred Holt Stone, "A Mississippian's View of Civil Rights, States Rights, and the Reconstruction Background," *Journal of Mississippi History* 10 (1948): 187; Stone, "Some Recent Race Problem Literature," 457; Alfred Holt Stone, *Material Wanted for an Economic History of the Negro* (Washington, DC: n.p., n.d.), 13.

16. Stone, "Mississippi's Constitution and Statutes in Reference to Freedmen, and Their Alleged Relation to the Reconstruction Acts and War Amendments," *Publications of the Mississippi Historical Society* 4 (1901): 159, 175–76; Alfred Holt Stone, *Studies in the American Race Problem* (New York: Doubleday, Page, 1908), 387, 357.

17. Alfred Holt Stone, "The Mulatto Factor in the Race Problem," *Atlantic Monthly* 91 (1903): 659.

18. Alfred Holt Stone, review of Carl Kelsey, *The Negro Farmer*, in *Publications of the Southern History Association* 8 (1904): 239; Stone, *Studies in the American Race Problem*, 368, 108, 359; Stone, "Fact and Tradition in Southern History," *Journal of Mississippi History*, 15.

19. Stone, *Studies in the American Race Problem*, 427, 428, 432, 398; Stone, "The Negro in the South," 170.

20. Stone, *Studies in the American Race Problem*, 235, 431; Stone, "The Negro in the South," 170; Stone, "Mississippi's Constitution and Statutes in Reference to Freedmen," 164.

21. Stone, "The Negro in the Yazoo-Mississippi Delta," 260, 262; Stone, "Fact and Tradition in Southern History," *Journal of Mississippi History*, 7.

22. Alfred Holt Stone, "A Plantation Experiment," *Quarterly Journal of Economics* 19 (1905): 272.

23. Stone, "A Plantation Experiment," 272.

24. Stone, "A Plantation Experiment," 274.

25. Alfred Holt Stone, "The Italian Cotton Grower: The Negro's Problem," *South Atlantic Quarterly* 4 (1905): 42–47.

26. Stone, *Studies in the American Race Problem*, 187; Du Bois, *The Autobiography of W. E. B. Du Bois*, 225; Stone, "The Negro and Agricultural Development," 10.

27. Alfred Holt Stone, "The Economic Future of the Negro: The Factor of White Competition," *Publications of the American Economic Association*, 3d ser., 7 (1906): 246; Stone, *Studies in the American Race Problem*, 163–64.

28. Stone, "Economic Future of the Negro," 257, 289.

29. Stone, "Mulatto Factor in the Race Problem," 660.

30. Alfred Holt Stone, "Status of the Free Negroes in Virginia Prior to 1861," 14, manuscript, n.d., Alfred Holt Stone Papers, University of Mississippi; Stone, *Studies in the American Race Problem*, 332.

31. Stone, "Responsibility of the Southern White Man to the Negro," 5, 16.

32. Stone, "Responsibility of the Southern White Man to the Negro," 11, 16–18.

33. Alfred Holt Stone, "Post Bellum Reconstruction, an American Experience," *Journal of Mississippi History* 3 (1941): 227–46; Stone, "A Mississippian's View of Civil Rights," 181–239, 229; Stone, "Post Bellum Reconstruction as an American Experience," 235–36; Alfred Holt Stone, "The Basis of White Political Control in Mississippi," *Journal of Mississippi History* 6 (1944): 226.

34. Stone, "A Mississippian's View of Civil Rights," 183; Stone, "The Basis of White Political Control in Mississippi," 225; Stone, "A Mississippian's View of Civil Rights," 192.

35. Stone, *Studies in the American Race Problem*, 91; Ulrich Bonnell Phillips, *American Negro Slavery: A Survey of the Supply, Employment and Control of Negro Labor as Determined by the Plantation Régime* (New York: D. Appleton, 1918), 401.

36. Stone, *Studies in the American Race Problem*, 235.

37. W. E. B. Du Bois, "Discussion of the Paper by Alfred H. Stone, 'Is Race Friction between Blacks and Whites in the United States Growing and Inevitable?'" *American Journal of Sociology* 13 (1908): 838.

SUGGESTED READINGS

Stone published widely on race relations and southern history. A convenient collection of nine of his essays is Alfred Holt Stone, *Studies in the American Race Problem* (New York: Doubleday, Page, 1908). No biography of Stone exists, but see John David Smith, "Alfred Holt Stone: Mississippi Planter and Archivist/Historian of

Slavery," *Journal of Mississippi History* 45 (1983): 262–70; and John David Smith, *An Old Creed for the New South: Proslavery Ideology and Historiography, 1865–1918* (1985; Athens: University of Georgia Press, 1991). A number of scholars include Stone and his plantation experiments in their analyses of late-nineteenth- and early-twentieth-century Mississippi history and culture. These include Robert L. Brandfon, *Cotton Kingdom of the New South: A History of the Yazoo Mississippi Delta from Reconstruction to the Twentieth Century* (Cambridge, MA: Harvard University Press, 1967); Neil R. McMillen, *Dark Journey: Black Mississippians in the Age of Jim Crow* (Urbana: University of Illinois Press, 1989); James C. Cobb, *The Most Southern Place on Earth: The Mississippi Delta and the Roots of Regional Identity* (New York: Oxford University Press, 1992); John C. Willis, *Forgotten Time: The Yazoo-Mississippi Delta after the Civil War* (Charlottesville: University Press of Virginia, 2000); and J. William Harris, *Deep Souths: Delta, Piedmont, and Sea Island Society in the Age of Segregation* (Baltimore: Johns Hopkins University Press, 2001). For a laudatory obituary that judged Stone the "stalwart champion of all that was conducive to the best interests of this section and our state," see *Jackson (Mississippi) Daily News*, May 12, 1955, reprinted in *Staple Cotton Review* 33 (1955): 1–3. To memorialize Stone, the *Staple Cotton Review* dedicated an entire issue in 1956 (vol. 34) to "Civil Rights and States' Rights," reprinting texts that celebrated states' rights, condemned Reconstruction, and criticized federal antilynching legislation.

5

Hester Calvert: Farm Wife

Rebecca Sharpless

Winnie Davis represented the well-educated, cultured, elite southern woman of the later years of the nineteenth century; Hester Calvert symbolized the more typical southern woman of that century and the first part of the next.

By contrast, Calvert's life included little formal education, marriage, frequent motherhood, and poverty. Her family's record as sharecroppers or tenant farmers resulted in many moves and much hardship. By necessity, the Calverts grew most of what they ate and made much of what they wore. About the only relief from the hot, demanding work in the cotton fields and the house came from Sunday church and visits afterward or occasional trips to a nearby town. But, in the end, her life proved both difficult and rewarding. The family tasted more success as time passed. A house with electricity seemed a godsend.

Hester Calvert lived as millions did in her time. Their stories usually remain untold or even forgotten, except by a few. Yet, in the end, their lives tell us just as much about the South, its people, and their outlooks as do accounts of the elite, like Davis or Alfred Holt Stone. For the history of Hester Calvert gives voice to the voiceless and shows the strength of the human spirit under adversity. Author Elizabeth Madox Roberts, in her Time of Man *(1926) called such people ones who constantly had "hopes ever defeated and ever renewed." Their lives, she wrote, reveal to us "the glory in the commonplace."*

Rebecca Sharpless is the director of the Institute for Oral History and senior lecturer in the department of history at Baylor University. She is the author of Fertile Ground, Narrow Choices: Women on Texas Cotton Farms, 1900–1940 *(1999) and coauthor of* Rock Beneath the Sand: Texas Country Churches *(2003).*

A husband, eight children, and the rhythms of cotton farming: these are the factors that shaped the life of Hester McClain Calvert. Daughter, wife, and sister of cotton farmers, Hester represents millions of southern women at the turn of the twentieth century who led their lives in relationship to their families and rarely had existences away from the farm. But these women are important because their families depended on them. A rural household without a wife and mother had a difficult, if not impossible, time.

In the story of Texas, the farm woman is an unsung heroine. The efforts of these women ensured that Texas led the United States in cotton production before World War II, growing one-third to one-fourth of the raw cotton for the entire nation. The mythic Texas is that of oil and cowboys, but it was agriculture that supplied most Texans with their living before World War II. Entire families worked hard to bring in the cotton crop, and the women labored in the fields as well as took care of their families' needs for food, clothing, and housing.

Cotton farming dominated much of the southern economy between the Civil War and World War II. The world wanted raw cotton from which to make cloth, and the southern climate and soil brought forth huge harvests to satisfy the demand. One writer declared cotton to be "one of the most important, if not the most important, articles of the world's commerce."[1] Most of the region's farm families, however, were poor. In Central Texas, for example, the majority of cotton farmers in 1900 did not own the land that they spent their lives working, and many did not even own the plows and mules that they used to break the ground. A large number of these tenant farmers and sharecroppers remained constantly indebted to the people who owned the land. Some lived in relative comfort, but most tenants and sharecroppers existed in various stages of deprivation, lacking suitable housing, clothing, and food for themselves and their numerous children. They almost never had any cash, and they lived on credit from year to year.

Until at least 1940, millions of men, women, and children in Texas and elsewhere in the South worked to bring in the cotton crop. Within this system, women played several crucial roles. A majority of Central Texas women not only worked in the fields but also raised vegetables to feed their household; they sewed their families' clothing so that they would not have to spend much money for those items and go further into debt to the landowner. And they bore the children who would be valuable agricultural laborers before they were even old enough to begin school. Farm women's lives were filled with hard work and not much pleasure, but most of them tried in good faith to meet their considerable responsibilities to their families.

Hester McClain Calvert is a good example of such a farm woman. She was born in Falls County, Texas, on December 6, 1878, and received a sixth-grade education in the Mooreville area. Despite a lack of formal schooling, she was an intelligent woman who remained an avid reader all her life. In 1904, at the then-advanced age of twenty-six, she married Robert L. Calvert, a farmer four years younger than she, who also lived in the Mooreville area. Both of their families had migrated to Texas from Mississippi after the Civil War. While Hester was born in Texas, Robert had been born back east and migrated as a child. When Hester and Robert were still children, Central Texas had been settled less than forty years. Although the Native Americans had been gone for at least thirty years, the rich prairie sod had been broken only recently, and life on the prairies beckoned to families such as the Calverts who were fleeing the destruction of the Civil War. They soon found, however, that their hopes were dashed, as little of the rich land was available for purchase, and they wound up working on land owned by other people. They, and most of their neighbors, were extremely poor, and no amount of hard work could remedy their situation. But young people such as Robert and Hester set forth bravely, believing that they could make a life for themselves and their children on a Texas cotton farm.

Like most farm women, Hester became a mother shortly after her marriage. Women in the rural South had virtually no access to birth control until the 1920s, and their families were consistently larger in number than those in other parts of the United States. Hester bore nine children, beginning with Myrtle in 1905, followed by Lillian in 1906, Thelma in 1908, Clark in 1910, Milas in 1911, Carlos in 1913, Royce in 1916, and Nadine in 1918. Clarence, born prematurely, died as a newborn in 1912. As she grew older and developed thyroid problems, pregnancy became harder for Hester. At the age of forty, she almost miscarried her daughter Nadine, and at the age of forty-five, she miscarried a tenth baby and nearly died from blood poisoning, more than fifteen years before the discovery of antibiotics. Throughout her difficult pregnancies, Hester remained on her feet. Her oldest daughter, Myrtle Calvert Dodd, remarked: "She couldn't stay in the bed. There was too many of us."[2]

Even with eight children, the Calvert household expanded to take in older relatives. The parents of Robert and Hester rotated among their adult children when they became too feeble to live alone. Growing too frail to farm, Robert's father, David Calvert, divided his farming tools among his sons. With his wife, Indiana, he left his farm in West Texas and returned to Central Texas. David and Indiana lived with Hester and Robert's family for the two years before David died in his late eighties. At that time, his wife, who was thirteen years younger, began circulating among her daughters' homes. Hester and her mother-in-law both worked hard at getting along despite the cramped quarters and the children bounding around them. Myrtle remembered, "Now, my grandmother knew to hold her tongue, but I've heard her say, 'If I's so-and-so, I wouldn't do so-and-so. I wouldn't let my younguns do so-and-so.' I've heard her say those things, but not to my mother. She knew when to say and when not to say. Very diplomatic." Hester's mother, Mary Adaline Strickland McClain, widowed years before, also rotated among her children. One grandparent often arrived shortly after the other had departed, making a congested household even more crowded.

Robert and Hester did not own land for the first twenty years of their marriage, and the family moved frequently. Sharecroppers and tenant farmers had little power within the economic system, but they often exercised their ability to change farms. The couple began their marriage on a farm near Lorena, in McLennan County. With their two oldest daughters, they followed his parents in 1908 to Jones County in West Texas, where cotton farming was opening up on the drier land. They remained there for two years, but, discouraged by a lack of rain, returned to Central Texas in 1910. Despite living next door to her in-laws, Hester missed her own family in Central Texas. Her widowed mother had bought a farm near the Woodlawn community near Bruceville, and two of Hester's brothers and sisters lived close by. When they came back, Hester was pleased to be among her people again.

With no land and few resources, the Calvert family continued to move for the next eighteen years across southern McLennan County. Their experiences show the range of situations available to a sharecropper or tenant farmer. They arrived back in Central Texas too late in the growing season of 1910 to find a suitable farm for the following year, and so they lived in a tiny house near Lorena owned by the Westbrooks, one of the wealthiest families in that part of Central Texas. Robert did odd jobs for the remainder of the crop year to support his family. The house on the Westbrook place was little more than an unpainted shack; Hester remained upset until her husband found screens to put on the windows to keep out flies and mosquitoes. Her daughter Myrtle recalled: "My mother just threw a fit when she saw that little house didn't have screens on it.... I can still remember when my mother said, 'Now listen, we're going to have screens. We can't live—my kids—with no screens.'" Like many of the houses in rural Texas, the Westbrook place had no electricity or running water; the family relied on kerosene lamps and brought water from a well.

The following year, they moved to the Attaway place near Hewitt, which had a large house, and remained there for two or three years. Robert then bought his own mules and tools and rose from the status of sharecropper to tenant farmer, and the family farmed for one year on the

McLaughlin place near Eddy. They next spent two years on the Connally farm at Long Branch, near Lorena, and then moved to the Stribling place at Hewitt, where they remained for five years, until 1921. The Stribling place was popular with the family, with its yellow paint, brown trim, carbide-burning electrical system, and indoor bathroom with a large tin bathtub. The Calverts fit eight children and two adults into three bedrooms: the two oldest girls in one, the parents and two youngest girls in the second one, and the four boys in the back room. When the Stribling farm came up for sale, the family urged Robert to buy it. He did not want to, however, declaring it not large enough. The Stribling farm passed to an outside buyer, and the family was forced to move once more.

To Hester's disappointment, they moved only a short distance to the Chapman place, which had more land but not as large or nice a house as the Stribling farm. The house on the Chapman place burned in the fall of 1927, with almost all of the Calverts' possessions. Neighbors donated food and furniture while the family lived in the basement of the vacant public school in Hewitt during the time that the Chapmans rebuilt the house. The next year, Robert and Hester bought a dairy farm near Bosqueville, five miles from Waco. They then moved to Waco, the county seat and a town of 56,000, in 1940, and Robert commuted to the dairy farm until his retirement in 1943.

With eight children, Hester spent almost all of her time meeting their needs. In this way, she was more fortunate than a number of women who had to balance child care with field work. Keeping a growing family supplied with proper food and clothing was more than a full-time job. Inevitably, some of the children became ill or injured, and she cared for them without the benefit of antibiotics or other medicines. To ward off colds, Hester made poultices of lard and turpentine or ammonia, pinning them to her children's undershirts. As the eight children grew up, bumps and bruises were common and were usually treated with kerosene. When one child brought an illness home, most of the others would contract it. For one entire winter, for example, measles passed from child to child in sequence. According to her daughter, Hester said, "I declare, we had measles up till spring!" The Calverts raised all of their children to adulthood except Clarence, who, as mentioned earlier, died shortly after his premature birth. In this way they fared better than many of their peers, who commonly lost at least one in every five children.

As did many of her counterparts, Hester sewed almost everything that she and her eight children wore. In the first years of her marriage, she borrowed sewing machines from her relatives but acquired her own upon the family's return to Central Texas in 1910. For her daughters, she made everything from flannel nightgowns to underwear to bloomers made of black sateen. The oldest ones handed down their clothing to the next ones.

Sometimes, Hester altered dresses for her daughters, making items over or dyeing them a different color. The boys wore store-bought denim overalls, but their mother sewed shirts and underwear. She even made costumes for her adolescent daughters to wear in a school program despite the fact that she considered the blue and green crinoline dresses far too skimpy for decency's sake. Hester also made items for the household, sewing sheets, pillowcases, and dishtowels from cotton yardgoods. From fabric scraps, she made two quilts per year, working in between daily tasks because the light was too dim at night for her to see her stitches. She kept geese and plucked their soft down feathers to fill pillows and mattresses.

Once it was made and worn, clothing had to be washed, and doing laundry was one of the heaviest, most unpleasant of farm women's tasks. At least once per year, the women cooked rancid lard, or rendered pork fat, with lye to make soap, boiling the lard in an open kettle over an open fire. They sometimes scented it with sweet-smelling spices. They poured the soft soap into pans and cut it into squares after it hardened. (Some of the poorest families even bathed with lye soap; others, like the Calverts, bought less harsh soap.) On washday, the women hauled water from a well or a creek to the yard of the house. They heated the water in a wash pot over an open flame and rubbed the clothes on a washboard. Each item then went through several tubs of rinse water. Men's heavy denim overalls, caked with mud and sweat from the cotton fields, were especially difficult to wash.

Like many Anglo women in Central Texas, Hester spent some of her family's hard-earned cash to hire help with the laundry. Across the region, African American women worked for low wages doing wash. When the Calverts lived on the Chapman place, an African American named Ada Richardson did their laundry, bringing her young son with her while she worked. Most women did their ironing with flat irons, or "sad irons," heated on the kitchen stove. Using the sad irons required some skill because the ironer could scorch the clean clothes or get soot on them from the stove. Most rural women did not have access to the electric irons that their city sisters enjoyed, and yearned for nicer possessions. As Myrtle said, "I didn't have things that I'd hear about. You know, I read the paper and read books, the [things] that they had. Of course, we all had the idea of going to town and having better things, and that's what most of us did."

Like virtually all southern farm women, Hester thought a great deal about meals for her family. The Calverts lived on the typical southern diet known as the three Ms: meat, meal, and molasses. The meat came mostly from hogs, which could be fed table scraps; it did not spoil as easily as beef or chicken. In every rural area, the men butchered hogs at the time of the first cold snap, using nature's refrigeration to keep the pork fresh. The women and children ground some of the meat and mixed it with salt, pepper, and sage, stuffing it into cloth casings or the butchered hog's intestines to make sausage.

Sausage casings were another of Hester's sewing tasks, made from wheat flour sacks. Her daughter said, "We didn't care for the sausage that was put in the intestines, so Mother made sacks. You saved your flour sacks from one year to the other, so she would have flour sacks to tear up and make sausage sacks out of them." The pork, particularly hams and bacon, would then be smoked or preserved with salt. Sometimes the supply lasted until the next year; at other times, families were left with no meat in their diet. As Myrtle commented, "When the sausage were gone, why, you did without."

Families used every part of the hog, pickling the feet and making loaves of jellied, chopped meat from the head. After the butchering, the next task was rendering lard. Hog fat was cooked into lard, which was stored from year to year and used for frying and for making biscuits and other baked goods. As poor as the Calverts were, they were better off than their African American neighbors. According to Myrtle, "They used to come and [say], 'Mrs. Calvert, you got any old grease?' You know, she would save old grease for the woman that washed for us. It would get kind of rancid, but, you know, she'd re-cook it and use it."

The "meal" of the three Ms was cornmeal. Southern farmers raised corn to feed their mules as well as their families. The men took part of their crop to a gristmill, sometimes paying the miller with a share of the ground meal. Families kept large amounts of cornmeal on hand, trying to store it in ways that would keep out weevils. Most farm women cooked cornbread at least once per day, a simple, hearty bread that could be made plain or elaborate depending on supplies of milk, eggs, and other ingredients. Hester also fried patties of cornmeal, which her children loved: "When she'd fry cornbread patties for supper, she couldn't hardly make enough. We kids loved them. . . . And you can imagine, especially when my grandparents were there, trying to make cornbread patties for supper. . . . I don't know how she stood it in the summertime, to get stuff ready over that hot stove, but she did." At the times of the year when the food supply was thinnest, the Calvert family lived on these cornmeal patties. And "molasses" was a variety of syrup made from sugarcane or sorghum.

Hester Calvert worked diligently to increase her family's diet beyond the three Ms. She supervised the planting of a large vegetable garden near the house, choosing beans, Irish potatoes, tomatoes, okra, turnips (used more for the greens than for the root), collard greens, and onions. Myrtle observed: "I remember my mother would say, 'We're going to plant this and plant that and plant the other thing.' Usually my mother bossed it, told what she wanted. If my father planted it, she would always say,

'Well, he planted too much of this or too much of that, or not enough of the other.'"

Families like the Calverts also depended upon wild fruits such as plums, grapes, and blackberries. While many owners had orchards of peach and plum trees, most tenants did not have access to them. The farmer who was lucky enough to be hired on a place with peach trees was ensured a rare treat for his family. "If we had one peach tree and plum tree, they were always so glad," Myrtle recalled. Her mother made jelly from the fruits that grew wild on the farm, standing over a woodstove in the summer heat. She also bought dried fruit. The stereotypical image of the farm wife with rows of canned goods on her pantry shelves did not ring true in Central Texas; most women canned nothing until after World War I, and Hester did not have any equipment for canning until the late 1920s. Families ate vegetables in season; there were no more until the next crop came in.

Farm women such as Hester also supplemented their families' diets by raising chickens for both eggs and meat. Chickens were easy to feed and water, and even the poorest households kept a few. They did not lay all year round, and families looked forward to the spring laying time, when eggs were plentiful. As the Calvert children grew, they had the task of gathering eggs each day and bringing them to their mother. Myrtle remembered an overabundance during the spring: "Mama would boil them and stuff them and fry them and any way in the world to get rid of them because you couldn't keep them very long." When farm women had a surplus of eggs, they often bartered them with traveling peddlers or town merchants for merchandise.

Hester raised turkeys as well—not an easy task, for they were stupid and easily injured. Myrtle told one of the family's favorite stories about their turkeys:

> When I was born, it was in May. And Mama had some turkey to come off with little turkeys, and you know, you put a little meat grease on top of their head to keep lice off. And my mother couldn't get out and do it, had my father to do it, and every one of them died. And my uncles just laughed so, said Papa had the idea, if a little bit did good, a lot would do more good, and he put too much on there and they died. He lost a whole setting of little turkeys. They laughed about that as long as most of them lived, about Bob greasing the turkeys.

When the turkeys survived, Robert took the doomed birds into Waco, the nearest town, to sell at holiday time. Hester used her turkey money to purchase Christmas gifts for the children.

Most rural families ate beef only occasionally; it spoiled easily. For the Calverts, roast beef remained a rare treat. Having dairy and meat products was difficult because most farm families had no refrigeration. They kept milk and butter cold by storing it in their well or in a cooler, a device with canvas-covered shelves that absorbed water from a pan; with a breeze, evaporation cooled the items. The Calverts eventually acquired a commercially manufactured icebox; even though they had to go into the nearby village of Hewitt to buy ice, they were extremely pleased to have it.

Until they bought the dairy farm, the Calverts usually had one or two cows, which made them more fortunate than many families in rural Texas and kept them supplied with milk, cream, and butter. However, butter making was a tedious chore, which the females in the house shared and despised. Myrtle observed: "My mother hated it. Nobody liked to churn. My sister Thelma used to read and churn and if Grandma's there, she'd say, 'Thelma, you're just slowing down. You've got to keep paying attention. Just get busy and churn! Get through with it!'" Extra butter also was taken by Robert to Waco to sell. With the proceeds, he bought rice, raisins, apples, and canned fruit such as peaches. The family loved the variety that store-bought food brought to their meals.

Hester prepared two hot meals per day. She cooked on a woodstove for most of her early marriage, with wood brought from the river bottom some distance away from the farm on the grassy prairie. For breakfast each morning, she made dozens of hot biscuits, served with homemade butter and jelly or syrup, bacon or ham, and sometimes scrambled eggs. Farm breakfasts were hearty, planned to sustain the family workers on their way to the fields. Dinner, the main meal of the day, was at noon. Robert always looked forward to dinner; relatives teased him about his punctuality in leaving the fields for the house at 11:30, when the nearby train blew its whistle. The midday meal usually consisted of some type of pork, cornbread, and whatever fresh vegetables were available, and sometimes dried beans. For supper, the evening meal, the Calverts ate bean or potato soup or a salad picked from the garden, with a fresh batch of cornbread. For some farm families, supper was cornbread crumbled into buttermilk. Cooking with children nearby sometimes was difficult. Myrtle remembered that one of her sisters accidentally knocked a sliver of Ivory soap into the soup: "And somebody got soup and said, 'Mama! What's the matter? This soup foams!' And we found out what had happened, couldn't eat it. Ruined the whole pot."

In the early part of the twentieth century, few families ate yeast bread or "light bread." Yeast was tricky to store, and breadmaking with yeast was time-consuming. Hester's sister-in-law made yeast bread, which her family consumed within a day or two. Robert also bought it in town as a treat for his family. The children all adored "light bread," but it had to be reserved for special occasions. Hester sometimes made chocolate pie or a flat, cookie-like cake known as a tea cake. She also baked a great deal at Christmas, hoarding eggs for her coconut and lemon cakes and various pies. From peaches, apples, and fresh or preserved berries, she made cobblers.

Life in rural Central Texas revolved around the seasons of the cotton crop. As a young woman, Hester worked in her parents' fields. The tasks of cotton cultivation changed little between the Civil War and World War II, and Hester's chores were identical to those done by her daughters thirty years later. As an adult, Hester did not take part in the actual field work, looking after her numerous children instead, but her daughters worked in the fields from the time that they were six or seven years old.

Hester labored diligently, however, to support the work of those out in the fields, cooking and caring for them. Cotton farming was extremely labor intensive, and it would not be completely mechanized until the 1950s. Robert, later assisted by his sons, prepared the land for planting in the late winter, then sowed the seed in early April. By late May, the young cotton would be ready for thinning and weeding in a process known as "chopping." The Calvert children began to help as soon as they could safely handle a sharp hoe, at the age of ten or eleven.

As the summer progressed, the cotton grew and ripened, moving toward the harvest that could start as early as August and might last as late as December, according to the weather. Hester began preparing for the harvest by sewing cotton-picking sacks. The pickers pulled long canvas sacks, secured with a strap over their shoulders, behind them as they moved down the long rows of cotton, pulling the white fibers from the hard boll. Hester also sewed fingerless gloves for her daughters to protect their hands from the prickly bolls.

Cotton picking was the time when the Calverts worked hardest, trying to bring in the harvest before rain could ruin the crop or other calamities befell it. They worked from first light until dark, with a meal break at the hottest part of the day. If a farm family could afford to, they hired help. African Americans and Mexicans, in particular, welcomed the wages, however meager, that picking cotton brought. Pickers were paid by the pound, and a good picker could average several hundred pounds per day. In many families, a daughter who was good at arithmetic waited by the cotton wagon and kept track of the pickers' daily yield. Once the wagon was full, the men took the cotton to the gin, and the women waited patiently at home for the news of what the family's income for the year would be. A poor harvest or low cotton prices meant a year of scraping by, making old clothes last a while longer, and not buying anything new for the house.

Life on the farm was more than hard work. Much of the farm people's socializing took place at church. Hester grew up as a Freewill Baptist but became a Methodist upon her marriage. As an adult, she sent her children to church regularly, but she herself attended only on special occasions. Her eardrum had burst when she was a child, and her hearing was significantly impaired. As a result, she remained at home much of the time, although she did attend the annual revival meetings sponsored by the

Christian churches—Baptist, Methodist, Church of Christ—in the Hewitt area. She took Sunday as her respite from cooking, preparing a meal on Saturday to serve on Sunday. Many rural women enjoyed belonging to the women's groups in their churches, but Hester's deafness prevented her from taking part. The Calverts hosted parties for their children, however, serving ice cream, cookies, and lemonade to the young people who lived in the area of their farm. The family loved music, and Hester played the organ despite her hearing loss.

Hester also liked trips into town. Before World War I, her trips were infrequent, perhaps only once per month or less. After the family bought a car, they traveled to Waco more regularly; the twenty-mile trip lasted about an hour. Once, Robert and Hester took all eight of their children to Waco to see a baseball game. They dressed in their Sunday clothes for the adventure. Myrtle remembered: "[Mama] probably wore her best dress and hat. Some of them said, why did she dress up so to come to the park? Well, I guess we thought you was supposed to. I don't know. But we wore our very best to go to the ballpark."

Robert began buying land in the 1920s, and the family moved to a dairy farm near Bosqueville in 1928. The family lived there until 1940, when they moved into Waco. Hester, who had lived in the country all of her life, adjusted immediately to living in Waco, with its shopping as well as electricity and running water. She enjoyed freedom from the responsibility of caring for livestock and raising crops. Myrtle confirmed that "she was thrilled. She was just ready to move to town. . . . She had a cousin just a few blocks from her that was real close, and they visited and she could walk to the little store and do things like that that was good for her." Her pleasure was short-lived, however, for Robert died in 1947. Hester then moved in with her oldest daughter, Myrtle Dodd, and lived in the Dodd household until her death on May 24, 1964.

As a southern farm wife, Hester Calvert never gained fame or fortune. For her husband and eight children, however, her efforts made a significant impact on their lives. The food that she cooked, the clothing that she sewed, and the care that she gave her family made the difference in the quality of their lives. The contributions of women like Hester made it possible for their children and grandchildren to grow and thrive amid the harsh circumstances of life in the rural South.

NOTES

1. William Bennett Bizzell, *Rural Texas* (New York, 1924), 156.
2. This and subsequent quotations are from Myrtle Calvert Dodd, Oral Memoirs of Myrtle Calvert Dodd (series of interviews by Rebecca Sharpless,

August 14–September 19, 1990, Waco, Texas; The Texas Collection, Baylor University).

SUGGESTED READINGS

Allen, Ruth. *The Labor of Women in the Production of Cotton*. Austin: University of Texas Press, 1931.
Bizzell, William Bennett. *Rural Texas*. New York: Macmillan, 1924.
Foley, Neil. *The White Scourge: Mexicans, Blacks, and Poor Whites in Texas Cotton Culture*. Berkeley: University of California Press, 1997.
Hagood, Margaret Jarman. *Mothers of the South: Portraiture of the White Tenant Farm Woman*. Chapel Hill: University of North Carolina Press, 1977.
Sharpless, Rebecca. *Fertile Ground, Narrow Choices: Women on Texas Cotton Farms, 1900–1940*. Chapel Hill: University of North Carolina Press, 1999.
Stimpson, Eddie, Jr. *My Remembers: A Black Sharecropper's Recollections of the Depression*. Denton: University of North Texas Press, 1996.

6

Ma Rainey: Mother of the Blues

S. Spencer Davis

Bill Malone and David Stricklin, in their Southern Music, American Music *(rev. ed. 2003), call music "one of the greatest natural resources of the South and one of its most valuable exports." Ragtime, the blues, jazz, gospel, hillbilly, country, folk music, protest songs, rock and roll, bluegrass—of whatever kind and by whatever name, music has been a vital part of the South, and the region in turn has been at the forefront of many musical styles. A history of country music without Jimmie Rodgers, or bluegrass without Bill Monroe, or rock and roll without Elvis Presley—southerners all—would be missing vital early chapters. So too with the blues and Ma Rainey of Georgia.*

From her southern roots, she became one of the first and certainly one of the best blues singers. Along the way, her life intersected with a score of influential musicians, black and white, including Bessie Smith, Louis Armstrong, and Tommy Dorsey. Different styles and musicians would influence each other, producing vibrant and fresh sounds. In that sense, the resultant music reflected a South of many parts and faces, each affecting the others, whether intentionally or not.

Much of southern music, and particularly the blues of Ma Rainey, gave those without a mainstream voice a way to express their hopes, fears, and frustrations. It provided an outlet for their feelings on a variety of subjects. The blues spoke to the South, with a distinctly southern accent.

Spencer Davis explains this complex, shadowy figure and places her in the context of her era—a time of segregation, minstrel shows, and sheet music, but also a time when the blues are born, records result, and radio begins.

Spencer Davis, a professor of history at Peru State College in Nebraska, is a specialist in African American intellectual and cultural history. He holds a Ph.D. from the University of Toronto.

Gertrude "Ma" Rainey is remembered today as second only to Bessie Smith among blues vocalists—a judgment that is at once accurate in the minor sense and yet inadequate as a full understanding of Rainey's career. She was the first professional singer to incorporate blues numbers into her act, and as an entertainer she was the greatest crowd-pleaser of the women singing blues. But even these substantial "firsts" are not the full measure of her achievements.

Gertrude Pridgett was born in Columbus, Georgia, in 1886, the second of the five children of Thomas and Ella Pridgett. Columbus was a town of 7,000. With its industry and location on the Chattahoochee River, it had attracted Thomas and Ella to migrate from their native Alabama.[1] No evidence beyond a baptism record describes Gertrude's youth, but undoubtedly she was singing at church and school events. At fourteen she sang in a local group called "The Bunch of Blackberries." Soon afterward, she must have begun to sing professionally. At eighteen she married William "Pa" Rainey, the manager and a performer in the Rabbit Foot Minstrels. They immediately worked together in the show as "Pa" and "Ma" Rainey, with an act combining comedy, singing, and dancing. Since Pa Rainey was substantially older than his eighteen-year-old bride, the match must have been as much professional as romantic.[2]

The situation of black entertainers in the first years of the last century was complex. A life of constant travel brought them into collision with the absurdities and indignities of segregation. Within the black community many religious believers frowned on secular music and looked on entertainers as Satan's assistants. The tangled cultural life of the nation put black entertainers in the dilemma of seeing their culture derided by Anglo-Saxon supremacists while their works were being adopted—or stolen—by white performers.[3]

Charles Dudley Warner, Mark Twain's coauthor on *The Gilded Age*, toured the South in 1888 and recorded his impressions in *On Horseback: A Tour in Virginia, North Carolina, and Tennessee*. In Asheville, North Carolina, Warner and a crowd of both races were entertained by Happy John. Once a slave of Wade Hampton, one of the largest and most famous slaveowners, and now appearing in Uncle Sam costume and blackface, Happy John sang and told stories. According to Warner, Happy John received the biggest response, from blacks in the audience as well as from whites, when his jokes were at the expense of his race. Warner, perhaps momentarily troubled by the situation, reached a conclusion that did not entirely disguise his anxiety. "I presume none of them analyzed the nature of his infectious gayety, nor thought of the pathos that lay so close to it, in the fact of his recent slavery, and the distinction of being one of Wade Hampton's [slaves], and the melancholy mirth of this light-hearted race's burlesque of itself."[4] The possibility of double-meaning in this stereotyped humor did not occur to Warner.

Happy John may not have been performing in the minstrel format, but there were similarities. The minstrel show is a strange American creation. White minstrel shows first appeared in the 1840s and created a sensation among white audiences. Most of them focused on plantation life, and many or most of them purported to depict "authentic" slave life. How white Americans could believe that is difficult to understand, given the fact that the actors were white people using burnt cork to blacken their faces. Their exaggerated physical movements helped to establish stereotypes that have persisted to this day.

By the middle of the 1850s black actors began to appear as minstrels, and they became firmly established as a part of the show business tradition by the 1870s. Showmen such as Charles Callender and J. H. Haverly were instrumental in making minstrels an integral part of show business. Black-owned companies also formed in the 1860s. Among the more important ones were the Brooker and Clayton Georgia Minstrels, a group that was very popular in the Northeast. Minstrels succeeded partly because they appealed to an essentially illiterate society, but their popularity was not limited to the unlettered. Prominent people, including Abraham Lincoln, reportedly found them very entertaining.

By the 1870s a separation occurred between black and white minstrels. Because black minstrels had the aura of authenticity, especially with "real Negroes," white shows moved away from portrayals of "realistic" plantation and black life to more lavish productions. They became more professional as well but continued to use African American culture as a major focus. Black minstrels flourished in the later decades of the nineteenth century and the first few decades of the twentieth.[5]

Thomas L. Riis, in his study of jazz, suggests a plausible explanation for the popularity of minstrels among whites and blacks alike. People have wondered why blacks would participate in and attend minstrel shows when portrayals were racist, degrading, and grotesque. He suggests that the actors and audiences of the day may not have seen them in the way that contemporary society does. In fact, he explains the low educational level of the country at the time and the importance of oral-cultural entertainments. In an oral culture, he believes, exaggeration and grotesque portrayals are necessary and are common in most nonliterate or semiliterate cultures. The exaggerations are needed to deliver the message, and the audience does not see the performances as degrading.[6]

Such was the minstrel tradition that Ma Rainey joined when she became a performer. Whether she was conscious of the subtleties of its historical and cultural significance is a moot point. She was essentially illiterate herself; and, if one accepts Riis's conjecture, she might not have seen it as degrading at all. Perhaps the Rabbit Foot Minstrels had no such figure as Happy John in their cast in 1904 when Ma Rainey joined the troupe, but minstrel shows, though they typically had black casts by that time, retained their stereotypes and the indignity of blackface. In the 1870s black minstrel shows and white minstrel shows had begun to diverge; the black entertainers included spirituals as well as stereotypes.[7] To play within but yet rise above the stereotypes was a difficult feat.

The Rabbit Foot Minstrels played only in the South, traveling in their own railroad car and playing one-nighters in their gigantic tent. The program included acrobats and a contortionist; eventually Ma Rainey was the star of the show. The Rabbit Foot Minstrels usually spent the winter in New Orleans, which gave her the chance to perform with some of the greats of New Orleans music such as Joe Oliver, Louis Armstrong, Sidney Bechet, and Kid Ory. In 1914, 1915, and 1916 she toured with Tolliver's Circus and Musical Extravaganza with the billing of "Rainey and Rainey, Assassinators of the Blues." In 1917 she created her own traveling show, Ma Rainey and Her Georgia Smart Set.

There is a fairly detailed account of that show. Rainey was short and heavyset; she had diamonds in her hair, gold-capped teeth, and heavy jewelry. In order to lighten the tone of her skin she used a great deal of skin cream and powder. Her humor, warm smile, and open sexuality compensated for her lack of classic features. Rainey played to all-black, segregated, and all-white audiences. If the audience was segregated, whites were seated on one side of the tent and blacks on the other side. Her show began with a band number followed by several numbers by male and female dancers. Next came two skits of ethnic humor, the first portraying a Japanese character and the second a black man stealing chickens. A fast number featuring the soubrette and the dancers was followed by another comedy routine. Then Ma Rainey came on stage, began with some comedy, sang half a dozen numbers including "Memphis Blues" and "Jelly Roll Blues," and ended with her specialty, "See See Rider Blues." The show closed with all the cast on stage for the finale.[8]

By this time, Rainey had been singing blues in her performances for a decade and was the preeminent female blues artist. She claimed that while she was working a tent show in Missouri in 1902, she overheard a young woman singing a strange lament about the man who left her. Taken by the unique sound, she learned the song and put it in her act. When asked what kind of song it was, she replied "the blues" and thus named the genre. It is unlikely that Rainey was in Missouri before 1904 and, therefore, equally unlikely that, in a moment of inspiration, she invented the label. But as an explanation of how Rainey became the first professional singer to put blues in a minstrel show, the story is more credible.[9]

The first sheet music with "blues" in the title was published in 1914 by a white band leader from Oklahoma, but the blues genre began almost certainly in the 1890s, almost certainly in the Mississippi Delta, and quite certainly among rural blacks. Defining the blues is more difficult. Blues began in the 1890s (or perhaps a little earlier) in the Delta—the heart of sharecropping, cotton-producing, rural Mississippi. The typical blues artist was a man singing and playing the guitar. The typical blues form was a twelve-bar, three-line stanza with the second line repeating the first (AAB) and the third line ending with the rhyme word. Blues singers drew on familiar lines from earlier songs, added their own, and used filler words or moans to complete lines. Blues numbers could change from one rendition to the next as lines were changed, or formulas from other numbers were added, or new stanzas were improvised. Blues lyrics focused on personal problems such as unfaithful lovers, whiskey, debts, and trouble with the law. The leading study of these original down-home blues finds surprisingly little social protest in them.[10]

Down-home blues were sung at picnics, on the porch, at the depot, and outside the barbershop. But to fit into the structure of the minstrel and tent shows, changes had to be made. Instrumental soloists could improvise, but too much improvising by vocalists would upset the band.[11] Rainey had to standardize the lyrics, but accompaniments had to be worked out for the band or small group.

In the late 1910s, Rainey's act changed. Pa Rainey, always a dim figure, dropped out of the picture. Ma Rainey was then a singles act. She may have spent a year in Mexico, but that is not confirmed. Within a year, however, she was back, entertaining southern black audiences. In 1922 and 1923 she worked with a pianist, usually Troy Snapp, accompanying her.[12] By this time the first recorded blues, Mamie Smith's "Crazy Blues," had appeared, and no doubt Rainey changed to keep up with the popularity of recorded blues—keep up, but never totally imitate. She remained closer to down-home blues than any of the other women recording classic (or vaudeville) blues in the 1920s.

On her own, Ma Rainey performed with many others, but she also befriended and assisted struggling entertainers. One of the most famous was Bessie Smith, who would overshadow Rainey in fame and popularity. In the beginning, however, Rainey gave her a start in the business. Their relationship may have been more than that. Smith later was well known for her bisexuality, and Rainey may have been bisexual as well. *Completely Queer* indicates that Rainey was a lesbian and that she introduced Bessie Smith to lesbian love. "Rainey was one of a number of legendary women singers associated with the Harlem Renaissance who were known to prefer women over men." This reference work also indicates that her nickname, Ma, referred to "the affection and nurturing she lavished on those around her."[13] Whatever her personal affairs may have been, her career flourished in the 1920s.

In 1920, Mamie Smith recorded "Crazy Blues" for Okeh Records. Its success persuaded record companies that there were profits to be made in "race" records. Other vaudeville singers who had the clear tone and distinct pronunciation of Mamie Smith were rushed into studios to record blues. In 1921 about fifty race records were released; by 1927 the number had soared to five hundred.[14] These blues—classic or vaudeville blues—were neither the down-home kind nor the blues of tent show veterans such as Ma Rainey and Bessie Smith. But, in 1923, both Smith and Rainey were recorded.

The phenomenal growth of radio in the 1920s created a crisis for the music industry. Record sales continued to decline throughout the decade. Since music could now be disseminated even to the most rural and unsophisticated audiences, record companies began to look for other entertainers who performed less well-known "folk" music. Company scouts fanned out across the country, especially the South, to find singers who would sound good on wax and whose talents could be promoted. One of the pioneers in this development was Ralph Peer, the man who first recorded Mamie Smith in 1920, but he became better known because he soon focused on recording country singers, including Jimmie Rodgers.

Mamie Smith's records for Okeh were successful and offered a potential new market for black singers—African Americans themselves who preferred to hear people of their own race perform music from their own culture.[15] Several recording companies created separate listings for songs designed for other races—meaning, almost always, African Americans. These became known as "race records." The term "race" in the 1920s was a badge of pride in the black community. "Although race records included spirituals, instrumentals, comedy, sermons, and even occasional classical arias, the biggest money was in the blues."[16] Okeh, Columbia, and Paramount set the pace for race records in the 1920s. Paramount had a black talent scout and recording director, J. Mayo Williams, who aggressively recruited black entertainers.[17]

In December 1923, at age thirty-seven, Rainey went to Chicago to record eight songs at Paramount Records. Despite its array of talent, Paramount was limited when compared to Columbia Records. Paramount recorded Rainey acoustically, "a crude process in which she sang into an enormous horn," and the results were primitive and disappointing.[18] That first session produced one hit, "Moonshine Blues." Rainey did most of her recording for Paramount in Chicago, where she kept an apartment, but in

1924 she had two Paramount recording sessions in New York. The backup musicians were among the stars of the jazz world: Fletcher Henderson, a leading New York band leader, on piano; Charlie Green on trombone; and, for the second session, Louis Armstrong on cornet. Of these six tracks, "See See Rider Blues" was the most important.[19]

With recording success came the opportunity to move from tent shows to the stages of the Theater Owners' Booking Agency (TOBA), the black vaudeville circuit. TOBA had been around since about 1907, but it really came into its own in the 1920s. The shows were targeted to black audiences, but on Thursday nights a separate performance was given for whites. The "Midnight Ramble" was a standard—a late show featuring the blues—unlike the regular performances that were more like white vaudeville in that various types of entertainment were provided. The typical TOBA show might include "comedy, circus acts, dramatic scenes, and pure vaudeville hokum as well as singing and dancing."[20] While TOBA stood for Theater Owners' Booking Agency, the performers often referred to it as "Tough on Black Artists," or, in more crude moments, "Tough on Black Asses." Even so, and despite low pay, hard work, and poor working conditions, TOBA offered regular employment for hundreds of black entertainers who would have had a difficult time arranging bookings for themselves.[21]

For her TOBA act, Rainey worked with Tommy Dorsey, a prominent musician in years to come, as pianist and music director. He put together and rehearsed a five-piece group, the Wildcats Jazz Band.[22] Evidently "jazz," like "blues," was an elastic and even indefinite term. The publicity photo of Rainey, Dorsey, and the rest of the Wildcats put them in awkward poses that nevertheless captured some of Rainey's energy.

Dorsey defined the connection between jazz and blues in several ways that help place Ma Rainey's music. He described jazz as music played at the better clubs; blues was played in Chicago in the back of saloons, at rent parties, and at buffet flats (unlicensed clubs set up in apartments and patronized by working-class people). Jazz was blues speeded up, a faster and flashier music; blues maintained a slower tempo to fit its sad mood.[23] Dorsey also described slowing down or dragging out popular tunes of the day to suit the taste of couples who wanted to "slow drag" or "shimmy" late at night.[24] Rainey's power over the audience is given in Dorsey's words:

> When she started singing, the gold in her teeth would sparkle. She was in the spotlight. She possessed her listeners; they swayed, they rocked, they moaned and groaned, as they felt the blues with her. A woman swooned who had lost her man. Men groaned who had given their week's pay to some woman who promised to be nice, but slipped away and couldn't be found at

the appointed time. By this time she was just about at the end of her song. She was "in her sins" as she bellowed out. The bass drum rolled like thunder and the stage lights flickered like forked lightning. . . . As the song ends, she feels an understanding with her audience. Their applause is a rich reward. She is in her glory. The house is hot. . . . By this time everybody is excited and enthusiastic. The applause thunders for one more number. Some woman screams out with a shrill cry of agony as the blues recalls sorrow because some man trifled with her and wounded her to the bone. [Ma Rainey] is ready now to take the encore as her closing song. Here she is, tired, sweaty, swaying from side to side, fatigued, but happy.[25]

Rainey's record sales and TOBA bookings were very successful through 1928, but at the end of that year conditions changed abruptly. Paramount decided not to renew her recording contract. The competition from sound movies, introduced in 1927, had sent the TOBA theaters into a steep decline, and in May 1929, Rainey quit the circuit with wages owed her. Thereafter came a series of desperate moves to keep her career going, but the Great Depression took its toll on her career as it had on many other black performers. Still she persevered, taking whatever engagements she could find. She toured with some of the tent repertory companies, but the Depression was destroying more prestigious careers than hers. Paramount Records went bankrupt in the early 1930s, black vaudeville died, and Ma Rainey quit the business.

In 1935 she returned to Georgia to her hometown of Columbus after the death of her sister Malissa; her mother died during the same year. Rainey purchased two theaters in Rome. During this time, she joined the Friendship Baptist Church where her brother, Thomas Pridgett, was a deacon. Her life in Georgia is not well known today, but clearly she dropped out of entertainment except for owning the theaters, and she essentially was forgotten in blues circles.

Rainey died on December 22, 1939, and was buried in Porterdale Cemetery in Columbus. She was only fifty-three years old; the cause of death was reported to be heart disease—not unexpected considering her lifestyle and weight. Her death went entirely unnoticed by the black press or by any other news medium. It seems especially ironic that her death certificate listed her occupation as housekeeping. One wonders if her neighbors were aware of her career in entertainment.[26]

Ma Rainey was a black woman and a professional entertainer. She played minstrel shows, tent shows, circuses, carnivals, clubs, theaters, and even a Texas cattle show. Wherever engagements were offered, she took them until, in the Great Depression, there were none. When wealthy white folks in Jackson, Mississippi, hired her, she serenaded at their homes. When black sharecroppers in Alabama were flooded out, she organized a fund-raising concert. She sang blues, popular tunes, and comedy numbers; she danced; she told jokes, often at her own expense and often ribald; she worked with partners in comedy routines. At times, she managed her road shows. She composed about one-third of the numbers she recorded.[27] She paid her musicians on time, treated them well, and never missed an engagement.

For all her versatility, Ma Rainey was most successful singing traditional blues—that is, songs employing many of the formulas and the loose organization of down-home blues but performed by a vocalist and small group as were vaudeville blues. In his poem celebrating the power of Ma Rainey over her audience, Sterling A. Brown tells how her rendition of "Backwater Blues" so perfectly expressed the tribulations of the audience that heads bowed and tears flowed.[28] Brown explained her appeal: "Ma Rainey was a tremendous figure. She wouldn't have to sing any words; she would moan, and the audience would moan with her." She dominated the stage. "She had them in the palm of her hand. I heard Bessie Smith also, but Ma Rainey was the greatest mistress of an audience."[29]

Her commanding presence was also reported by Jack Dupree: "She was really an ugly woman, but when she opened her mouth—that was it! You forgot everything. She knew how to sing those blues, and she got right into your heart. What a personality she had. One of the greatest of all singers."[30] Almost everyone who saw her perform agreed that she was a "blues queen" who, like so many others, acted the part. Strong, unpredictable, and "volcanic," she spoke her mind. She was "soft-hearted and generous; but she was a tigress when roused."[31]

In her recorded blues, Rainey touched upon all the causes of heartache and anguish—unfaithful lovers, violent men, poverty, debt, jail time, alcoholism—of women abandoned, betrayed, or overpowered by life's problems. But in some of her numbers she portrayed aggressive, violent, lustful women—those sinning rather than those sinned against. Thus, in "Bared Home Blues," written by Louie Austin, Rainey's "Mama" matches "Papa," vice for unblushing vice.[32] In "Black Dust Blues," she is a woman who has stolen another one's man but pays the price through the effect of the voodoo potion placed in her house.[33]

In his path-breaking analysis of French folk tales, Robert Darnton discovered a world of constant poverty, death, hunger, starvation, injustice, and cruelty. The poor survived only by tricking others; in such a world the eradication of personal and social problems was inconceivable.[34] Reading the lyrics to Ma Rainey's blues can create the same sense of global despair. But when we turn from the lyrics on the printed page to the recordings, the power of her voice and the gusto in her delivery come into play. The sadness and hurt do not disappear but undergo a transformation. The sheer waste and inwardness of suffering are overcome; artistry gives meaning to the pain of a world we must take as we find it. For Ralph Ellison this was the outrageous, inexplicable truth of African American culture.[35] Many artists represent Ellison's insight as well as Ma Rainey, but none represents it better.

NOTES

1. Hettie Jones, *Big Star Fallin' Mama*, rev. ed. (New York: Viking Penguin, 1995), 19–21.
2. Sandra Lieb, *Mother of the Blues* (Amherst: University of Massachusetts Press, 1981), 4–5.
3. W. C. Handy, *Father of the Blues* (New York: Collier, 1969). Chapters 1–4 describe the conflict between religion and secular music.
4. Quoted in Alton Hornsby Jr., ed., *In the Cage: Eyewitness Accounts of the Freed Negro in Southern Society, 1877–1929* (Chicago: Quadrangle, 1971), 140–42; quote on 142.
5. Lieb, *Mother of the Blues*, 4–7; Thomas L. Riis, *Just before Jazz: Black Musical Theater in New York, 1890–1915* (Washington, DC: Smithsonian Institution Press, 1989), 4–5.
6. Riis, *Just before Jazz*, 5–7.
7. Lieb, *Mother of the Blues*, xiii, 5.
8. Lieb, *Mother of the Blues*, 10–13.
9. Lieb, *Mother of the Blues*, 3–5.
10. Jeff Todd Titon, *Early Downhome Blues*, rev. ed. (Chapel Hill: University of North Carolina Press, 1994).
11. For the problems created by an improvising soloist in Mahara's Minstrel Show, see Handy, *Father of the Blues*, 40–41.
12. Lieb, *Mother of the Blues*, 18–25.
13. Steve Hogan and Lee Hudson, *Completely Queer: The Gay and Lesbian Encyclopedia* (New York: Henry Holt, 1998), 471.
14. Titon, *Early Downhome Blues*, 200.
15. Bill C. Malone, *Country Music U.S.A.*, rev. ed. (Austin: University of Texas Press, 1985), 34–35.
16. Lieb, *Mother of the Blues*, 21.
17. Lieb, *Mother of the Blues*, 21.
18. Lieb, *Mother of the Blues*, 22.
19. Lieb, *Mother of the Blues*, 10, 26, 178.
20. Lieb, *Mother of the Blues*, 27.
21. Lieb, *Mother of the Blues*, 26–27.
22. Paramount Records talent man J. Mayo "Ink" Williams paired Dorsey with Rainey. Lieb, *Mother of the Blues*, 29; Michael W. Harris, *The Rise of Gospel Blues* (New York: Oxford University Press, 1992), 86–87.
23. Harris, *Rise of Gospel Blues*, 53.
24. Harris, *Rise of Gospel Blues*, 59.
25. Harris, *Rise of Gospel Blues*, 89–90.

26. Darlene Clark Hine, ed., *Black Women in America: An Historical Encyclopedia*, 2 vols. (Brooklyn, NY: Carlson, 1993), 960; John A. Garraty and Mark C. Carnes, eds., *American National Biography* (New York: Oxford University Press, 1999), 18:80.

27. More accurately, she was listed on the copyright as composer or co-composer of these numbers.

28. Sterling A. Brown, "Ma Rainey," in *The Collected Poems of Sterling A. Brown*, ed. Michael S. Harper (New York: Harper & Row, 1980), 62–63.

29. Quoted in Derrick Stewart-Baxter, *Ma Rainey and the Classic Blues Singers* (New York: Stein and Day, 1970), 42.

30. Stewart-Baxter, *Ma Rainey*.

31. Stewart-Baxter, *Ma Rainey*.

32. Angela Y. Davis, *Blue Legacies and Black Feminism* (New York: Pantheon, 1998), 200–201. Davis provides the words to all the songs of Rainey and Bessie Smith, a tremendous aid to scholars, but the interpretive section of her book is another matter.

33. Davis, *Blue Legacies*, 203.

34. Robert Darnton, *The Great Cat Massacre* (New York: Basic, 1984), chap. 1.

35. Ralph Ellison, in *Collected Essays of Ralph Ellison*, ed. John Callahan (New York: Random House, 1995).

SUGGESTED READINGS

Albertson, Charles. *Bessie*. Rev. ed. New Haven, CT: Yale University Press, 2003.
Armstrong, Louis. *Satchmo*. New York: Da Capo, 1986.
Cohn, Lawrence, ed. *Nothing but the Blues*. New York: Abbeville, 1993.
Davis, Angela Y. *Blues Legacies and Black Feminism*. New York: Pantheon, 1998.
Floyd, Samuel A., Jr. *The Power of Black Music*. New York: Oxford University Press, 1995.
Handy, W. C. *Father of the Blues*. New York: Collier, 1969.
Lieb, Sandra. *Mother of the Blues*. Amherst: University of Massachusetts Press, 1981.
Malone, Bill C. *Country Music U.S.A*. Rev. ed. Austin: University of Texas Press, 1985.
Morgan, Thomas L., and William Barlow. *From Cakewalks to Concert Halls*. Washington, DC: Elliott & Clark, 1992.
Oliver, Paul. *The Story of the Blues*. Boston: Northeastern University Press, 1997.
Oliver, Paul, et al. *The New Grove Dictionary: Gospel, Blues, and Jazz*. New York: Norton, 1986.
Riis, Thomas L. *Just before Jazz*. Washington, DC: Smithsonian Institution Press, 1989.
Southern, Eileen. *The Music of Black Americans*. 3d ed. New York: Norton, 1997.
Stewart-Baxter, Derrick. *Ma Rainey and the Classic Blues Singers*. New York: Stein & Day, 1970.
Titon, Jeff Todd. *Early Downhome Blues*. Rev. ed. Chapel Hill: University of North Carolina Press, 1994.

7

Dizzy Dean: Baseball's Quintessential Southerner

William J. Marshall

Sports are an important part of southern life and southern history. Some of those sports have remained almost unchanged over the centuries, such as hunting and fishing, and continue to be a staple of the rural and small-town southern lifestyle. Older sports, such as horseracing, have changed over time and go on yet, while newer ones, such as NASCAR racing, have risen in popularity.

But most of those are more individual in their focus. After the Civil War, more organized team sports began to make an important impact on what people of the South did for recreation and, even more, on what they watched for enjoyment. The first major sport in the region was not football, which would later become immensely popular, or basketball, which would gain fans over the years, but rather baseball. Born before the Civil War, baseball grew in popularity during the war and matured in the late nineteenth century. Heat, segregation, and the size of southern cities kept major league teams away for a long time, except on the southern periphery, until Houston started a team in 1966 and the Braves moved to Atlanta in 1968.

But all across the region for a century before that, in small towns and large, people of all races played the sport. It proved immensely popular, and each state contributed southern-born players to the major leagues and to the Baseball Hall of Fame—whether Hank Aaron of Alabama, Brooks Robinson of Arkansas, Steve Carlton of Florida, Ty Cobb of Georgia, Pee Wee Reese of Kentucky, Mel Ott of Louisiana, Cool Papa Bell of Mississippi, Catfish Hunter of North Carolina, Mickey Mantle of Oklahoma, Larry Doby of South Carolina, Turkey Stearnes of Tennessee, Nolan Ryan of Texas, or Eppa Rixey of Virginia. Frequently baseball spoke with a southern accent.

One of those players was Jay Hanna "Dizzy" Dean. His career as a pitcher often strengthened then-existing American stereotypes of the rural South, yet his time as a baseball announcer helped break down regional differences, as he became popular across the nation. His story shows the role sports played in individual lives, and how sports helped bring the South into the American consciousness.

William J. Marshall is curator of manuscripts in the Division of Special Collections and Digital Programs in the University of Kentucky Libraries system. He is the author of Baseball's Pivotal Era, 1945–1951, *which won the 2000 Seymour Medal awarded by the Society of American Baseball Research.*

There is a little of Dizzy Dean in all of us. Some people crave attention, adulation, and appreciation. Many want to appear fearless, self-confident, and, in their worst moments, even brash, often as a means of hiding insecurities. The ability to set the record straight, however, without retribution or significant consequence, with a verbal barb, a quick punch, or a fastball aimed at an opponent's temple remains an unrealized desire for most. Moreover, to toe the rubber, hand encircled around a small slightly soiled and scuffed baseball, awaiting the catcher's signal, knowing that the hitter will not connect with your 97-mile-per-hour fastball, is a situation and feeling unknown to most. Add a few taunting remarks, a rich southern twang, and an earnest grin, and you have Dizzy Dean.

Jay Hanna "Dizzy" Dean grew up poor. Born on January 16, 1910, Dizzy was the fourth of five children (two of whom died in early childhood) born to Alma and Albert Dean. He was preceded into adulthood by a mentally challenged brother, Elmer, born in 1908, and followed by brother Paul, born in 1913. Dean's father was a sawmill laborer and later a sharecropper who picked cotton for a living and played baseball when time permitted. Earlier Dean ancestors hailed from Tennessee and Missouri, where as Jacksonian Democrats they supported the Union during the Civil War. Albert Dean was a frustrated ballplayer—good enough to play sandlot baseball but not skilled enough to sign a professional contract. He married Alma Nelson in Lucas, Arkansas, a small rural community located in the Arkansas River Valley between the Oauchita and Ozark mountain ranges. The town, which often failed to appear on maps, consisted of a general store, a cotton gin, a church, and frustrated hopes.

During Dizzy Dean's early years the family lived in a cabin, sharecropping for rent. While shoes and clothes might be scarce, according to the father the family did not want for anything. "Plain grub made the boys," he recalled in 1934. "They was raised on corn bread, sweet potatoes, peanuts, and milk."[1] In 1916 Dizzy began school. Never a strong student, Dean

Dizzy Dean. *Courtesy of Brace Photo*

made it into the second grade before the death of his mother from tuberculosis in 1918 interrupted his schooling. It was a hiatus that was only intermittently filled thereafter. Later Dizzy claimed, "If I'd went to the third grade, I'da passed my old man. I didn't want to show Paw up."[2]

Albert Dean later remarried, to Cora Parham, a widow with three children of her own. Not long after, in 1919, the new family moved to Chicklah, Arkansas, a small community northwest of Little Rock, where they rented from a cotton farmer. As a child laborer Jay Hanna Dean would arise early in the morning and often pick more than three hundred pounds of cotton a day. It was at Chicklah that Dean also returned to school—an experience that also demonstrated Dizzy's stubbornness. At Chicklah's one-room school the young boy was forced to stand for hours facing a blackboard with his nose pressed to the surface because of his refusal to learn to read.

Baseball, not education, was the first love of the Dean children. When not working, they would play constantly with sock balls and sticks as their main equipment. Dizzy and brother Paul honed their pitching arms. In 1922, Dizzy pitched in his first formal nine-inning game, earning a win for a Belleville team against Sulphur Springs. Using an imitation Walter Johnson windup, an above average fastball, and a cocky attitude, the young man already knew that he was good. A year or two later the Deans moved to Oklahoma to pick cotton near such communities as Okemah, Purcell, and Spaulding. By 1924, Dizzy looked old for his age—a big, rawboned kid wearing overalls, a blue shirt, and no shoes. He came across as good-natured, cheerful, and gregarious. School continued to beckon, but only during baseball season. Showing up at school without lunch pails, pencils, or paper, Paul and Dizzy attended mostly on Fridays because rules dictated that players be in school on game days. To their classmates they were known as "the dumb Deans" or the "once-a-weekenders."[3] Nevertheless, as players both kids were in demand. In 1926, the Spaulding school system assigned Paul to the fifth grade and Dizzy to the seventh. That allowed Dizzy to throw his fastball for the high school team. During the last tournament of the season, pitching barefoot in his overalls, the durable young pitcher defeated three teams in a single day.

By late 1926, Dean had grown weary of life as a cotton picker. Even though underage (his father signed papers attesting that the sixteen-year-old was eighteen), he left home and enlisted in the U.S. Army at Fort Sam Houston, Texas. Assigned to the Third Wagon Company of the Second Infantry Division, Dean could have been the prototype for Mac Hyman's classic novel *No Time for Sergeants*. Not unlike Hyman's Georgia bumpkin, Will Stockdale, Dean was naive, innocent, outgoing, humorous, and honest almost to a fault. By his own admission and those of others, he was a poor soldier. Indeed, his first sergeant, William H. Barnett, noted, "That boy couldn't pour piss out of a boot with directions on the heel."[4] Deemed too inept to become a teamster, the young man was placed on permanent KP (kitchen police) to mop floors, prepare food, and wash dishes. Unlike the fictional Stockdale, however, Dean could pitch. When word of his prowess reached the manager of the 12th Regimental Team, the fort's best baseball team, Dean was transferred to the 12th Field Artillery and assigned to the Battery C kitchen as a cook. Later the army even sent him to cooks and bakers school. Dean's kitchen antics led to his nickname. One afternoon a sergeant caught Dean flinging freshly peeled potatoes at garbage can lids. "You dizzy son of a bitch," he exclaimed.[5] The nickname stuck.

Jay Hanna Dean became the fort's star pitcher, wowing onlookers with his strikeout performances—accounts of which appeared in the San Antonio papers. While he pitched for two post teams during the week, he slipped off on Sundays as a mercenary to pitch for semipro teams. Worried about Dean possibly losing effectiveness or getting hurt in a brawl, his sergeant made Dean promise to stay on the army base. Several times, when he failed to keep his word, Dean ended up in the guardhouse. Dizzy's stay in the army was cut short when the San Antonio Public Service Company bought up the remainder of his enlistment so it could hire him to play on its own team, a practice not uncommon in the peacetime army of the 1920s. The date was March 15, 1929, seven months before the start of the Great Depression. Working a real nine-to-five day job, Dean pitched on weekends for the company and instantly helped his team win the city league and go to the state finals. At one point Dizzy reeled off sixteen wins in a row—a feat which drew the attention of Don Curtis, a part-time scout with the Houston Buffaloes, a farm club of the St. Louis Cardinals.

Dean signed a professional contract for $300 a month. In the spring of 1930 Houston placed Dean with the St. Joseph (Missouri) Saints—a lower-level Cardinal farm club in the Western League. Dizzy arrived at the Saints training camp in Shawnee, Oklahoma, with no luggage, soiled clothing, and a smudged face. Apparently he had cashed in his $8 train ticket and had ridden the rails to camp like a hobo. At Shawnee, Cardinals general manager Branch Rickey got his first look at Dizzy Dean. Rickey, an astute judge of talent, had invented the farm system that developed young players. He stockpiled talented players and led the small-market Cardinals to several pennants in the 1920s. Watching the young pitcher convinced him that the Cardinals not only had a great prospect, but one who might be in the class of the great Christy Matthewson. Rickey, however, received a quick dose of Dizzy's "charm" and self-assurance later that evening. While sitting reading a newspaper in the lobby of the hotel, Rickey was greeted by Dean with a "Hello, Branch." Dean asked, "When're you takin' me to join the Cardinals? I can win the pennant up there for you, Branch." Taken aback by Dean's brashness and familiarity, Rickey rose and replied gravely, "Mr. Dean, I don't know when or where you're going. The men in charge will decide and let you know. Meanwhile, Mr. Dean, I'd like to continue reading my paper."[6]

Dizzy Dean backed up his statements with results, however. Though playing for a mediocre team, Dizzy fashioned a 17-8 record with a 3.69 earned run average and 134 strikeouts in 217 innings. Before one of his starts, he called up the manager of an opposing team and said, "This here is Dizzy Dean. I'm gonna pitch against your club this afternoon and hold them to two or three hits."[7] Dean held them to two. Dizzy would also frequently ask hitters where they wanted the ball, then throw it there and retire them anyway. A success on the field, Dean had problems off it, where his total lack of sophistication got him into constant difficulty. His rural southern country roots did little to prepare him for life in rural southern or midwestern towns. He discovered the allure of women and reportedly saw a different one each night regardless of reputation. Dean also stayed out beyond curfew; he lived in several hotels simultaneously without ever checking out of any of them (the team settled the bills); he continually lost his clothes or threw them away when they got too dirty to wear, and he left rental cars parked on the street without ever returning them or paying for them. Money was also simply expendable and while at St. Joseph he accumulated more than $2,500 in debts. He seemed totally irresponsible.

In August 1930, the Cardinals summoned Dean to play at a higher level—with Houston, a club fighting for the Texas League pennant. Even though the team finished third, Dean ended the season sensationally with an 8-2 record and recorded an impressive number of strikeouts. At the end of September, the St. Louis Cardinals, playing a series against the Giants in New York, called him up to the major leagues. Arriving in town with another rookie player from Houston, Dean asked to borrow a shirt because the two suitcases he brought with him were full of books on the Wild West. On September 28, Dean made his major league pitching debut at the Cardinals' Sportsman's Park and won 3-1. After watching the Cardinals lose the World Series to the Philadelphia Athletics from the bench (he was not on the roster), Dean had the audacity to ask Branch Rickey for a raise and bragged that he would outdraw Babe Ruth. "By Judas Priest!" Rickey later noted, "If there were more like him in baseball, just one, as God is my judge, I'd get out of the game."[8]

Rebuffed by Rickey, Dean returned to the minor leagues at St. Joseph. He continued to refer to himself as "the great Dean," and told reporters that he would win for the Cardinals soon. Announcing that he would return to San Antonio to live with his family, he noted that he was taking his sixteen-year-old brother Paul to camp with him. "And next to me, I think he'll be the greatest pitcher in the world."⁹ Instead, to keep Dizzy Dean out of trouble, Branch Rickey arranged for his young pitcher to stay during the off-season with the St. Joseph team's business manager in Charleston, Missouri, a quiet little town in the southeastern part of the state. Though Dean attended every dance he could and learned to play contract bridge, shoot a rifle, drive a car, and fly a plane (he was involved in a Piper Cub crash), he grew supremely bored. For entertainment he developed a simulated baseball game by throwing coal into his host's furnace—a practice that turned the home into a winter oven.

Moreover, per Branch Rickey's orders, Dean received only a meager allowance. To compensate, Dizzy would open tabs at the local drugstore and other businesses and tell them that the Cardinals would reimburse them. Dean became so upset over his poor financial condition that he insisted on seeing Rickey. After his meeting with the Cardinal executive, he was obviously dispirited. "A fine friend you are!" he told his host on their way home. "All I wanted was a hundred an' fifty dollars, an' all I got was a lecture on sex."¹⁰ The young pitcher had fallen in love with a high school girl, but Rickey counseled him that his machinations were premature. Dean continued to be a handful for the Cardinals. "Dean is like an oil burner without a governor," Rickey confided to newspaperman J. Roy Stockton. "If we could get a governor for him, he would be the greatest pitcher in the world."¹¹

Unable to keep Dean in check, Rickey sent him to Florida several days before the Cardinals' 1931 spring training reporting date. In Bradenton Dizzy continued his free-spending ways—reputedly spending most of his 1931 salary before the season started. When financially embarrassed, he passed bad checks or signed Branch Rickey's name. Rickey put Dean on a dollar-a-day allowance and a repayment plan, and instructed Bradenton merchants not to extend him credit. Unfortunately for Dean, his lackadaisical attitude extended to the baseball field. He had difficulty making 10:00 A.M. practices and he refused to obey Cardinal manager Gabby Street—an "old school" disciplinarian. Though there is little doubt Dean would have been an asset to the Cardinals, they returned the wayward pitcher to the minor league team at Houston several weeks into the 1931 season.

Dean won his first five games at Houston (including two shutouts), was decked twice by Dallas catcher Al Todd in a brawl on the field, and, on June 15, 1931, married a twenty-four-year-old Mississippi shop girl named Patricia Nash. She had been married twice before and had a questionable reputation. Dean's marriage to Pat Nash, however, proved to be propitious—she became his mother figure, his personal adviser, his lifelong partner, and his constant companion. Moreover, she organized and "civilized" him. As she told the press not long after, "I'm his banker, bookkeeper, manager, and girlfriend."¹² Dizzy's success on the field continued, as he fashioned a 26-10 record, led the Texas League with a 304 strikeouts, and took his team to the 1931 Dixie World Series against Birmingham from the Southern League. Although Dean lost two games to the Barons, his participation allowed the Dean family to reunite with brother Elmer. Five years earlier, the family had lost track of the mentally challenged son when he became separated from his brother Paul and his father on a trip. Now Dizzy learned that a farm worker in Plumerville, Arkansas, had seen his Dixie World Series picture in the paper and was telling everyone that he was Dizzy Dean's brother.

The Cardinals won the 1931 National League pennant without Dizzy Dean and he barely made the roster for 1932. Dean did so with good, if not meek, behavior and by following the manager's rules. Dean did not make his first start until May 3, when he beat the Cincinnati Reds 9-0. By June Dizzy had a 4-2 record, but the team was playing poorly. Furthermore, his good behavior ended when he decided that he was underpaid. When his request for a salary increase was not met, he left the team in Philadelphia and took a train home to St. Louis. In addition, Dean petitioned Commissioner Kenesaw Mountain Landis claiming that he was underage (not yet twenty-one) when he signed his contract, thus making the contract invalid and entitling him to his unconditional release. Dean actually was twenty-two at the time—a fact supported by several legal documents, including his marriage license. Although initially concerned by Dean's allegation, upon receiving evidence to the contrary, Branch Rickey turned Dean's actions into a positive publicity opportunity for the Cardinals. Once the evidence was presented, the commissioner severely admonished Dean, and the Cardinals compromised by sending money to Dean's wife and father. Dean wrote a published letter of contrition and rejoined the team. When Dean returned to the Cardinals, he told writer J. Roy Stockton that he had overheard Rickey tell Cardinals owner Sam Breadon "that the publicity from the run-out could not have been purchased for $100,000."[13]

Money continued to be an issue for Dean. Later in the season during two different road series, he feigned earaches to avoid traveling to Cincinnati, where a legal suit over a tailor's bill awaited him. Once the Cardinals paid the tailor, Dean quickly "recovered." Money also concerned the Cardinals. As the Depression deepened, Cardinal gate receipts plummeted. During the 1932 season Dean became such a draw that the Cardinals routinely pitched him in the second game of doubleheaders to ensure fans would stay to consume more Sportsman's Park concessions. After a brief run at the league leaders in August, the Cardinals folded, finishing in seventh place. Dean nevertheless ended with an 18-15 record, a 3.30 earned run average, and a league-leading 191 strikeouts. The Cardinals posted a $75,895 loss in 1932 largely because of poor attendance and poor performance on the field.

The 1932 season revealed Dean's humor when, much to the dismay of purists, he appeared at a rodeo and roped a calf. In another instance, Dean was traveling with a New York writer when they passed a filling station. After a brief pause Dean exclaimed, "I don't see how they do it!" After receiving a quizzical look from the writer, Dizzy continued, "It puzzles me how they know what corners are good for filling stations. Just how did these fellows know there was gas and oil under here?"[14] In spite of his much publicized humor, Dean was unpopular among opposing players and teams. As a pitcher he quickly developed a reputation as a "head hunter." On the mound he was simply mean. Former teammate Leo Durocher recalled that Dizzy especially disliked batters who methodically dug a hole for their back foot before stepping into the batter's box. Dean would wait patiently for the hitter to finish and then would yell, "You all done? You comfortable?" and then throw a ball aimed at their temple.[15] In one instance Dean dusted seven Giants in a row during an exhibition game because they had hit him liberally during the previous inning. In another famous incident, which took place in 1932, Dizzy Dean beaned weak-hitting Brooklyn Dodger catcher Clyde Sukeforth. Dean was enraged about blowing a 3-1 lead and the fact Sukeforth had previously hit a double off him. When Sukeforth went down and failed to get up, Dean took refuge in the Cardinal dugout—which several enraged Dodger players interpreted as an act of cowardice. Sukeforth, who was one of the Dodgers' most popular players and was later instrumental in the signing of Jackie Robinson in 1945, recovered. Dean, who was not punished by league president John Heydler, later apologized, "Shit-fire Sukey, I didn't mean to hurt you. The ball plumb got away from me."[16] Few, including Sukeforth, believed him.

In 1933, as the Depression deepened, the Cardinals finished in fifth place playing before just 256,171 fans—their weakest attendance in fourteen years. Nevertheless, Dizzy Dean solidified his position as one of the best pitchers in the National League as he finished with a 20-18 win-loss record, led the league in complete games with 26 and in strikeouts with 199. On July 30, 1933, Dean also established a new single game strikeout record, setting down seventeen Cubs in an 8-2 victory over Chicago at Sportsman's Park. In another instance, Dean promised a group of children in a hospital ward that he would strike out Giants slugger Bill Terry with the bases loaded. That afternoon, he purposely loaded the bases against the Giants and with Terry at bat made good on his promise, beating them 2-1. September 17, 1933, was Dizzy Dean Day at Sportsman's Park and he received a new Buick and other gifts. Nevertheless, Dean's season was marred by several events, including fights with ex-teammate Paul Derringer and Cardinal outfielder Joe Medwick. Dizzy was also instrumental in the firing of manager Gabby Street, who by midseason had lost control of his players. As Rickey biographer Arthur Mann noted, "Rampant disobedience in 1932 became open revolution in 1933."[17] For his part, Dean purposely missed two exhibition games. Dean's antics sent the message that he was bigger than the manager and bigger than the team.

Gabby Street was replaced in midseason by second basemen Frankie Frisch—one of his chief tormentors and severest critics. Frisch, a Fordham graduate who loved gardening and classical music, possessed a pointed sense of humor and well-deserved reputation for an acidic foul mouth. While he did not turn the Cardinals into a contender in 1933, his nononsense approach succeeded in getting the most from his players. As 1934 dawned, the Cardinals team (eventually known as the Gas House Gang) began to gel. At shortstop the Cardinals had acquired infielder Leo Durocher in 1933. Not known for his hitting (Babe Ruth called him "the all-American out"), Durocher was an excellent fielder and a fiery competitor who knew the game well. Off the field Durocher was a pool shark whose friends included crooks and gamblers.

The most visible star on the Cardinals before Dizzy Dean's arrival had been Oklahoman Johnny "Pepper" Martin—a talented third baseman who hustled incessantly and had a insatiable desire to win. Martin, who wore no shirt, no sanitary socks, no underwear, and no jock strap under his uniform, was almost always dirty and disheveled-looking. Nicknamed "the wild horse of the Osage," the show-off Martin represented the heart and spirit of the club. "The best thing a manager could have is nine Pepper Martins on the field," once noted Frankie Frisch.[18] Another cog was outfielder Joe "Ducky" Medwick, a gifted athlete who spoke fluent Hungarian (his parents were from Budapest). The gruff, pugnacious Medwick could hit for power. Other important players included first baseman James "Rip" Collins, outfielders Ernie Orsatti, Jack Rothrock, and Chick Fullis, catchers Virgil "Spud" Davis and Bill DeLancey, and utility player Burgess Whitehead, the first Phi Beta Kappa scholar in baseball.

Significant pitchers on the squad included James "Tex" Carleton, a blunt but talented Texas Christian University graduate, and left-handers Bill Walker and William "Wild Bill" Hallahan. In addition, at the beginning of 1934 Dizzy was joined by another Dean, for brother Paul had made a name for himself winning nineteen games in the minors the previous season. Initially known as "Harpo" after the silent Marx brother and then "Daffy," a term coined to complement Dizzy, Paul was as introverted as his brother was outgoing. Together, this group of rough-and-tumble, dirty-uniformed, mostly rural southern young men became known as the Gas House Gang. The name was coined by cartoonist Willard Mullin in a caricature appearing in the *New York World* in early 1935 depicting the Cardinals as a migrant group from the wrong side of the tracks. In this case Mullin was referring to the South, as St. Louis was the closest major league city to the heart of Dixie and the Cardinals were the South's team.

Even before the beginning of the 1934 season, Dizzy Dean predicted that the Cardinals would win the National League pennant and that he and his brother Paul would win forty-five games between them. Dizzy, who became famous for his boasts, once noted that "it ain't bragging if you can back 'em up."[19] Nevertheless, experts considered the Cardinals a long shot to win the pennant and favored the Giants and the Cubs. It was in 1934 that Giant manager Bill Terry, when asked about the Dodgers' chances, had replied, "Brooklyn? Are they still in the league?" The Cardinals, who were in first place by a game on June 1, performed according to Dizzy Dean's script by becoming a bona fide contender in the race. They were led by the Deans, who appeared in thirty-one of the team's first fifty-two games.

Problems arose in June when the Deans decided to test manager Frankie Frisch and the Cardinals over their salaries. Paul Dean signed a contract in the spring of 1934 for $3,000 and Dizzy was making $7,500. The Cardinals were known for their poor salaries, and Dizzy Dean, who was beginning to demonstrate the clever calculating side of his persona, saw an opportunity to take advantage of the Cardinals' dependence on the brothers' pitching. Dizzy complained of a chronic sore arm and refused to pitch in the second game of a Sunday doubleheader on June 2. Realizing that this ploy was about salaries, Frisch held his ground, telling the brothers that could leave the team and return home if they did not wish to play. The brothers yielded and the issue abated.

The Deans took on the Cardinals again in early August. After both pitchers lost tough games in a doubleheader, they purposely missed a train to Detroit, where the Cardinals were scheduled to play an exhibition game with the Tigers. A crowd of over 40,000 fans, who had specifically come to see the Dean brothers pitch, was greatly disappointed by their absence. In the Cardinals clubhouse before their next regularly scheduled game, Frisch announced that he was fining Dizzy $100 and Paul $50 for missing the game. Dizzy exploded with indignation and almost destroyed the clubhouse. He tore up two of his own uniforms and vowed that he would never play for the Cardinals again. Refusing to lose control of his team, Frisch suspended both players. When Breadon and Rickey stood fast behind Frisch, Paul Dean paid his fine and was reinstated. Dizzy Dean left the team and took his case to baseball commissioner Judge Kenesaw Mountain Landis in Chicago. At the hearing Frisch, Breadon, Rickey, and several Cardinal players testified against Dizzy, and Judge Landis upheld the Cardinals' suspension of Dean and their fines.

Following the hearing, Manager Frisch told one newspaper reporter that "there are ten million people out of work in this country, yet Dizzy

Dean is willing to sacrifice a daily income of approximately $50 to fill the role of a play-boy."[20] After glumly telling reporters that the Cardinals were taking advantage of the brothers, Dizzy admitted that he was "whipped." According to one writer, the Dean brothers' rebellion actually "crystallized the team spirit, made possible the spectacular pennant drive, and made Frankie Frisch."[21] Although the Deans' antics caused resentment among the Cardinal players, their success on the playing field lessened the negative impact of their actions as they led the team to twenty wins in their final twenty-five games. Five days after his return, Dean pitched a shutout against the Giants for his twenty-second win of the season. Later in September, the Dean brothers pitched the Cardinals to a doubleheader win over the Giants in the Polo Grounds in front of 62,573 fans—an all-time Polo Grounds attendance record. Moreover, they did the same to Casey Stengel's Brooklyn Dodgers with Dizzy winning the first game, allowing only three hits, while Paul threw a no-hitter in the second contest. "Why didn't you tell me you wuz going to pitch a no-hitter?" Dean reputedly asked his brother after the game. "I would have too."[22]

Throughout the last days of September, Frankie Frisch employed an erratic pitching rotation featuring the Deans. The brothers pitched eleven times in the team's final ten games, with Paul winning his nineteenth game on September 29 and Dizzy his thirtieth on the last day of the 1934 season. While the Deans exceeded Dizzy's outlandish prediction of forty-five wins at the beginning of the season, it was the Brooklyn Dodgers who helped catapult the Cardinals to the pennant by taking their last two games of the season against the Giants. Manager Casey Stengel, who remembered Bill Terry's preseason remarks, had little sympathy for the Giants. When told that Terry was humiliated by the outcome of the race, he noted, "So he feels bad, huh? How do you think I felt when he made fun of my ball club last spring?"[23]

After winning the National League, the Cardinals faced the Detroit Tigers in the 1934 World Series. When asked by a sportswriter who would win the series, the pitcher confidently replied, "Me and Paul."[24] Indeed, that was exactly what happened, for the brothers won four games and the Cardinals took the series 4-3 over the Tigers. The series was famous for two incidents. In game four, Dizzy Dean entered the game as a pinch runner and was knocked unconscious when he was hit in the head by an infielder's throw while attempting to break up a double play. Although not seriously injured, Dean himself would later joke that a St. Louis newspaper ran a headline which read, "X-rays of Dean's Head Show Nothing."[25] The second incident occurred in game seven. After a rough slide and an on-the-field altercation between the Cardinals' Joe Medwick and the Tigers' Marv Owen, Tiger fans halted the game when they bombarded

Medwick with garbage after he ran out to left field to begin the next half-inning. To prevent a riot, Judge Landis removed Medwick from the game.

By 1935 Dizzy Dean was a public figure—as well known in the United States as Great Britain's King George V, President Franklin D. Roosevelt, humorist Will Rogers, and aviator Charles Lindbergh. Nowhere was he more popular than in the South—St. Louis was considered a southern town. Its pace of life was slower, it had a southern charm that no other major league city boasted, and it had agrarian ties to a large region stretching south through the Mississippi Valley and west into Oklahoma and Texas. Agrarians, townsfolk, and southerners in general identified with the Cardinals and with Dizzy Dean. He was one of them—the sharecropper's son who surmounted the Depression with his baseball success. He made them laugh, was willing to fight on or off the field for what he believed, and usually had their sympathy in his quests for higher wages. His victories on the mound made them proud, and, even more, he helped them temporarily forget their woes.

The World Series win and the Dean brothers' fascinating eccentricities represented a publicist's dream and the St. Louis Cardinals helped make Dizzy Dean marketing's darling. Moreover, with Babe Ruth's playing skills quickly diminishing and his release by the Yankees at the beginning of 1935, Dean now became baseball's biggest attraction. Not only did he cash in on the World Series—his share was $5,000—he also participated in a lucrative barnstorming trip and made numerous radio appearances. He endorsed tobacco products, breakfast cereals, clothing, watches, a harmonica, writing tablets, and games; he even appeared in a weeklong show at New York's Roxy Theater. In the spring of 1935, Dean signed an $18,000 contract, and with Patricia Dean controlling his finances, he was not just solvent but suddenly awash in income.

Prosperity was fleeting, for during the 1935 season Dean succeeded in squandering many of his gains, and he lost endorsements and fan support in the process. In Pittsburgh Dean became enraged when an adverse call by an umpire led to three Pirate runs. Childishly, in front of thousands of fans who came to see him pitch, Dean purposely lobbed the ball into the Pirate hitters who took advantage of his generosity. Boos erupted from the stands and many fans left in disgust. After being lifted by manager Frisch, Dean initiated an ugly scene in the dugout. Another incident occurred when the Cardinals played an exhibition game in St. Paul, Minnesota. Although neither of the Deans was scheduled to pitch, the game's promoters expected them to appear. Instead, when asked to greet the crowd on the public address system or simply take a bow, the Deans remained in the dugout the entire time. Local writers wrote scathing columns charging the Deans with being big-headed and ungrateful. Dean also had a run-in with a promoter in Chattanooga, which led Judge Landis to fine Dizzy $100.

Dean also publicly stated that he would not pitch to his catcher Virgil Davis because he lacked confidence in Davis's catching ability. In spite of Dizzy's success on the field, all of these antics angered the fans.

Between 1935 and 1937 the Gas House Gang continued to be one of baseball's most exciting teams, but pennants eluded them. Dizzy Dean won twenty-eight games in 1935 and twenty-four in 1936. He was on his way to another stellar season in 1937 when Earl Averill hit a line drive that broke Dean's toe during the All-Star game. "Your big toe is fractured," reported the doctor. "No it ain't," replied Dean. "It's broke."[26] Determined to continue pitching, Dizzy permanently hurt his arm while favoring his toe. In 1938 Dean's stock tumbled—Branch Rickey was now looking for a buyer and J. Edgar Hoover reported that a Dean kidnapping had been averted because the kidnappers believed that the Cardinals would no longer pay a $50,000 ransom for the damaged hurler's return. Nevertheless, the Cardinals traded Dean to the Chicago Cubs for three players and $185,000. Dean would win only seventeen games in a Cubs uniform before his career ended in 1941. His golden arm simply failed him. In 1941, Cubs owner Phil Wrigley signed Dean as a coach.

Dizzy Dean did not remain a coach very long. A month later he signed with the Falstaff Brewing Company to team up with Johnny O'Hara to announce the St. Louis Cardinals and St. Louis Browns home games (away games were not covered) at $10,000 per year. When asked why he was willing to take a chance on announcing, he replied, "There ain't no future in coachin', and I can make enough speakin' into them microphones to put me on easy street in a couple of years."[27] Dean followed other successful players such as Jack Graney, Waite Hoyt, and Harry Heilmann in making the transition from field to microphone. Vowing that his new responsibility would not change him, he noted further, "I'm just gonna speak plain ol' ordinary pinto bean English."[28]

Dean, while nervous about announcing, made his debut on July 10, 1941. It was his immediate good fortune to attract a large audience because he began announcing during Joe DiMaggio's famous fifty-six-game hitting streak. Once listeners tuned into Dean, they were hooked. He was a natural. He peppered his broadcasts with homespun humor, wild stories, opinions on everything from cooking to world events, and a delicious sense of irreverence. Moreover, he knew enough about baseball—particularly the game within a game, the struggle between pitcher and hitter—to provide insight into what was happening on the field. His sayings and language also entertained his listeners. Runners "slud" into second; batters "swang"; pitchers "throwed"; balls "karmed" off the wall; infielders made "airs" and "sists"; "umparrs" made bad calls; and the "ketcher" dropped the ball. Pronunciations of names also proved challenging for Dean. He gave up on Chico Carrasquel—calling him "the hitter with three Ks in his name." Stan Musial became "Moo-zell," Phil Rizzuto was "Rizoota," and Walker Cooper was "Cupper." His personalized vocabulary also included "blue darters" for line drives, "dyin' quails" for sinking liners, and "a can of corn" for a catch made on a pop fly. He also became famous for malapropisms and redundant phrases such as "the score is nothin'-nothin' and nobody's winning."[29]

Soon he captured more than 80 percent of the Cardinals' listening audience (there were competing broadcasts). Dean became the center of the broadcast with baseball becoming the secondary attraction. He was extroverted, attractive, loquacious, knowledgeable, entertaining, and unpredictable. He rooted heartily for the home team but could be outrageously opinionated or critical when he saw something he did not like. When the game slowed down, he became an entertainer, singing his favorite song—"The Wabash Cannonball"—or a hymn or some other tune. In addition, he was an excellent salesman for Falstaff and Griesedieck beers and other products.

Nevertheless, Dean was not everyone's favorite announcer. In 1942, a year in which the Cardinals won another pennant, Dean was named the baseball announcer with the worst diction and the St. Louis Board of Education urged Falstaff to remove Dean from the air. Dean replied, "A lot of folks that ain't saying ain't, ain't eatin'." Moreover, in 1944—the only year in which the two St. Louis teams met in the World Series—Judge Landis blocked Dean from announcing the games because his poor syntax was not suitable for national broadcasts, even though paradoxically the *Sporting News* named Dean announcer of the year. "How can the commissar say I ain't eligible to broadcast?" Dean complained. "I ain't never met anybody that didn't know what ain't means."[30] Dean also raised eyebrows when he openly campaigned on the air for the reelection of President Roosevelt. Stations on St. Louis networks immediately broadcast disclaimers noting that Dean's opinions were his own.

Dean's most serious challenge came in 1946 during the so-called school marms' uprising, when national columnist Leonard Lyons reported that a group of Missouri schoolteachers had complained to the Federal Communications Commission that Dean's misuse of the English language was having a bad influence on their pupils' grammar and syntax. Dean fans flooded St. Louis radio stations in protest and the *St. Louis Globe Democrat* and Norman Cousins, the editor of the prestigious *Saturday Review*, also weighed in on Dean's side. Cousins eloquently noted that "abuse of English is the standard occupational disease of the national pastime—a disease which, if cured, would do irreparable damage to the patient."[31] When all was said and done, the English Teachers Association of Missouri denied that the complaint had come from them and the furor died.

In 1947 a decision by a sponsor split the broadcasts, leaving Harry Caray and Gabby Street as the Cardinals' announcers and Dean and Johnny O'Hara with the Browns. Dean became so disillusioned with the Browns' poor field performance that he donned a uniform and made a one-game comeback as he pitched for the team in their final game of the season against the Chicago White Sox. He acquitted himself well, yielding only four hits and no runs in three innings. He had to quit the contest because of a leg injury he incurred while sliding into third base. In 1950, the New York Yankees saved Dean from the Browns when they asked him to join the team's baseball telecasts as a pre- and postgame interviewer and broadcaster. Although Dean developed a modest cult following among New York television watchers, many viewed him as a curiosity. One television critic wrote, "When it comes to using back-country expressions the Diz has it all over Red Barber, and if his grammar goes astray it's not obtrusive. Dizzy also knows his TV. He doesn't talk too much."[32] In 1951 Dizzy Dean returned to St. Louis to team with Buddy Blattner for St. Louis Browns' games and Al Helfer on Mutual's *Game of the Day*. For the first time Dean's southern twang and brand of announcing were carried nationwide, and he was an instant success.

In 1953 the Falstaff Brewing Company added the first regularly televised national broadcasts of baseball on ABC's *Game of the Week* to Dizzy Dean's busy schedule. While the telecasts were blacked out in baseball's eleven major league markets and the network could only telecast American League games from three cities, viewers in the rest of the nation could watch major league baseball for the first time. Thus television watchers in San Francisco, Houston, Dallas-Fort Worth, Minneapolis-St. Paul, Milwaukee, Kansas City, New Orleans, Atlanta, and Miami, and most of the territory in between, were introduced to major league baseball by Dizzy Dean. The program proved an immediate success as 75 percent of all sets in use on Saturdays in 1953 in non–major league market cities were tuned to the *Game of the Week*. Between 1953 and 1966 Dean established a national allegiance not replicated since. Bill MacPhail, the director of CBS Sports (the *Game of the Week* switched to CBS in 1955) simply stated that "watching Dizzy Dean was a religion. An absolute religion."[33] As the first of his two broadcast partners, Buddy Blattner, explained, Dean "didn't simply provide the program, he *was* the program."[34]

Dean took to television as quickly as his viewers took to his broadcasts. He filled the downtime baseball provided with warmth, homespun philosophy, humor, stories, and fun. He developed a public persona that was affable, down-to-earth, and folksy. Moreover, as one writer noted, he maintained a "pennant-winning smile and spoke with a voice marinated in chicken-fried gravy."[35] He realized the entertainment value of his broadcasts and noted in 1955 that "the thing I have to guard against is improvement. If I start talking better, they'll throw me out."[36] Fans across America loved him because they could identify with him—he spoke their language in an idiom they easily understood. Listeners, including Blattner and subsequent partner Pee Wee Reese, became "Pod-nuh" as if they were part of the broadcasts too. Dean's appeal to America's heartland was undeniable.

He was in the vanguard of a cadre of southern baseball announcers regularly heard on regional or national radio and television broadcasts during the 1940s and 1950s. Led by Red Barber from Florida via Alabama, this group included Mel Allen from Alabama, Jimmy Dudley from Virginia, Lindsey Nelson of Tennessee, and Georgian Ernie Harwell. Together through the airwaves they brought a southern vernacular into homes across America. The familiarity of their words, sayings, and personalities helped reintroduce southern culture into the mainstream of American society. Although he was the least articulate of these men, Dizzy Dean was by far the most effective in achieving this subtle reconciliation.

Dizzy Dean's run on the *Game of the Week* ended with the 1966 season, when the production switched to NBC and the network decided that Curt Gowdy should do the games. Dean now retired to his farm near his wife's hometown of Bond, Mississippi, and continued to serve as a spokesman for the Falstaff Brewing Company. Through Patricia Dean's financial genius, he was now a wealthy man. Inducted into baseball's Hall of Fame in 1953, Dean attended old-timer's games and baseball banquets, made guest appearances on radio and television, did commercials, endorsed products, and spent much of the remainder of his time fishing and hunting. The only dark side of his legacy was his penchant for gambling. In 1948 he was called into Commissioner A. B. "Happy" Chandler's office and presented with evidence that he was betting on baseball while broadcasting from the radio booth. Dean pledged to quit and Chandler let him off with a warning. In 1970 Dean was caught up in a gambling scandal that ended with the arrest of several gamblers. Newspaper reports concluded that Dean was "victimized and utilized by various elements of the bookmaking world without his knowledge."[37] Dean died on July 17, 1974, while on a golf and gambling trip in South Lake Tahoe, Nevada.

Dizzy Dean was the quintessential southerner. Born in Arkansas and raised there and in Oklahoma, he was a rural, uneducated farm boy who was the son of a poor cotton sharecropper. Considered a hick or a rube during his teens and twenties, he appeared gullible, provincial, and unsophisticated. His introduction to society belied his poor background, lack of education, and worldliness. As soon as Dean opened his mouth, people knew he was from the South, for his speech pattern was definitely southern.

His habits, outlook, likes and dislikes, and eccentricities were southern as well. He built his radio broadcasts on his familiarity with things rural and southern—music, food, cooking, and language. He was a spinner of yarns, stories, and jokes that typically had southern themes. "Old Diz" was a builder and creator of myths, including those about himself. Even though his early life experience was that of an itinerant, he remained deeply southern in his later adherence to the importance of place.

Dizzy Dean overcame his southern history. Assured and full of self-admiration, he would not accept frustration, failure, or defeat. He never considered himself a loser. He never knew a Lost Cause—especially if it pertained to him. In many respects, he overcame the South's tragic experience and heritage. Dean's fresh innocence and immediate success appealed to a people caught up in the depths of depression and personal despair. He was a success story they could understand, if not emulate. Dizzy provided them with hope. As a professional baseball player, Dean made enough money so that he was no longer shackled to anyone. Free to exercise his opinion and to do almost as he pleased, he showed himself to be audacious, ridiculous, ambitious, and humorous—a persona he purposely developed. His sense of well-being allowed him to act superior both on and off the field.

Dean was rarely associated with the greatest burden of southern history—race. He simply ignored segregation and the civil rights movement, in public at least. Though he lived in the heart of the South during the turbulent 1960s, he believed that a discussion on civil rights did not belong in the television or radio booth, even though he was broadcasting a sport that was in the forefront of integration. Weak attempts by civil rights groups to remove Dean were ignored.

As a broadcaster, Dean's humorous personality, his love of baseball, and the southern flavor he added to the game are forever etched in the memories of millions who listened to and watched his broadcasts. Thus, long after his voice was stilled, his legacy lives on.

NOTES

1. Vince Staten, *Ol' Diz: A Biography of Dizzy Dean* (New York: HarperCollins, 1992), 16.
2. Bill McGoogan and Kyle Chrichton, "The Dean Murder Case," *Colliers Magazine*, September 18, 1943, 76.
3. Staten, *Ol' Diz*, 27.
4. Robert Gregory, *Dizzy Dean and Baseball during the Great Depression* (New York: Viking, 1992), 20.
5. Gregory, *Dizzy Dean*, 32.

6. Arthur Mann, *Branch Rickey: American in Action* (Boston: Houghton Mifflin, 1957), 159.
7. Curt Smith, *America's Dizzy Dean* (St. Louis: Bethany, 1978), 24.
8. John J. Monteleone, *Branch Rickey's Little Blue Book: Wit and Strategy from Baseball's Last Wise Man* (New York: Macmillan, 1995), 117.
9. Smith, *America's Dizzy Dean*, 26.
10. Mann, *Rickey*, 163.
11. Staten, *Ol' Diz*, 60.
12. Gregory, *Dizzy Dean*, 65.
13. J. Roy Stockton, "Me and Paul," *Saturday Evening Post*, March 16, 1935, 104.
14. Smith, *America's Dizzy Dean*, 42.
15. Leo Durocher with Ed Linn, *Nice Guys Finish Last* (New York: Simon & Schuster, 1975), 85.
16. Gregory, *Dizzy Dean*, 92.
17. Mann, *Rickey*, 180.
18. Doug Feldmann, *Dizzy and the Gas House Gang: The 1934 St. Louis Cardinals and Depression-Era Baseball* (Jefferson, NC: McFarland, 2000), 46.
19. Smith, *America's Dizzy Dean*, 50.
20. Feldmann, *Dizzy*, 108–9.
21. Stockton, "Me and Paul," 104.
22. Peter Golenbock, *The Spirit of St. Louis: A History of the St. Louis Cardinals and Browns* (New York: HarperEntertainment, 2001), 180.
23. Golenbock, *Spirit of St. Louis*, 182.
24. Stockton, "Me and Paul," 105.
25. Staten, *Ol' Diz*, 145. None of the St. Louis or Detroit papers ran that headline.
26. Smith, *America's Dizzy Dean*, 104.
27. Gregory, *Dizzy Dean*, 363.
28. Gregory, *Dizzy Dean*, 364.
29. Curt Smith, *Voices of the Game* (New York: Simon & Schuster, 1992), 102.
30. Smith, *Voices of the Game*, 104.
31. Norman Cousins, *Saturday Review of Literature*, August 3, 1946, 16.
32. Gregory, *Dizzy Dean*, 375.
33. Smith, *Voices of the Game*, 3.
34. Smith, *Voices of the Game*, 145.
35. Gregory, *Dizzy Dean*, 387.
36. Smith, *Voices of the Game*, 150.
37. *Lexington Leader*, January 5, 1970, 15.

SUGGESTED READINGS

Alexander, Charles C. *Our Game: An American Baseball History*. New York: Henry Holt, 1991.

Feldmann, Doug. *Dizzy and the Gas House Gang: The 1934 St. Louis Cardinals and Depression-Era Baseball*. Jefferson, NC: McFarland, 2000.

Gregory, Robert. *Diz: Dizzy Dean and Baseball during the Great Depression*. New York: Viking, 1992.
Miller, Patrick B., ed. *The Sporting World of the Modern South*. Urbana: University of Illinois Press, 2002.
Smith, Curt. *America's Dizzy Dean*. St. Louis: Bethany, 1978.
———. *Voices of the Game*. New York: Simon & Schuster, 1992.
Staten, Vince. *Ol' Diz: A Biography of Dizzy Dean*. New York: HarperCollins, 1992.
Voigt, David Q. *American Baseball*. 3 vols. University Park: Pennsylvania State University Press, 1983.

8

Eleanor Copenhaver Anderson and the Industrial Department of the National Board YWCA: Toward a New Social Order in Dixie

Margaret Ripley Wolfe

From the time of her birth in 1896 until her death in 1985, Eleanor Copenhaver Anderson and her South experienced tremendous change. During her formative years, many southern states had elected demagogues. While such men as Ben Tillman and Coleman Blease of South Carolina, or James K. Vardaman and Theodore Bilbo of Mississippi, or Tom Watson and Eugene Talmadge of Georgia all varied in their characteristics, most used a colorful campaign style that featured often-irresponsible promises, couched in strident terms that frequently centered on racial rhetoric. Bilbo, who once shot a black man on a streetcar, wrote a book entitled Take Your Choice: Separation or Mongrelization; *Blease called for the "inferior race" to be wiped from the Earth. Many such demagogues did try to help poor whites in their states, although few focused on improving the lot of African Americans. More conservative politicians gave even stronger support to the status quo (though often with less emphasis on racial arguments) but did little to help workers of either race. As a result, Anderson's South of the 1920s and 1930s stood poised to experience the change that came only slowly over the years.*

In contrast to the elected leaders whose dedication to reform seemed hesitant or even nonexistent, a cadre of southerners continued to work, often quietly, to change and improve the system. They sought to bring better lives for workers, blacks, women, and others. While the greatest transformation would come from another generation, Eleanor Copenhaver Anderson and those like her kept the torch of reform burning, to be passed on for others to carry. *Margaret Ripley Wolfe shows how Anderson investigated working conditions, wrote reports that formed the basis for action, supported educational progress, and more—usually with little recognition and often with much controversy. Frequently forgotten in their time, people like her only now are receiving deserved notice for their courage and actions.*

Margaret Ripley Wolfe, Professor of History Emerita and Senior Faculty Affiliate, East Tennessee State University, is the author of numerous scholarly publications and professional papers, among them Daughters of Canaan: A Saga of Southern Women *(1995). She is a former president of the Southern Association for Women Historians (1984). The author gratefully acknowledges grants from the Research Development Committee, East Tennessee State University, Johnson City, and the Southern Regional Education Board, Atlanta, as well as an Appalachian Studies Fellowship funded by the Andrew Mellon Foundation and administered by Berea College, Berea, Kentucky.*

The life of social activist Eleanor Copenhaver Anderson spanned almost ninety years. It began in the Jim Crow Dixie of the 1890s and ended in the desegregated South of the 1980s. During Eleanor's childhood and youth, a conservative Democratic party prevailed, grandfather clauses and lynchings kept blacks at bay, mill owners closed ranks with planters to control poor whites, and men consigned women to second-class citizenship. Before her death, she witnessed the resurgence of a two-party system, the development of an improved work environment, and significant strides toward equal opportunity for blacks and women. This transformation owed no small debt to a cadre of indigenous southern liberals and radicals of the interwar period who envisaged a new social order.[1]

During much of the first half of the twentieth century, even as bigotry had full sway and racism ran rampant, southern liberals and radicals in league with their counterparts from elsewhere in the nation laid the foundations for the reformation of the region. They challenged—indeed threatened—the very pillars on which southern society had rested. A roll call of southern Old Left activists includes such names as Lois MacDonald, Louise Leonard McLaren, Zilphia Johnson Horton, Myles Horton, Don West, James Dombrowski, Howard Kester, and Claude Clossee Williams and such organizations as the Young Women's Christian Association (YWCA), the Southern Summer School for Women Workers (SSSWW), Highlander Folk School, and Commonwealth College. Together, individuals and agencies like these forged a loose network that attempted to transcend race and class. They shared the notion of a more humane society—although not always a common vision of how best to achieve it. To greater and lesser degrees, race relations, women's issues, and labor problems all attracted the attention

Eleanor Copenhaver Anderson in the 1930s. *Courtesy of the Copenhaver Family; print in the possession of Margaret Ripley Wolfe*

of social activists of the interwar period; but just as civil rights took center stage after World War II, the plight of workers reigned supreme during the interwar period.[2]

Eleanor Copenhaver Anderson not only kept company with southern liberals and radicals of the interwar period but also qualified as a second-generation southern feminist, a representative of the generation between the suffragists and the civil rights activists. Although she became the fourth and last wife of writer Sherwood Anderson, Eleanor had a commitment to social activism that antedated by several years their first acquaintance in 1928 and their subsequent marriage in 1933. Even then, Eleanor struggled to maintain a separate identity as a professional. When Sherwood pressured her to use his name, she proved reluctant, retaining her own at first and then gradually signing off as Eleanor Copenhaver Anderson.[3] Friends and family alike have suggested that she had the capacity to assume several different personas, ranging from the helpless southern belle to the big-city sophisticate.[4] This chameleon-like quality undoubtedly served her well in the emotionally charged environment of southern labor relations during the 1920s and 1930s. For approximately twenty-five years, longer than any other YWCA national staff member, she remained deeply involved with the work of the Industrial Department. For some thirteen years, commencing in 1925, she served as regional secretary for the South; in 1938 she became the Industrial Department's national executive secretary. From its inception following World War I until its phaseout just after World War II, the Industrial Department, operating out of headquarters in New York City, functioned as the most radical and most controversial experiment ever to operate under the auspices of the YWCA.[5]

Born on June 15, 1896, in Marion, Virginia, a small valley town in the mountainous southwestern portion of the state and the seat of Smyth County, Eleanor was the first of the five offspring of B. E. Copenhaver and Laura Lu Scherer Copenhaver. B. E. served for many years as superintendent of schools in Smyth County and cut a swath in local political circles; Laura Lu taught at Marion College and assumed a position of leadership in the Lutheran church and on the Marion social scene.[6] The baby girl born at Rosemont, the family home, carried the bloodlines of two well-respected valley families that traced their ancestry to forebears who had come to America during the eighteenth century. Thomas Copenhaver arrived in 1728, and Jacob Daniel Scherer in 1752.[7] Eleanor's maternal grandfather, the Reverend J. J. Scherer Sr., a Lutheran minister and one of several clergymen in his family, founded Marion Female College in 1873.[8]

Eleanor Copenhaver Anderson's heritage, therefore, included a firm sense of civic and religious duty, a commitment to education, and an identification with independent-minded female relatives. Already steeped in the tradition of single-sex education as a result of her family's connections with Marion Female College, Eleanor graduated from Westhampton College in Richmond, a Baptist institution for women, in 1917. She had begun her college career at Marion College but transferred to Westhampton College when it was founded in 1914. Immediately after graduating from college, she did a stint as a high school teacher in Marion and then enrolled at Bryn Mawr College, completing a two-year social economy program there in 1920. The entire tradition of women's colleges with their impelling sense of mission had a profound impact on Eleanor's life as well as on those of many other college-educated women of her generation.[9]

While enrolled at Bryn Mawr College, Eleanor spent a summer as camp director for College Settlement in New York City and found her calling in community organizing. After earning her certificate in social economy, she joined the professional staff of the National Board YWCA as a field secretary for the south central region; her name first appeared on the September 1920 roster.[10] Within three years, Eleanor had become attached to the Industrial Department. It provided her entrée into labor education and served as her vehicle for social activism.[11] By the end of the decade, Eleanor had established herself in a career and made her mark in labor education. She was in her early thirties—independent, confident, and poised. All the same, the adjective most often used to describe her by those who knew her back home in Marion was "self-effacing." She avoided talking about herself and her work when she vacationed or visited in Virginia. Friends and relatives reported that "she knew who she was" and did not find it necessary to engage in self-promotion.[12]

Although Eleanor was short of stature and had an average figure, some considered her pretty with her black hair, usually cut short, and her lovely skin, medium to dark in tone. One friend remembered that she had always looked forward to seeing Eleanor step off the train in Marion wearing what was believed to be the latest fashion from the "Big Apple," but another acquaintance considered her more the "YWCA executive type" and not a really fashionable sort. No longer just a small-town southern girl, she was a New Yorker and "very cosmopolitan," a phrase that she reportedly used frequently to describe those she admired and knew in the social whirl of New York City.[13]

The National Board YWCA, identified as it had been with evangelical Protestantism, provided an institutional shield, if sometimes a bit reluctantly, for Eleanor Copenhaver Anderson and like-minded colleagues in the Industrial Department. It must have been an effective cover, for even Eleanor's family seemed relatively uninformed about her work. In December 1931 Sherwood Anderson claimed that they had a "sort of half-formed picture" of her "as a weak little Christian gal, helping factory girls to say the Lord's prayer."[14] The *Chicago Daily News* once described her as "a traveling religious worker" and "a petite and charming southerner."[15] Lois MacDonald, cofounder of the SSSWW, described Eleanor as "sort of volatile. [She] was a very small person physically and very vigorous and, the word I use is volatile. I'm not sure that's just the word, she was an intense kind of person."[16] Lucy P. Carner, who headed the National Board YWCA Industrial Department during the 1920s, considered Eleanor the best of her staff.[17]

Brooks Spivey Creedy, also a National Board YWCA industrial secretary and a colleague, has provided perhaps the most complete description of Eleanor in action: "one of the great people I've ever known . . . a very glamorous figure." Creedy added that "she had a great deal of sophistication . . . a southern born lady . . . one of the warmest people that . . . ever walked the earth." And she elaborated: "One of the most unbelievably generous women. Bright, giving an effect of great disorganization, which was an effect only, since she was well organized . . . a terribly elliptical talker, by which I mean she would make quantum leaps from one point to another . . . an innovative person." According to Creedy, Eleanor possessed "an absolutely encyclopedic knowledge of people and movements, and where the sources of power were." She was "a real organizer in that sense [and knew] where to go for things."[18]

Possessed of what seemed to be boundless energy, Eleanor Copenhaver, along with other National Board YWCA industrial secretaries, kept up a grueling travel schedule. During 1928–1929, for example, Eleanor made seventy-one local visits to industrial sites largely in the South and attended eleven major conferences, ranging from regional to international at such disparate locations as Institute, West Virginia, and Budapest, Hungary.[19] Duties included visiting and assisting local YWCAs, investigating working conditions, organizing and overseeing conferences, and serving on numerous boards and committees. On the job her keen intellect permeated her no-nonsense reports to the National Board. Direct and analytical, they provided first-rate assessments of the southern social climate.

Not unlike other white southern liberals and radicals of the 1920s and 1930s, Eleanor Copenhaver Anderson seemed drawn to secular social activism because institutional religion, traditional ministries, and evangelical Protestantism failed to meet the challenges posed by race relations and labor conditions in Dixie. Many of the southern-born social activists of the interwar period had experienced a religious odyssey to radicalism, among them Claude Clossee Williams, Howard Kester, James Dombrowski, and Myles Horton. Some—Horton, Kester, and Dombrowski—had been influenced by Reinhold Niebuhr of Union Theological Seminary; others cited Dr. Alva W. Taylor of Vanderbilt School of Religion as their source of inspiration; most had YWCA or Young Men's Christian Association (YMCA) connections. Well versed in the trappings and substance of the social gospel, they doubted the ability of religion alone to produce their new social order. Above all, their peculiar cultural heritage shaped their responses to the social challenges of their times.

Southern liberals and radicals had ties with and sometimes came under the influence of activists and intellectuals in the North and abroad, and their causes received financial support from outside the region as well as from within. Those committed to the status quo in Dixie often exaggerated the involvement of nonsoutherners in the efforts to foment change. Eleanor Copenhaver Anderson wrote that the South represented "an interest-zone for organizations of national scope which were casting about for new worlds to conquer" and that "this sudden invasion of the sacred soil of the South by professional putterers with multitudinous motives has been a cause of annoyance to some southerners" but "a source of amusement" to the more sophisticated. "Sensitivity to outside interference has been exaggerated by mill management to make people who were trying to improve conditions keep their hands off." In addition to the YWCA, whose work with industrial workers in the South antedated that of the others by several years, Eleanor considered the involvement of the following organizations particularly significant during the labor disputes that punctuated the late 1920s: the Women's Trade Union League, the American Civil Liberties Union, the League for Industrial Democracy, the Emergency Committee for Strikers Relief, the Conference for Progressive Labor Action, the National Textile Workers Union, and the American Federation of Labor.[20]

In 1927 the American Labor Education Service (ALES) had come into existence as an independent umbrella organization committed to female workers' education. Earlier that year, Bryn Mawr Summer School, the Wisconsin Summer School, the Barnard Summer School, and the Vineyard Shore School formed the Affiliated Summer Schools, a clearinghouse for coordinating recruitment, publicity, and finances. The Southern Summer School allied with this organization but never formally affiliated with it. ALES, in turn, owed its origins to the Affiliated Summer Schools but evolved into an independent entity. The National Board YWCA's concern for women workers antedated the beginnings of ALES and the summer school movement, and, not surprisingly, the summer schools and ALES had strong ties to the YWCA. Neither the staff and board of ALES, the respective summer schools, nor the National Board YWCA promoted particular unions, but they shared the general goals of the American labor movement.[21]

The South of the interwar period provided an immense challenge for organized labor, and the region's economy garnered considerable attention. President Franklin Delano Roosevelt asserted during the late 1930s that the region represented "the Nation's No. 1 economic problem—the

Nation's problem, not merely the South's."²² Almost a decade earlier, A. J. Muste, chairman of the faculty at Brookwood Labor College and vice president of the American Federation of Teachers, had predicted that "the fate of labor in the United States [would], to a large extent, be settled by developments in the South." He argued that if southern workers remained "unenlightened and subservient . . . they [would] retard, if not destroy, the conditions achieved by labor in other sections of the country."²³ Other activists of the 1920s and 1930s surely shared Muste's point of view, for they focused a great deal of attention on southern labor and worker education in Dixie.

In response to the query, What do workers want in education? Hilda W. Smith, the first director of the Bryn Mawr School for Women Workers and later a specialist in workers' education with the New Deal's Works Progress Administration, declared in 1933: "It is evident that they want instruction which will illuminate for them every-day questions of the economic world; give them a broad background for the understanding of current labor problems, increase their power of expression in writing and speaking, and develop ability for independent thinking which may be translated into terms of constructive social action."²⁴

Southern liberals and radicals and their institutions addressed themselves to these issues precisely. Commonwealth College targeted tenant farmers and coal miners; Highlander started with destitute woodcutters, miners, and mill workers in Tennessee; the National Board YWCA, through its Industrial Department and its ties to local associations and their programs for women laborers, concentrated on factory workers; and the SSSWW initially focused its entire effort on working-class females. Although the SSSWW, founded by Louise Leonard of Pennsylvania (Louise Leonard McLaren after her marriage) and Lois MacDonald of South Carolina in 1927, was not a permanent residential operation, students viewed it as *a place* where they could speak their minds. Largely an outgrowth of YWCA activities and founded by individuals with strong YWCA connections (Leonard had been an industrial secretary for the National Board YWCA), the SSSWW, according to historian Mary Evans Frederickson, "offered working-class women an ideological vision of a new social order, and the tools to work for the creation of an industrial democracy." Describing the unique position of the YWCA in the South, Frederickson wrote that "no other organization was at once an intrinsic community institution and tied to a national network [with the possible exception of the YMCA] which channeled progressive ideas to southern women in local Associations."²⁵ Espousing collective action in general, the National Board YWCA Industrial Department and the SSSWW endorsed no particular unions; Highlander Folk School, however, occasionally did so and was directly involved at one time with the Congress of Industrial Organizations. All of these organizations offered instruction from a left-of-center perspective, used dramatics and music, developed abilities in public speaking, and taught students to draft statements, print leaflets, and disseminate information.

Labor education in the South during the 1920s and 1930s often involved a retreat to nature as a respite from noisy mills and the daily monotony and strain of human existence. Location played a role in the ritualistic, almost mystical tactics in Dixie; training sessions took on the aura of monasticism in remote enclaves. Isolation also carried with it a relatively low risk of hostile interference. Mena, Arkansas, the site of Commonwealth College, and Monteagle, Tennessee, home of Highlander, could hardly be considered major stopping points on the avenues of civilization. In the South, where evangelical religion had been such a vital force, ritualistic practices, albeit secular, proved particularly effective. Union organizers sometimes tapped the reservoir of religious emotionalism through music as did the workers themselves, who set their own repetitive words to old gospel favorites and hymns. Indigenous activists understood fully the power of religion in southern society, encouraged ritualism, and employed religious analogies to produce the desired results.

At the 1934 YWCA businesswomen's conference, for example, those in attendance recited a "litany" (the word that was actually used) compiled from comments they had offered about what the ten-day gathering had meant to each of them. "I believe in my oneness with the workers of the world," they incanted; "I believe in the interdependence of nations and races." Afterward, the entire group "sang the Negro national anthem and went down to the water to sing taps." According to a participant, "the entire Negro staff [presumably custodial and culinary] had come out and were singing for us 'God be with you till we meet again,' 'Lord, I want to be like Jesus,' and 'Ain't going to study war no more.'"[26]

Although a variety of liberal and radical organizations concerned themselves generally with the plight of labor in Dixie, the YWCA and SSSWW committed themselves specifically to female workers. The weeklong sessions of the YWCA for female industrial workers convened in such places as Camp Merriewoode at Sapphire, North Carolina; Camp Chelan at Sellersburg, Indiana (near Louisville, Kentucky); and Lincoln's Academy at Kings Mountain, North Carolina. The business and professional women occasionally used Camp Nakanawa at Mayland, Tennessee. The SSSWW conducted its first term in 1927 at Sweet Briar College in Virginia. Thereafter, the six-week annual programs went forward in North Carolina at such places as Burnsville, Arden, Little Switzerland, Brevard, and Skyland. Over the course of their existence, the Y's separate conferences for industrial workers, on the one hand, and business and professional women, on the other, and the SSSWW camps—organized, attended, taught, and financed mostly by women—touched the lives of hundreds directly and thousands indirectly. Through a steady correspondence with local Y chapters and camp alumnae, organizers forged a network of socially conscious women.

Outlines for courses, lists of speakers, and official reports provide evidence of a philosophical challenge to southern conservatism. Studying labor history, speaking in public, and preparing pamphlets, flyers, and yearbooks provided practical lessons in organizing techniques. Discussions of black literature and history and the presence of an occasional black visitor raised doubts about the rationale for segregation. The young women in attendance had the advantage of physical examinations and medical treatments; their nutritional deficiencies received temporary attention. Courses in personal hygiene offered information about birth control and routine feminine health care; some sessions afforded the opportunity for discussion of adult female–male relationships. Organizers understood full well that unless women had some control over their own reproductive capacity, they could hardly shape their personal lives, much less build a new social order in Dixie.

Although reformers sometimes held highly visionary notions during this period, they also employed practical methodology and possessed an uncanny ability to identify and cultivate potential leadership among workers. Adults who had already been dismissed as hopeless by traditional pedagogues sometimes provided eager students for labor educators. Individuals and agencies committed to worker education ran the gamut from moderately liberal to radical. Given the National Board YWCA's commitment to a new social order in Dixie and its pioneering efforts and skillful approach to labor education in the South, occasional criticism from other liberals and radicals must have proved particularly galling.

Lucien Koch, for example, the director of Commonwealth College during the early 1930s, denigrated the efforts of those he considered more moderate than Commonwealth and himself. "In America, Y.W.C.A. industrial secretaries have been reading Carl Sandburg to waitresses for years, trade unions have carried on educational programs, liberal groups have held their summer camps, and universities have sponsored extension lectures for the proletariat," Koch railed. "Under the catch-all label of labor education the coal miner has had Browning rammed down his throat, the machinist has been told of the value of unionization (and of the necessity of paying dues) and the girls in the hosiery mills have learned how to avoid split infinitives and paint their own lamp shades."[27]

While Koch's criticism suggests some of the bickering that occurred among interwar liberals and radicals, it hardly speaks to the complexity of the Y's activities or the commitment of its professional staff. The Industrial Department of the National Board YWCA, the Y's agency for worker education, largely owed its existence to Florence Simms. She had become the YWCA national industrial secretary in 1904 and, until her death in 1923, played a key role in shaping the commitment of the National Board to labor and in creating the Industrial Department. "The more abundant life," a euphemism used by Simms, meant an interest in industrial workers and the concept of a more inclusive membership. The first national conference of industrial girls met in Washington, DC, in 1919. It adopted resolutions urging the YWCA to "consider and present to its National Board a set of standards for women in industry such as an 8-hour law, prohibition of night work, the right of labor to organize" and to work toward "the passage of such laws as will make possible the carrying out of these standards."[28]

By 1920 the YWCA in convention at Cleveland, Ohio, adopted resolutions regarding "social ideals," which basically followed those suggested by the 1919 Washington conference and recognized the rights of workers to organize. This action came on the heels of a similar position taken by the Federal Council of Churches of Christ in America at a special 1919 meeting also held in Cleveland. At a YWCA convention in Hot Springs, Arkansas, in 1922, the industrial membership, made up of women and girls employed in industry, participated in all of the affairs of the organization for the first time. This element recommended a study of industrial employment and presented Simms with the opportunity to educate the entire membership to the special problems of females in industry.[29]

The "factory girls," as they were often called, proved more strident than most of the middle- and upper-class membership. Legends persist at the YWCA headquarters of women in the upper echelon of the organization who had moved or been maneuvered into positions philosophically, politically, and economically at variance with their own husbands. The rift between members who just wanted to believe in Jesus Christ and the social activists who wanted to practice His teachings left scars, and official records of the organization suggest that these differences remained unresolved for the duration of the Industrial Department's existence.

The industrial work of the National Board went forward under the leadership of professional staffers. Industrial secretaries out of New York City and the factory girls who belonged to local chapters of the Y, sometimes found themselves at odds with the club women-philanthropists who held ranking positions on the National Board. Eleanor Copenhaver Anderson operated in this organizational maze during the 1920s and 1930s. That "factory girls" continued to be catalysts for social change seems evident. In a 1936 diary entry, for example, Eleanor Copenhaver Anderson mentioned a High Point, North Carolina, council meeting, where the "industrial girls" had seemed "bent on [having a] Negro girl as well as [a Negro] leader at [their] conference." Apparently the same was true of the Charlotte council. "It will be hell to pay in New York," Eleanor wrote, "but a real sophisticated decision."[30]

As southern industrial secretary for the National Board YWCA, Eleanor Copenhaver Anderson had a front-row seat for the general labor unrest that punctuated the late 1920s and early 1930s. Anderson, a native southerner and a keen student of the region, wrote in 1929, a year viewed as a milestone by liberals, radicals, and fellow travelers of the interwar period, that "the traditional southern mind held several sacred doctrines." These included "a worship of aristocracy and belief in the divine right of the aristocracy to rule," the "assumption that the aristocracy knew what was best for the 'poor white trash' and lower economic groups," and the knowledge that the region possessed a "huge, untapped labor supply from the farms." The labor unrest that broke across the Upper South during the late 1920s seemed to suggest that the "revolution" had commenced. Eleanor Copenhaver wrote that "students in the South see in the upheavals . . . a mass movement touching many kinds of people, which they liken in its potentialities to the Reformation or the Renaissance. It is hard to convey to the outsider who has not watched the South from the inside for the last ten years, the magnitude and subtlety of this revolution." Even the most casual observers, she claimed, "had detected restlessness for some time past, but few of them prophesized that general disturbances would come so soon."[31]

The strikes commenced in 1929 at German-owned rayon plants in Elizabethton, Tennessee, where a walkout of women workers led by Margaret Bowen precipitated a general strike. Developments at Elizabethton and the series of strikes that followed put the lie to New South propaganda with its resounding paeans to docile southern labor. At Gastonia, North Carolina, Ella Mae Wiggins, the National Textile Workers Union's (NTWU) most effective local organizer, was shot to death. At Danville, Virginia, some 15,000 people, including 4,000 workers and their dependents, faced a prolonged strike that involved bloodshed. Major disturbances also occurred during these years at Marion, North Carolina. Company gunmen there fired on striking workers, shooting them in the back as they fled from tear gas; when the smoke cleared, six had died and twenty-five lay wounded. When none of the local ministers who were under the influence of the company dared offer a word at the funerals, an old mountain preacher, Cicero Queen, appeared, dropped to his knees, and prayed, "Oh Lord Jesus Christ, here are men in their coffins. . . . I trust though, O God, that these friends will go to a better place than this mill village or any other place in Carolina."[32] Eleanor Copenhaver Anderson wrote that "visitors to Marion after the massacre felt that the blood of the martyrs there would become the seed of the new social order."[33]

In the great human continuum, the struggles of these years contributed to long-term gains. The influence of the press and the power of public opinion affected the political realm. Nevertheless, the labor struggles that occurred in the South during the interwar period took heavy personal tolls on workers, in the short term sometimes wrecking individual lives. The consequences of collective action ran the gamut from lost pay to permanent layoffs, from physical injuries to deaths. Blacklisting not infrequently followed unemployed strikers and union members from one industrial enclave to another. Anderson visited Elizabethton, Tennessee, during the 1929 strike and followed developments there almost daily. In a letter to the editor of the *New York Times* written on May 22 of that year she observed that "one of the many surprising factors in the situation in the Carolinas and in Tennessee has been the amount of sympathy shown for the cause of the workers by the middle-class groups in many Southern Communities." "To the best of my knowledge," she wrote, "in spite of many provocations the workers have been orderly, sober and restrained." What was happening to native-born workers in mountain towns profoundly and personally affected Anderson. "I grew up in the Southern Appalachians," she explained.[34]

Obvious class distinctions existed between the workers on the front lines and many of the region's liberals and radicals, but even the most timid advocates of constructive change in Dixie ran risks. Not all southern liberals and radicals of this era stood on picket lines and confronted gun thugs—although some did—but danger of one kind or another never lurked far from them. In 1921 during the course of her work, Eleanor Copenhaver Anderson had been accosted by southern Klansmen.[35] The conferences that she organized sometimes received threats as well. In addition to attempts at physical intimidation, the old order employed psychological weapons. The Communist bugaboo haunted the benighted South; conservatives and reactionaries brandished it as a weapon against their enemies. Not surprisingly, Anderson drew the attention of the Special Committee on Un-American Activities in the U.S. House of Representatives. Both her name and her husband's appeared often enough in the committee's official proceedings to qualify them for what amounted to a veritable hit list of American liberals and radicals.[36] Being targeted by congressional committees was in itself cause for considerable consternation, and Eleanor's situation was exacerbated by her concern that all of this attention could adversely affect the career of her brother, Randolph Copenhaver, a physician and career army officer.[37]

The red-baiting and witch-hunts of the 1930s, 1940s, and 1950s took its toll on the Old Left, and Eleanor Copenhaver Anderson was no exception. Furthermore, she experienced some severe personal losses. In 1941 Sherwood Anderson died suddenly and prematurely of peritonitis while

Eleanor and he were on a trip to South America; her mother, Laura Lu Scherer Copenhaver, had died some four months earlier. Eleanor continued her work with the National Board YWCA, although the Industrial Department as a separate entity ceased to exist. During World War II, she traveled about the country, investigating conditions of women workers in defense industries. In 1947 she received an appointment to work with a YWCA-sponsored labor project in Italy. Although she had accumulated approximately thirty years of service with the National Board, she was terminated in 1950, which proved to be a watershed in her life. In the lengthy citation that the organization presented her, the officials hailed her as "an interpreter of and a resource on matters pertaining to labor and the labor movement," adding, "It is not often in one small and very modest person there is found so fine a mind and so zealous a spirit." Eleanor's recorded comments, though brief, clearly showed her bitterness. "The 'Y' would never give me any time off," she wrote, "and now they have fired me."[38]

The specifics of the YWCA's actions remain unclear, but the organization had entered into a period of retrenchment and cut others on its staff as well as Eleanor. Furthermore, red-baiters and witch-hunters of the era targeted Y professionals who had been associated with labor education and organizing, and no one had stronger connections than she did. Finally, during a stint of approximately two years in Italy, from 1947 to 1949, working on the YWCA-sponsored labor project, Eleanor had erred; in her handling of the organization's accounts, she authorized an unsecured loan to an individual involved with a factory being nurtured by the Y and he absconded. All of these circumstances coalesced to make her termination an easier decision than it might otherwise have been. Volunteer officers as well as paid administrators were anxious to demonstrate their conservatism in an organization under political fire from the extreme right.

Eleanor returned to the Y during the 1950s to work with the United Community Defense Services project and stayed on in one capacity or another until her retirement in 1961. As long as her health permitted, she spent her winters in her New York City apartment and returned to Virginia for her summers at Rosemont, the Copenhaver family home in Marion, and Ripshin, the home and farm in Grayson County that she had shared with Sherwood Anderson. She maintained ties to liberal organizations throughout the remainder of her life while carefully preserving Sherwood Anderson's literary estate, managing it carefully to reap its financial potential, and fostering scholarship pertaining to his life and his work. She also acted as chief executive officer for the family handicrafts and furniture-making business, Laura Copenhaver Industries, and became the titular head and ruling matriarch of the Copenhaver clan. When she died in 1985, at the age of eighty-nine, her cremated remains came to rest beside her husband in a cemetery on Round Hill in Marion, Virginia. His monument, bearing the inscription "Life not death is the great adventure," presides over them.

NOTES

1. The facts and interpretations in this chapter are based on extensive research in manuscript collections, which include the following: National Board YWCA Records in the Sophia Smith Collection, Smith College, Northampton, Massachusetts, and at the Library and Archives, YWCA of the U.S.A., New York City; the Bertha C. Reynolds Papers also in the Sophia Smith Collection at Smith College; the Southern Summer School Papers, American Labor Education Service (ALES) Records, Labor-Management Documentation Center, Martin P. Catherwood Library, Cornell University, Ithaca, New York; Highlander Research and Education Center Collection, New Market, Tennessee (originals with the State Historical Society of Wisconsin; the collection contains materials pertaining to Commonwealth College, Mena, Arkansas); the Sherwood Anderson Collection, Midwest Manuscripts Division, Newberry Library, Chicago; and Southern Oral History Transcripts, Southern Historical Collection, Wilson Library, University of North Carolina, Chapel Hill. The author has also had access to materials in the possession of members of the Scherer-Copenhaver family. Professors Charles E. Modlin and Hilbert H. Campbell, English Department, Virginia Polytechnic Institute and State University, Blacksburg, have shared their memories of Eleanor Copenhaver Anderson and their insights. Professor Campbell allowed the author to make copies of Eleanor's diaries from the 1930s, which are in his possession.

2. For a useful overview of the liberals and radicals of the interwar period but one that gives scant attention to women activists, see John Egerton's prize-winning book, *Speak Now against the Day: The Generation before the Civil Rights Movement in the South* (New York: Knopf, 1994).

3. For purposes of simplification in the text, Eleanor Copenhaver Anderson will either be identified by her first name, Eleanor, or her married surname, Anderson; in the notes, her name will appear as it does in the documents being cited.

4. Interview, Charles E. Modlin and Hilbert H. Campbell, professors of English and Sherwood Anderson authorities, May 21, 1992, Blacksburg, Virginia; interview, Mrs. Randolph (Lois C. "Cookie") Copenhaver, Eleanor Copenhaver Anderson's sister-in-law, and Mrs. David (Virginia) Greear, a family friend, February 7, 1992, Marion, Virginia. Unless otherwise noted, all interviews were conducted by the author.

5. Mary Van Kleeck, "Florence Simms," *Womans Press*, April 1923, 192–94; Richard Roberts, *Florence Simms: A Biography* (New York: Woman's Press, 1926), 177–92; typescript of four pages (6–10), identified as historical background for Industrial Study, YWCA of the U.S.A.; and Annabel M. Stewart, *The Industrial Work of the Y.W.C.A.* (New York: Womans Press, 1937), 10. "The Woman's Press" appeared with and without an apostrophe; the author has punctuated it as it appeared at respective times.

6. Charles E. Modlin and Hilbert H. Campbell, "An Interview with Mrs. Sherwood Anderson," in Hilbert H. Campbell and Charles E. Modlin, eds., *Sherwood Anderson: Centennial Studies* (Troy, NY: Whitston Publishing Company, 1976), 69–70; interview, Carolyn Sheffey, neighbor of the Copenhavers, February 8, 1992, Marion, Virginia.

7. Mildred Copenhaver and Robert Madison Copenhaver Jr., comps., *The Copenhaver Family of Smyth County, Virginia* (Radford, VA: Commonwealth Press, 1981), holds to the German origin of the Copenhavers. A loose clipping from *Presbyterian Survey*, containing an obituary of Laura Scherer Copenhaver, associates them with Denmark; the latter is in the possession of Mary Grace Scherer Taylor, Richmond, Virginia.

8. Thomas W. West, *Marion College, 1873–1967* (Strasburg, VA: Shenandoah, 1970), 1, 7–33.

9. See Claire Millhiser Rosenbaum, *A Gem of a College: The History of Westhampton College, 1914–1989* (Richmond, VA: William Byrd Press for Westhampton College of the University of Virginia, 1989); and Virginia Wolf Briscoe, "Bryn Mawr College Traditions: Women's Rituals as Expressive Behavior" (Ph.D. diss., University of Pennsylvania, 1981). See also Allen F. Davis, *Spearheads for Reform: The Social Settlements and the Progressive Movement, 1890–1941*, Urban Life in America Series, ed. Richard C. Wade (New York: Oxford University Press, 1968; Oxford University Press paperback, 1970), 33.

10. *Association Monthly* 14 (September 1920); staff listings; and the roster for November 1920, YWCA of the U.S.A.

11. File—Industrial Reports, 1923, YWCA of the U.S.A. See also Modlin and Campbell, "An Interview with Mrs. Sherwood Anderson," 68.

12. Sheffey interview; Modlin and Campbell interview; and Copenhaver and Greear interview.

13. Sheffey interview; and Copenhaver and Greear, interview.

14. Charles E. Modlin, ed., *Sherwood Anderson's Love Letters to Eleanor Copenhaver Anderson* (Athens: University of Georgia Press, 1989), 207.

15. *Chicago Daily News*, March 31, 1962.

16. Interview, Lois MacDonald, conducted by Mary Frederickson, August 25, 1977; transcribed by Jean Houston for the Southern Oral History Program.

17. Liselotte Bendix Stern, conversation, July 26, 1992, New York City.

18. Brooks Spivey Creedy, interview by Mary Frederickson, July 14, 1975; transcribed by Gerry Cohen for the Southern Oral History Program.

19. Eleanor Copenhaver, "Biennial Report for 1928–1929," 1, National Board YWCA Papers, Box 25, Sophia Smith Collection.

20. Copenhaver, "Biennial Report for 1928–1929," 5–6.

21. See Doris Cohen Brody, "American Labor Education Service, 1927–1962: An Organization for Workers' Education" (Ph.D. diss., Cornell University, 1973); and Eleanor Coit, "American Labor Education Service: Historical Notes, 1927–1962" (typescript), ALES Records, Box 125.

22. National Emergency Council, *Report on Economic Conditions in the South* (Washington, DC: Government Printing Office, 1938), 1.

23. A. J. Muste quoted in *Southern Summer School for Women Workers in Industry* (Baltimore, MD: Printed by Center Office, 1929), ALES Records, Box 12.

24. Hilda W. Smith, "A Summary of Workers' Education," address at Temple University, May 10, 1938, Highlander Records, Reel 1.

25. Mary Evans Frederickson, "A Place to Speak Our Minds: The Southern Summer School for Women Workers" (Ph.D. diss., University of North Carolina, 1981), 9, 46.

26. Report of Executive of Business Girls Conference, 1934, National Board YWCA Records, Box 6, Sophia Smith Collection.

27. Lucien Koch, "Do Workers Need a 'Different' Education?" Highlander Collection, Reel 8.

28. Van Kleeck, "Florence Simms," 192–94; Roberts, *Florence Simms*, 177–292; unnumbered typescript (6–10), identified as historical background for Industrial Study, YWCA of the U.S.A.; and Stewart, *Industrial Work of the Y.W.C.A.*, 10.

29. *Report of the National Board of the Young Women's Christian Associations of the United States of America to the Sixth National Convention at Cleveland, Ohio, April 13–20, 1920*, 14–15, 90–93; National Young Women's Christian Association, *Proceedings of the Sixth National Convention, Cleveland, Ohio, April 13–20, 1920*, 95–115; copies from the YWCA of the U.S.A.

30. Eleanor Copenhaver Anderson Diary, January 4–5, 1936.

31. Copenhaver, "Biennial Report for 1928–1929," 1–2.

32. For an overview of the labor unrest and strikes that hit the South during 1929 and 1930, see Tom Tippett, *When Southern Labor Stirs* (New York: Jonathan Cape and Harrison Smith, 1931). See also John A. Salmond, *Gastonia, 1929: The Story of the Loray Mill Strike* (Chapel Hill: University of North Carolina Press, 1995); and Jacquelyn Dowd Hall, "Disorderly Women: Gender and Labor Militancy in the Appalachian South," *Journal of American History* 73 (1986): 354–82. The Cicero Queen quotation is from Tippett, *When Southern Labor Stirs*, 144.

33. Copenhaver, "Biennial Report for 1929–1930," 9.

34. *New York Times*, May 26, 1929.

35. Modlin, *Sherwood Anderson's Love Letters to Eleanor Copenhaver Anderson*, xiv.

36. For examples, see Congress, House, Special Committee on Un-American Activities, *Investigation of Un-American Propaganda Activities in the United States*, 75th Cong., 3d sess., August 1938, 379, 530–31, 538–39, 557, 565, 568, and 569; Congress, House, Special Committee on Un-American Activities, *Investigation of Un-American Propaganda Activities in the United States*, 78th Cong., 1st sess., March–April 1943, 3105, 3147–48, 3163, 3179, and 3190; Congress, House, Special Committee on Un-American Activities, *Investigation of Un-American Propaganda Activities in the United States*, 78th Cong., 2d sess., September–October 1944, 10,298, 10,301, 10,304, 10,341, 10,345, 10,346, 10,347, and 10,348; and House, Committee on Un-American Activities, *Investigation of Communist Activities in the Los Angeles Area—Part 8*, 83d Cong., 1st sess., November 1953, 3639, 3670, and 3688. Existing evidence does not lend itself to the conclusion that either Sherwood or Eleanor was a Communist.

37. Modlin and Campbell interview.

38. Minutes, National Board YWCA, June 7, 1950, YWCA of the U.S.A.; Eleanor Copenhaver Anderson to Stanley Pargellis, February 14, 1950, Correspondence File, Sherwood Anderson Collection.

SUGGESTED READINGS

This chapter is based largely on primary sources. Published works pertinent to southern liberals and radicals of the interwar period include: John Egerton, *Speak Now against the Day: The Generation before the Civil Rights Movement in the South* (New York: Knopf, 1994); Hollinger F. Barnard, ed., *Outside the Magic Circle: The Autobiography of Virginia Foster Durr* (Tuscaloosa: University of Alabama Press, 1985); John M. Glen, *Highlander: No Ordinary School, 1932–1962* (Lexington: University Press of Kentucky, 1988); John A. Salmond, *Miss Lucy of the CIO: The Life and Times of Lucy Randolph Mason, 1882–1959* (Athens: University of Georgia Press, 1988); Robert F. Martin, *Howard Kester and the Struggle for Social Justice in the South, 1904–1977* (Charlottesville: University Press of Virginia, 1991); and Frank T. Adams, *James A. Dombrowski: An American Heretic, 1897–1983* (Knoxville: University of Tennessee Press, 1992).

For the southern labor situation, see Tom Tippett, *When Southern Labor Stirs* (New York: Jonathan Cape and Harrison Smith, 1931); Jacquelyn Dowd Hall et al., *Like a Family: The Making of a Southern Cotton Mill World* (Chapel Hill: University of North Carolina Press, 1987); and John A. Salmond, *Gastonia, 1929: The Story of the Loray Mill Strike* (Chapel Hill: University of North Carolina Press, 1995).

The following afford insights into the marriage of Eleanor Copenhaver and Sherwood Anderson: Charles E. Modlin, ed., *Sherwood Anderson's Love Letters to Eleanor Copenhaver Anderson* (Athens: University of Georgia Press, 1989); and Ray Lewis White, ed., *Sherwood Anderson's Secret Love Letters: For Eleanor, a Letter a Day* (Baton Rouge: Louisiana State University Press, 1991).

9

Harland Sanders: The Man Who Would Be Colonel

John Ed Pearce

Business became a staple of the New South, as the career of Asa Candler and Coca-Cola showed. In the twentieth century, the focus of those efforts went many different ways. Delta Airlines developed out of its Atlanta hub, while Ted Turner built a media fortune there as well. From Arkansas, Sam Walton took his Wal-Mart success to greater levels. Southern initiatives grew into national and even international success stories.

Over the years, southern food has been both praised and damned. At one time the endless diet of "hogs, hominy, and hoecakes" earned deserved criticism for its lack of variety and nutrition. At other times, however, the foodways of the region have garnered high praise. But whether the debate centers on Goo-Goo Clusters or grits, mint juleps or moon pies, chitterlings or country ham, southern foodways have been crucial to explaining the region and its people.

Colonel Harland Sanders took a southern dish, called it Kentucky Fried Chicken, and combined that strength with the fledgling fast-food industry to produce a product and a marketing strategy that took a southern staple worldwide.

But his story represents more than that. For the Colonel's saga also reveals that business successes do not occur overnight or without work. His life shows the value of persistence in all stages of life. It reveals that image and reality often differ significantly as well. The story presented by Pulitzer Prize–winning journalist John Ed Pearce is a straightforward one, but a story that also reveals much about success and failure in the business world of the twentieth-century South. It offers a case study of how personality shaped one of the New South's success stories.

John Ed Pearce served for a half century as a reporter, editorial writer, associate editor, and columnist for the Louisville Courier-Journal. *While there, he was a corecipient of the Pulitzer Prize. Currently he writes columns for the* Lexington Herald-Leader. *The author of eight books, he has written, among others,* The Colonel *(1982),* Divide and Dissent: Kentucky Politics, 1930-1963 *(1987), and* Days of Darkness: The Feuds of Eastern Kentucky *(1994).*

Harland Sanders always wanted to be somebody, to do something great. He wanted to be recognized when he walked down the street, have people notice when he stepped into a room. He wanted to be rich and famous but longed for the fame more than the wealth. And he reached his goal, though not as Harland Sanders.

He did not get a running start toward his goal. He was born on September 9, 1890, in a thin-walled, four-room shack beside a country road three miles east of Henryville, Indiana, the oldest of three children born to Margaret Ann and Wilbert D. Sanders. His father, a mild, affectionate man, tried to make a living as a farmer but fell, breaking his back and a leg, and had to give up farming. For two years he worked as a butcher in Henryville, just eking out a living. Then one afternoon in the summer of 1895 he came home with a fever, lay down, and died. Attempting to care for the three children, his widow tried for several months to make a living by sewing and doing housework for neighbors, but such work proved difficult to find. She finally took a job in the tomato-canning plant in Henryville, leaving five-year-old Harland to look after his brother and sister.

In the winter Harland went to school, which he did not like and for which he showed little aptitude, and during summer months he took care of his siblings, freeing his mother to work in the cannery. When he was ten, his mother "hired him out" to farmer Charlie Norris, who offered two dollars a month "and keep" if the boy proved satisfactory. He did not. Put to work cutting weeds, Harland spent much of his time sitting and watching rabbits in the fence rows. At the end of the month, Norris said, "Here's your two dollars. Now get your stuff. You're not worth a daggone." Even worse was the tongue lashing he got from his mother. "It looks like you'll never amount to anything," she said. "I guess I'll never be able to count on you." Her words stung. "After that," Harland said later, "I never got fired from another job." Actually, he never lost a job again for being lazy. When, the following summer, he was given a job on the farm of Henry Monk for four dollars a month and keep, he worked himself glassy-eyed following a plow from dark to dark, after which he helped with the chores. But he stuck to it and at the end of summer, Monk said, "You did all right, boy. You want a job next summer, I'll see if I can find something for you." Harland returned home heavy with pride and with money in his pocket. He was twelve.

The happy homecoming did not last long. His mother had been keeping company with a burly truck gardener named William Broaddus and, tired of supporting the family by herself, she married him. This proved unfortunate for Harland. Broaddus did not take to the self-assertive (and probably jealous) youngster and finally "just kicked me all over the kitchen." This show of hostility sent Harland scuttling to the barn for the night. The next morning, with his mother's approval, he packed what belongings he had and headed for New Albany, home of his uncle, Dick Dunlevy, who, his mother told him, would take care of him. She was right. Dunlevy not only offered him shelter but helped him find a job. It was another farm job, but Harland preferred it to school. However, he sensed that he was not going to make the big time following a plow. When Uncle Dick advised him to apply for a job as fare collector for the New Albany Street Car Company, he did so and soon walked the aisles in a uniform complete with a billed cap, calling out "Fares, please!"

But he still felt he was not on the track to great things, and when a passenger told him that the army was looking for young fellows to serve in Cuba, he went down to the quartermaster depot and signed up, giving his age as twenty-one, although he was actually several months shy of sixteen. With a group of would-be warriors, he went by train to Norfolk, where he embarked on the worst voyage of his life. Not only was he deathly seasick—he had never been on a body of water wider than the Ohio River—but he was assigned to help care for a shipment of mules, also headed for Cuba, and the smell mercilessly exacerbated his nausea. Fortunately the Cuban crisis had been settled about the time he arrived in Havana, and when the army announced that any new recruit who wanted to go home could sign out, he signed. It involved a cruise to New Orleans, where he caught a steamboat up the Mississippi, a body of water he could cope with.

After hopping freight trains around the South for a summer, Harland wound up in Sheffield, Alabama, where, he remembered, his Uncle John lived. It happened that his brother Clarence was also living with Uncle John, having fled home and Mr. Broaddus. Uncle John worked for the Southern Railroad, and Harland soon found work in the railway roundhouse, where he became a blacksmith's helper, a job he loathed. But one morning he heard a locomotive engineer telling the trainmaster that his fireman was sick. Harland struck while the iron was hot.

"Mister," he said to the engineer, "I can fire that engine."

"You ever fired?" the man asked.

"No," Harland admitted, "but I can try, and you ain't got nobody else."

He got the job, worked all day learning the tricks of balance and timing, and the next morning the trainmaster pointed to a waiting locomotive. "You want to be a fireman," he said, "well, there's your run."

So Harland became a genuine railroad man. He was only twenty, but at five feet ten and 185 pounds, he was strong and farm hardened. Sadly, he was also developing a habit of opening his mouth when he should not and barging in where caution would not tread. He became active in the rail union and jumped to the defense of a union member who had been wrongly fired (and saved the man's job). But soon afterward he found himself fired. This was a doubly serious matter because, a few months earlier, he had met and married a tall, solidly built, quiet girl named Josephine King, of Jasper, Alabama. He quickly bounced from the Southern to the Norfolk and Western, but the young couple had set up housekeeping in Tuscumbia, Alabama, and the N&W did not run to Alabama. Harland wrote frequently and sent money home to Josephine, but the marriage grew strained.

It had been somewhat strained from the beginning. The young couple had two children, Margaret and Harland Jr., in the first two years. But Josephine did not feel well during her pregnancies and did not respond happily to married life. Harland chafed at her lack of physical affection but remained devoted and attentive from long distance. Soon, however, he received a letter from Josephine's brother informing him that Josephine had gone home to live with her parents in Jasper. Harland was outraged, especially since Josephine took the two children and sold their scant furniture.

"I figured she didn't have any right to take my children and give away my furniture," said Harland, but he admitted that "I didn't know anything to do about it." Eventually, like other fathers faced with similar circumstances, he devised a plan: he would kidnap the children. So on a hot summer day he sneaked up on the King home, where Josephine was staying, and hid in the field behind the house, waiting for the children to come out to play. But they did not appear, the sun grew hotter, and Harland sweated among the weeds. Finally, feeling foolish, he got up and walked to the house, where his father-in-law had sat watching him, and announced that he had come to see his family. His father-in-law said he had figured as much.

Harland and Josephine were reconciled. They stayed together for thirty-seven years, but he later reflected that "things were never the same between us." He got a job firing on the Illinois Central line but got into a fight with his engineer and was again fired. He was forced to take a post as a lowly section hand, doing manual labor. Josephine moved back to live with her parents. Another daughter, Mildred, was born shortly.

Determined to get a grip on the ladder of success, Harland began taking correspondence courses in law. Though handicapped by his scanty education, he had become something of a reader and now bent to the task with his usual stubbornness. Had he avoided conflict, Harland could well have become a successful trial lawyer. He was a gifted orator and actor.

But he also had a temper. In court, he won damages for a client injured on the job, but when the client demanded the check for his damages, Harland refused to hand it over until the client paid him his fee. The matter should have been decided in his office. Instead, he and the client exchanged words and then blows before the startled eyes of those in the courtroom. Harland was seized by deputies, charged with assault and battery, and lodged in jail. The incident destroyed his fledgling practice.

Harland was now thirty-one years old. He had been working twenty years, had a wife and three children, and was about out of money. He was also burdened with his brother Clarence, who, as Harland admitted, was "boozing himself to death." Sending Josephine and the children once more to her parents in Jasper, he went with Clarence to Louisville, where he planned to seek help from his relatives across the river in New Albany. Again, his Uncle Dick Dunlevy proved helpful. The small town of New Washington, Indiana, had lost its barber, offering, Harland decided, opportunity. He found some used barber equipment in Louisville, piled it into a Franklin automobile he had bought, and established Clarence in the vacant barbershop, ignoring Clarence's plaint that he knew nothing of barbering. "Just cut the hair that's too long, and put on plenty of tonic," Harland told him. "Their wives will like the smell and tell them it looks nice." Soon Clarence became a successful and respected fixture in town.

Harland did not immediately do as well and again became a lowly section hand with the Pennsylvania Railroad. But upon hearing that the Prudential Life Insurance Company was looking for a salesman, he bought a gray suit, black shoes, and white shirt, in which he presented himself to the Prudential office with the announcement that they were "looking at the best insurance salesman in the state of Indiana." Impressed with his brass and needing a salesman to replace the old one who had quit in disgust, Prudential hired him.

Harland faced a hard task, but he devised a plan. Going door-to-door as a "representative of a firm conducting a survey," he asked if the household had insurance. If not, he returned the next day to offer that opportunity. He did so well that the company soon promoted him to assistant supervisor of the industrial division, with a salary of $17.50 a week. At the end of thirteen months, he was transferred back to the office and given a whole division, but again his ego got in his way. Asked to turn in his reports and collections before leaving the industrial division, he refused to comply until he got his commission. Instead, he got fired.

He moved across the river to Louisville, started selling insurance for Mutual Benefit of New Jersey, and became an active member of the Young Businessman's Club. But he tired of selling insurance and looked for greener pastures. Noticing that traffic clogged the two-lane bridge between New Albany and Louisville, backing up in numbers the antique ferry could not handle, Harland sensed opportunity. He quickly formed a ferryboat company, announced construction of a steel-hulled ferry that would carry fifteen cars and 150 people at ten cents a person, and within thirty days had sold enough stock to finance the venture and pay himself a hefty $20,000 commission. The ferry was an instant success, and Harland found himself a member of the Rotary Club. But he was not satisfied. The Roaring Twenties were in full roar. America and the South seemed to be getting richer and richer, but Harland was missing the parade. Resignedly, he went back to selling insurance but then heard that the Michelin Tire Company needed a salesman. He applied, made his usual presentation, and promptly got the job, with all of Kentucky as his territory. With every car on the road as a prospect, he received a guarantee of $750 a month. "Actually," he admitted later, "I had a guarantee of $750 if I made my quota, and naturally I always made my quota." He also established dealerships across the state and "humped them to keep the tires rolling." He and Josephine bought a small white house sitting on a rise of a hill in Jessamine County, south of Lexington. There was a large barn on the property, where he threw "big feeds" for his dealers and prospects. On Saturdays, when farmers poured in to county seat towns for Court Day or Mule Day, he would put on his "bib suit," the one used by Michelin in its ads, and swagger through the courthouse crowd, challenging local tire dealers to a contest that, he promised, would prove the superiority of Michelin tubes. He would ask two husky farm boys to pump away, invite the crowd to count the strokes each boy used to inflate the tube, and warn them to stand back to keep from being hit with rubber flying from the other tire. By the time the first tube exploded, a big crowd was usually watching, and the Michelin invariably won. Harland was learning how to attract and hold a crowd. He became convinced that within him was a natural leader of men, meant for great things.

But once more the roller coaster stalled. He had given Harland Jr. an old Ford to drive to school in Nicholasville, about seven miles away, but on this particular morning the Ford refused to start. Finally they hitched it to a Maxwell automobile and started towing it to a garage. But as Harland started onto the rickety bridge across Jessamine Creek, the bridge collapsed, dropping him and the Maxwell about forty feet into the creek, where it landed on its top, its front end under water. Harland managed to get out and clambered up the bank, muddy and bleeding from a head wound. His scalp was split from his forehead to the top of his head, and blood ran down his face and into his eyes. Neighbors rushed to the creek bank and began hollering for someone to get a doctor.

"You wait till I say get a doctor before you go getting a doctor," Harland shouted. Taking his split scalp in his hands, he pressed it back in place. "Just pushed it back together, you see, and held it there until it dried," he recounted. "The blood dried in just a few minutes. Grew back pretty as anything. It was two or three weeks before I could wash it, but there never was a scar, except when it gets cold it turns sort of blue."

But more than his scalp had been hurt. The Maxwell, when they finally dragged it out of the creek, was a total wreck. And without a car, he could not manage his job. He could have gotten another car—the company would probably have furnished him with one. But for some reason, he did not. A week after the accident, he took a bus to call on one last customer in order to make his monthly quota and then left the company. "Just felt it was time," he said.

Shortly after the first of the year, Harland hitchhiked to Louisville to look for a job. He caught a ride with a man who introduced himself as Mr. Gardner, a division manager for Standard Oil of Kentucky. Harland, never bashful, poured out the story of his misfortune, and Gardner, apparently impressed, asked him if he thought he could run a filling station. He explained that he had a man running the Standard Oil station in Nicholasville but was not happy with him. He asked Harland if he would like to try it. "I sure would," he replied.

It seemed made to order. Harland's new station was located on Main Street, and the couple bought a white frame house across the street. It seemed ideal, but the first weeks proved difficult. The man who had operated the station before him had been popular, and a lot of people resented it when Harland took his place. In his first week he pumped just three and a half gallons of gas.

But this time he was patient. He cleaned the place until it sparkled, put up a new sign, and began giving more service than people had known before. He started wiping windshields, checking tires, and giving away air without being asked. He put up a big sign: FREE AIR. Within six months he was pumping more gas than any station in Kentucky, and officials in Louisville brought new men down to see how he did it. "I just told them to use their heads, their imagination, like I was doing," he said modestly.

But storm clouds gathered. Months before the stock market crash of 1929 sent warnings of the approaching Depression, a ruinous drought hit Kentucky. Farm prices began to slide. Grocery, feed, hardware, and clothing stores felt the drop in buying and laid off help. As the weeks went by, business at the Standard station went slowly downhill. "I finally sold my grease rack, just to pay the rent. But it was no go. I had to give it up," said Sanders.

Once more, Harland was down, seriously down, with no job but a home, wife, and three children to support. One daughter had been accepted by Berea College in nearby Madison County, and another would soon follow. Since the girls lived outside the Berea territory, they could not live in a dormitory, so Josephine rented an apartment where she and the girls lived most of the year. This arrangement seems strange. If Harland had enough influence to have the girls admitted, it seems he could certainly have gained them rooms in the dormitory. Perhaps he did not want to. Harland Sanders loved women and later gained a reputation for philandering. Josephine, on the other hand, was a withdrawn, taciturn woman who found her husband's sexual demands unbearable.

Now, in 1930, with the Depression settling like a blight, Harland found himself against the wall, unemployed, like one of every four adult males. But the good work he had done in Nicholasville soon paid dividends. A major highway ran from Lexington through Corbin, and a branch extended through Cumberland Gap. The Shell Oil Company decided that the location could support a station in spite of the Depression and, having heard of Harland's record, offered to give him the station rent free. He would pay an extra penny a gallon in lieu of rent. He grabbed the offer.

Corbin presented a sharp contrast to the placid, farm-oriented Nicholasville. A railroad and coal town located in the foothills of the eastern Kentucky mountains that had gained a bloody reputation for mine wars, moonshine whiskey, bootlegging, and pistol justice, Corbin was a bustling town of six thousand people, with its quota of churches, civic clubs, and a booster spirit fed by the chamber of commerce. North Corbin, however, resembled a sprawl of small stores, filling stations, modest homes, and establishments suspected of selling illegal moonshine whiskey. Miners, railroad workers, and farm toughs brawled on weekends, while deputies tried vainly to restrain high spirits and federal revenue agents tried to check the flow of illegal spirits. No one seemed to give thought to the salesmen, businessmen, and tourists on the highways.

Into this rowdy environment Harland moved in the summer of 1930. He found that the road curved as it approached his station, so that drivers saw the station across the road before his they saw his.

"Fellow named Ancel McVey had the station across from mine," said Harland. "Nice a fellow as you would want to meet, but he didn't work at his station much. Spent a lot of time playing the mandolin. He could play it, too. Fellows would come down of an evening, bring a guitar or fiddle, and they would play. And he had this hog, sort of a pet, that he kept there at the station, and he kept this puddle of water for it to wallow in. I coulda told him it didn't look too good."

Unlike McVey, Harland worked. He put in an air compressor to give customers free air, and when the workmen put in the line, he had them dig a little trench across the road and run a line over so that McVey could have air, too.

"That made a hit with him," he remembered, "and when he decided to quit, he let me have his place for 25 dollars a month, and later sold it to me reasonable."

But within months, tragedy struck. Harland Jr. began to complain of a sore throat, and the local doctor diagnosed sore tonsils. Harland took him to the hospital in Richmond, fifty miles north of Corbin, where a doctor removed the tonsils. But Sanders's son seemed to recover very slowly. With Josephine and the girls in Berea, there was no one to look after him but Harland, who had the station to run. So he drove him to a health resort in Martinsville, Indiana, making arrangements to come back for him in a week. But on the way back to get him, Harland stopped to see his mother, who greeted him in tears with the news that Harland Jr. was dead. The doctor explained to Harland that the boy had apparently picked up a streptococcus, blood poisoning had set in, and he had developed blood clots that had killed him. Harland took him to Henryville and buried him. He and Josephine had grown too far apart to be of much comfort to each other over the loss of their only son.

Back in Corbin, Harland threw himself into operating the filling station and began advertising, although not in the usual way. He used the sides of barns. Shell furnished the paint, Harland painted the side of the barn, and a helper put in the lettering.

"My gas business almost doubled," he said proudly. Asked why he chose barns rather than the usual signboards, he explained that "good old boys riding around like to shoot up signboards, but if they thought there might be a cow or mule on the other side of the sign, they wouldn't blast away like they liked to." Harland himself kept a pistol on the shelf below the cash register and a shotgun in his bedroom. He might never have used the pistol had it not been for his advertising campaign.

About a half mile south of his station stood a highly visible concrete wall along a railroad. Harland decided to use it. His sign was simply a large arrow with the words "North to Lexington" on it. It made no mention of his station, but the arrow led traffic past it. It also diverted traffic from the station of a competitor, Matt Stewart, who had opened a Standard Oil station down the road a short time before. Stewart had a reputation as a dangerous man who owned a gun and would use it. He charged that Harland's sign was illegal, since it was painted on railroad property. Railroad officials later testified that they did not care and had neither permitted nor forbidden the sign.

A truck driver soon stopped and told Harland that Matt Stewart had painted over the sign with creosote, which was hard to remove and impossible to paint over. Harland got some rags and gasoline, scrubbed off the creosote, repainted the sign, and paid a social call on Stewart. Accounts of what transpired differed, but either Sanders or Stewart promised to "blow your goddam head off" if more sign activity occurred.

On the morning of May 7, 1931, Harland was visited by Robert Gibson, Shell Oil district manager, and H. D. Shelburne, a Shell supervisor. As the three stood talking outside the station, a trucker passed and called out, "Hey, Sanders. Matt Stewart's painting over your sign again." Once Harland explained his trouble to the company officials, they decided to pay Stewart a call and found him on a ladder painting over the sign. "Well, you sonofabitch," yelled Harland. "I see you done it again." Stewart jumped down from the ladder. Someone pulled a gun. Five shots were fired and Gibson fell, mortally wounded. Shelburne jumped from the car and opened fire on Stewart. Harland said later that he saw Gibson's gun and picked it up. Stewart said Sanders pulled the gun from his own pocket. The police report said simply, "All of them were armed."

Stewart jumped over a wall and started toward Harland. Harland shot him in the shoulder and at the same time, Shelburne hit Stewart in the shoulder. "Don't shoot, Sanders!" Stewart called. "You've killed me!" Stewart lived and went to the hospital before he was put in jail. He was later shot and killed in a gunfight with a sheriff's deputy. Charges filed against Harland and Shelburne were dismissed, but the incident had a strange aftermath. Harland went to Stewart's attractive daughter, Ona May, apologized for his part in the tragedy, and offered to help her if he ever could. Later he did.

But fortune was about to smile on Harland Sanders, though it took awhile showing itself. One day a traveling salesman said to him, "Damn! There ain't a decent place around here to eat." "I'm afraid you're right, friend," Harland replied, but the exchange set him to thinking.

"It came to me that the one thing I could do was cook," he said. "And I figured I couldn't do any worse than the people running these places around town." So he bought a piece of linoleum to fit the small room off his office, brought out the dining room table and chairs (he and Josephine were living in rooms behind the station), put them in the room, and started serving meals to anyone who asked. When a driver pulled in and asked where he could get a good meal, Harland would tell him, "Right here, friend, if you don't mind plain home cooking."

It was not fancy and was served boardinghouse style, with bowls of food from which the diners helped themselves. Truckers and tourists headed for Florida partook of country ham, pot roast, or fried chicken with mashed potatoes, fresh vegetables, and milk gravy. Harland did not have much equipment—a four-burner stove, a refrigerator, and the family china and silverware. But the food was good and word spread. Soon people stopped not for gas or free air, but for the food. Sanders put up a large sign proclaiming Sanders Shell Station and Café (later Sanders Café and Service Station).

With the restaurant booming, Sanders became active in civic affairs and joined the Rotary Club, the chamber of commerce, and the Masons. He became a one-man lobby for road improvement and railed against fellow

Rotarians for failing to see the gold in tourism. More important, Ancel McVey decided to retire and rented his station to Harland. It not only had a better location, but also a big side room and a vacant lot for expansion. Harland threw himself into the job of remodeling and expanding his new establishment, turning the side room into a real restaurant, with six tables, each seating four to six people. And he filled in the hog wallow.

But success brought problems. Running both a filling station and a restaurant proved difficult. Not only did Harland have to man the pumps, wipe windshields, check tires and batteries, sweep out cars, and give directions, but he also planned menus, shopped, cooked, waited tables, watched the cash register, and, when business was done, washed the dishes, emptied the garbage, checked supplies, and set the tables for breakfast. He had to have help, but with the Depression deepening, he hesitated to spend an unnecessary penny. Finally he had no choice and hired his first waitress, Nell Ray. It proved to be one of the most far-reaching things he ever did. In October 1932, when Nell was sick and could not go to work, he asked her sister, Claudia, to take her place. Divorced and with two small children, Claudia accepted.

"I always liked to hire widows with children because they needed work and there wasn't any foolishness about them," Harland admitted. Claudia filled the bill. "I don't remember exactly what I thought of him," she said later. "He seemed nice and friendly. Oh, he had a temper. He had that. He hollered at me, but I didn't let it worry me. It was either that or go away, and I needed the work."

Depression or not, the business was growing fast. Typically, to save a dollar, Harland went to North Carolina, bought some wide poplar boards, and made booths. "People took to them right off. Feeling of privacy, you see." By trial and error, he learned the restaurant business.

In 1935 his mother died, and the loss hit Harland hard. He regretted not spending more time with her and, as a way of repentance, vowed to live a more moral life. He began to devote time to the Christian Church. About that time, a man came into the restaurant worried because his wife was in labor and he could not find a doctor. Harland drove to his home and delivered the baby himself. Word got around, and he became quite a midwife. He also became involved with the Galilean Children's Home, an orphanage near Corbin, home to eighty children run by a minister known as Brother Vogel. On Sundays during summer months, Harland would take two ice-cream freezers out to the home and let the children eat their fill, and at Christmastime he closed the restaurant and treated them to what was undoubtedly their best meal of the year. That experience, though, ended rather sadly when three girls from the home went to a minister in town and reported that Brother Vogel had made a practice of sexually exploiting the teenage girls, threatening to expel them if they reported it. Vogel had been keeping, in effect, a teenage harem. He went to prison and left a bitterly disillusioned Sanders behind.

At about the same time, Harland became involved in politics. He worked for the election of A. B. "Happy" Chandler to the governorship, but, after winning, Chandler rewarded local politicians and forgot those who had worked for him. When a personable young attorney from Lexington named John Young Brown ran against Chandler's choice of a successor, Harland backed Brown. Brown lost, but the two men remained friends. Chandler did, however, name Harland Sanders an honorary Kentucky Colonel. Curiously, Sanders did not take the award seriously and even lost the certificate.

The growing popularity of the restaurant persuaded Harland that he should start a chain, and he invested substantially in a restaurant in Cumberland and another in Richmond. Neither succeeded. Cumberland was in depressed coal region, and miners could hardly eat at home, much less eat out. In the college town of Richmond, students, like the miners, could not afford to eat out, and the restaurant was not on a main highway. This did not discourage Harland, who decided, in the spring of 1937, to go into the motel business. The decision was well timed. Most tourist camps of the time were fairly primitive affairs, offering little in the way of sanitation or comfort. Harland determined that his would be different. And it was.

Being Harland Sanders, he could not just go to the bank, borrow some money, and hire a contractor. He bought the lumber from a friend, bargained with his gasoline supplier for the brick (paying him an extra penny on the gallon until the debt was liquidated), and gave another friend a percentage of the business in return for the furnishings. It proved to be a sound investment for all. Starting with a small investment, Harland soon had a modern motel with well-furnished, clean rooms and soundproof walls that allowed considerable privacy. He charged $2.50 a room per night and, in a gesture toward morality, would not rent to anyone living within a hundred miles. The motel made money from the day it opened. Harland changed his sign, again, to read Sanders Court.

But Harland could not be satisfied, even with running a profitable establishment that had a sound reputation. He constantly worried about his costs, about the fact that he had so many people on his payroll—cooks, waitresses, dishwashers, cleaning women, pump help. Yet he was becoming a recognized business leader in the Corbin-London area, as he attended restaurant conventions and lobbied the state legislature for road improvements.

But it was not enough. He built a new motel in Asheville, North Carolina, and sent Claudia down to run it. It was a sign of his regard for her business acumen, as well as of the bond growing between them. Claudia could handle the cash register, run the dining room, and take care of the court when Harland was away. And she was not intimidated by his temper and foul language. But again, the new venture proved unsuccessful; the trade was too seasonal and Asheville already had good eating places. He had to sell it.

Then one day a hardware merchant called on him, said he had something to show him.

"What's that thing?" asked Harland.

"Pressure cooker," said the man. (It was one of the first Presto cookers and is now on display in the Sanders Museum in Louisville.) "Put your beans in with a piece of meat, cover them with water, and cook them ten minutes."

Harland, who soaked beans overnight and cooked them most of the day, was dubious but agreed to try it when the man said he could bring it back if he did not like it. That night after work, he put on a pot of beans. He cooked them for ten minutes and told the cook to sample them. "Be durned," the cook said, "they're good." He then cooked some carrots and cabbage. Good again. The next day Harland went back to the hardware store. "All right, I'll keep it," he said. "While I'm at it, might as well get a couple more."

Everything went well until he tried frying chicken. The chicken came out either crusty or soggy, and he would not serve it. He "raised hell" with the hardware dealer, who told him to consult the manual. It still did not work. A friend, Eulah Gordon, had given him a recipe for fried chicken and he began experimenting, using that. (In studying his success, people overlook the fact that Harland Sanders was a great cook. He understood the effects of heat on the texture and taste of food, the art of mingling flavors, the art of temperature control.) One day a man from Michigan stopped by and asked for "some of that fried chicken like I got the last time I was through here." That got Harland's attention. Previously his menu had featured country ham. ("Not worth it, but mighty good," the menu read.) But maybe fried chicken was the answer. He had turned fifty in 1940 and was afraid that he would never be completely successful. He went to work.

Unfortunately World War II erupted. Rationing made it difficult to operate the restaurant and dried up the traffic on the highway. Claudia, along with three other women, went to work in a restaurant in Seattle, where wartime industry kept the economy humming. Harland, in the meantime, had hired Ona May, daughter of his old adversary Matt Stewart. She had married H. F. Leddington, one of Claudia's brothers. Ona May demonstrated quickly that she could run the restaurant as well as Harland could, and he turned it over to her.

He had other troubles. His marriage had hit bottom. His daughters posed a problem, and Harland alternately gushed and raged, trying to enforce a puritanical discipline for which he was hardly exemplary. One daughter was headstrong and regarded in Corbin as "a wild one." Harland once sat in his car and cried uncontrollably. "Those girls are going to kill me," he sobbed.

The war ended and business revived. Harland again tried to branch out. Taking advantage of the GI Bill, which paid for veterans' training, he opened a flying school with ten airplanes. He also started a bricklayers school. But the booming economy absorbed all the potential bricklayers and not enough veterans wanted to fly. The bricklayers school closed. He sold his remaining planes at a loss of $38,000. Harland reluctantly went back to the kitchen.

He was still trying to solve the fried chicken problem. The trouble was that if he cooked the chicken when the customer ordered it, it took too long and the customer got restless. If he cooked it ahead of time, it got cold or too much remained unused. The pressure cooker could fry, but he had not found the right cooking oil, the right procedure.

In 1947 Harland and Josephine divorced, and in 1949 he married Claudia, as he had long desired. Her calmness, loving nature, and compromising ability helped steady his life. The year 1949 brought another event that redirected Harland's life. Governor Lawrence Wetherby, with whom Harland had become friendly, gave Harland another Kentucky Colonel's commission. This time Sanders framed it. And over the next few years Harland Sanders slowly faded and Colonel Sanders was born.

Harland began referring to himself as Colonel Harland Sanders. He signed his name Col. Harland Sanders. His hair was turning white, and he let it grow long while cultivating a mustache and a short goatee. He began wearing a black string tie. "Everybody just accepted it," said businessman Bob Blair. "If he wanted to be Colonel, it was all right with us." Then one day in the chamber of commerce office, Lorene Hodge said to him, "You ought to do something about that beard; bleach it to match your hair. Go over to Lorayne's and have her do it." "I didn't think he would do it, but he did. Lorayne did a good job, and anytime it would start growing back red, he'd go back and she'd do it again." At that time, Harland began to wear his white suit and black tie, summer and winter. Gradually Harland was fading into the past.

Harland finally mastered the secret of frying chicken There was nothing mysterious about Eulah Gordon's recipe; it depended heavily on commercial seasoning salt that contained herbs and spices, to which Harland added his own. (Old-timers in the company said the secret was nothing more than confectioners salt. Whatever it was, it did the trick.) His cooking procedure was similarly simple—dip the chicken in a "wash" of eggs and milk and roll it in his own special flour, to which the special mix of herbs and spices was added. He prefried it (a procedure he later abandoned), then cooked it under fifteen pounds of pressure for seven minutes in oil at 250 degrees.

In 1952 the Colonel took off time to attend the Restaurant Association convention in Chicago, where he met Leon "Pete" Harman, owner of the Dew Drop Inn in Salt Lake City. Pete was thirty-two, the Colonel sixty-two, but neither smoked or drank and thus spent some time together. Despite the age difference, they formed a friendship that would last throughout the Colonel's life. Three months later, the Colonel decided to attend a conference of the Christian Church in Sydney, Australia (he said he was going in hopes of curing his habit of using foul language). He stopped to see Harman and accepted an invitation to dinner, on the condition that he be allowed to fix it. Not surprisingly, after rummaging through Harman's restaurant kitchen for ingredients, the Colonel served the family his fried chicken. When the Harmans praised the meal, the Colonel was elated. "I'll fix you up with pressure cookers," he proposed, "and show your cook how to fix it and sell you my secret recipe. We'll agree on the price."

To his surprise, Harman did not leap to the bait, but he did not press him. On his trip he spent much of his time thinking about his plan to sell his chicken and what he should call it. He finally decided on Colonel Sanders' Kentucky Fried Chicken. He planned to incorporate as soon as he got home. Sanders also thought that he had better copyright the name, too, and his picture, Colonel suit and all. On his return, Claudia met him and they stopped by to see Pete Harman again. He found Harman enthusiastic about the idea of selling the fried chicken and suggested that the Colonel franchise his cooking process and charge each franchisee a few cents for each chicken sold. By the time they got to Corbin, the Colonel had his franchising plan pretty well in mind.

"I could see it wasn't going to be easy," he admitted. "I couldn't give a franchise to any old greasy spoon. And I knew the chicken had to be cooked the way I told them to cook it if it was going to be as popular as it could be. And how was I going to check on how many chickens a man sold using my recipe? I couldn't. In the long run it was just going to be a matter of getting honest people. I figured if I got honest people, a handshake would be all the contract I'd need."

But there was business to care for. His third motel and restaurant—in Georgetown, Kentucky—was not doing well: good town, poor location, and no Colonel to run it. And he still had Sanders Court to operate. According to people working for him, he grew extremely irritable, almost tyrannical.

"I hated working there," said Norma Crawford, wife of publisher Jim Lee Crawford. "I was a student at Transylvania at the time, and mothers didn't mind their daughters working there; it was a nice place. Sanders paid just what he had to, but the tips were good and I needed the money for college, so I stuck. He had a violent temper and a vile tongue. If anything went wrong, he took it out on the girls. He was just plain mean."

He was also superstitious. In 1952 at a convention in Chicago, a fortuneteller offered to devise a horoscope for any diner who wished. The Colonel, insisting that he put no stock in such things, asked for a reading, and the woman told him that between June 28 and 30 of the following year he would get a large sum of money and be offered an even larger sum. Sure enough, the next June 28 a man paid the Colonel $29,000 for his lease on the Georgetown motel and restaurant. Two days later a man from Cynthiana offered him $164,000 for Sanders Court. The Colonel turned it down, figuring business was too good to let go. But the incident left him with a belief in astrology, which almost had disastrous results.

Sanders Court felt the loss when Ona May quit. She was not dissatisfied; she just wanted to be on her own and opened a restaurant in downtown Corbin. She then moved to Lexington and, with the Colonel's help, bought a better place. "I owned fifty percent, the Colonel owned fifty," she explained. "I always knew I could count on him."

The Colonel had been wanting to start selling franchises, and in 1954 he finally took the leap. Driving through Louisville, he stopped to see his old friends Carl and Margaret Kaelin at their restaurant on Newburg Road to eat one of their famous cheeseburgers. (It was a secret that the cheeseburger, not chicken, was the Colonel's favorite food.) When he left, he had another franchisee.

To speed the franchising effort, the Colonel devised a plan, an act. He would wear his Colonel outfit, Claudia would dress in an old-fashioned southern belle outfit, complete with hoopskirts, and they would circulate among the diners in a restaurant where Kentucky Fried Chicken was served, encouraging the customers to try some. Claudia was not overjoyed ("that hoopskirt and all wasn't my idea, I can tell you that, but I went along"). The Colonel loved it. It was like being onstage.

But while they were grinning their way among the tables, misfortune was taking shape back at the Court. Initial plans for the new interstate highway system had suggested that there would be an interchange near his court. The prospect of increased traffic was a main reason he had turned down the generous offer for the restaurant in 1953. But then it was announced that the old highway would be rebuilt and rerouted, with the interchange about four miles west of his motel. No golden traffic flow would result.

It was a devastating blow. Frantically the Colonel put the court up for sale. He got no takers. Desperate, he finally sold it at auction for $75,000. That and the negligible amounts trickling in from franchises were all he had. He was now sixty-five years old and had drawn his first social security check for $105. Sixty-five seemed a little late to be starting over, but he had no choice. He decided that he needed a more central location for his business, so he sold his home, paid off his debts, and moved to a big white-brick home in Shelbyville, Kentucky. Then he loaded a few pressure cookers, a few timers, and packages of his secret herbs and spices into the trunk of his white Cadillac and hit the road, telling himself that he could make one more start. "Hell," he said. "I had to."

Colonel Sanders knew that selling, like acting, is basically an emotional exercise. The salesman sells himself as much as his product, and it took all of the confidence and perseverance built up over the years to meet the challenge he now faced. He had led a strenuous life, and the years were beginning to take their toll. He had to wear his reading glasses all the time. His arthritis hurt when he drove, as he sought to keep his accounts and worried about money. He often slept in his car at night to save motel rates, waking stiff and sore in the morning, and shaved in a restaurant restroom. The Colonel then combed his hair and readied himself to go out and sell an owner on the virtues and value of Kentucky Fried Chicken.

He was not always successful, but after six months on the road he had amassed a good file of franchises. Back in Shelbyville, Claudia operated KFC out of the Sanders home. Equipment and supplies were shipped to franchisees from an old warehouse. But the woman who had kept the books in Corbin did not want to move, and bills and records piled up. A nephew and grandson handled shipments, and a new hire, Maureen McGuire, finally brought order to the office.

Sales came slowly, but they came. Pete Harman, to whom the Colonel had given the territory of Utah and Montana, was issuing franchises under an agreement in which the Colonel got a percentage of sales and customers for his flour and herbs and spices. One of Sanders' daughters worked in the office, while another franchised in Florida. It was a family affair. By 1958, almost fifty restaurants around the Midwest featured huge signs advertising Colonel Sanders' Kentucky Fried Chicken. By the end of the year the old confidence was flowing again. The Colonel knew he was going to make it big.

He had more than a hundred franchises in 1963, when he ran into his old friend John Y. Brown and began discussing the old days when Brown was a struggling young lawyer and the Colonel was pumping gas in Corbin. Sanders asked Brown to join him as company attorney. Brown demurred but suggested that the Colonel see his son, John Y. Jr., who was not long out of law school and practicing in Louisville. It was a sensible suggestion. Tall, handsome, and athletic, John Y. Brown Jr. had a record of success. At the University of Kentucky he had been a golf and swimming champion while working his way through school selling the *Encyclopedia Britannica* in eastern Kentucky. By the time he finished law school, he was making $26,000 a year and Britannica offered him $75,000 to join the national sales force. He declined, saying he could not see himself selling books all of his life. After opening his law office in Louisville, he won nine of his first cases, but few people thought he would go far in the law. He remained too obviously the salesman, the promoter. When he appeared on television in support of his father's campaign for the U.S. Senate, many newsmen said that the most interesting thing about the race was John's emergence as a potential candidate. He worked in publicity in Edward Breathitt's successful battle against Happy Chandler for governor. And on Derby Day 1963, he met Colonel Harland Sanders.

In his usual blunt fashion, Sanders proposed that John Y. become his corporate counsel, but they were both too busy shaking hands and slapping backs to talk seriously. John told him that when the campaign ended he would come to see him, which he did.

"He wanted me to handle real estate matters for him," Brown recalled. "I didn't know anything about real estate, but we sat around talking, and he reached into a desk drawer and pulled out a bunch of uncashed checks, royalties people were paying on his chicken. I asked him what kind of sales force he had and he said, 'Hell, I don't sell. If people want my chicken they can come to me now. I don't have to go to them.' I said to myself, Brown, you'd better pull up a chair and sit in."

Sanders mentioned that he was thinking about a chain of barbecue stands. "I didn't know anything about barbecue," said Brown later, "but I was interested in the promotional aspects of the business, franchising, so I told him I'd raise the money and put up the barbecue place and we'd be partners. He agreed."

John found a vacant store on Louisville's Preston Street. He and his wife, Ellie, decorated it. "Funny the way things turn out," mused Brown. "A young man named Jimmy Cavanaugh had moved into the office just above mine; he was married to a girl named Cindy who had been Ellie's roommate in college, so we got to be friends. When I confided what I was trying to do, he introduced me to a fellow from Nashville who he said might help me." Thus John Y. met Jack Massey. They liked each other immediately. Massey, sixty-two, had no desire to retire and was looking for ways to invest the money he had made in the surgical supply business. He loaned John $16,000 to launch his barbecue place, named Porky Pig House. John's contract with the Colonel allowed him to sell not only barbecue but also Kentucky Fried Chicken. After sixty days John studied the books and found that he was selling 20 percent barbecue and 80 percent chicken. "It occurred to me that when I went to the store, I ate chicken, and it was damn good chicken," he said. "I knew then that I was in the wrong end of the right business."

Just then John ran into a remarried Ona May, the Colonel's former assistant in Corbin. Ona May and her husband, Joe Barbati, were managing a restaurant in Lexington, making $75 a week. John offered them the same money and a partnership in the Porky Pig. They accepted, and John turned his energies toward Kentucky Fried Chicken. The circle of connections grew wider.

While John was wondering how to get into the chicken business, Colonel Sanders was exhausting himself trying to expand his business.

"We kept everything in the warehouse," recalled Maureen McGuire, "and shipped direct to the franchisee, usually by truck—pressure cookers, warming ovens, filters, seasonings, all supplies like buckets, napkins, spatulas. The Colonel designed and built everything from buckets to spatulas, and if a man got a franchise, he had to buy from us. Spices, seasonings came in little plastic twenty-six-ounce bags. That would mix with twenty-five pounds of flour, about an ounce to a pound. An order would come in, I would write it out and put it in a basket [and it would then go] to the warehouse for shipping. That got unhandy, so we got Durkee's Foods to mix the spices, and when we got bigger we had a contract with Stange to put seasoning in the flour and ship it."

And this was the heart of a multimillion-dollar business; no one knew exactly how big it was. The Colonel was on the road most of the time, promoting franchises in Canada and England and spending about half his time in those offices. A lot of expensive equipment was involved, so John Y. Brown mentioned to Jack Massey that perhaps they could do some business with the Colonel financing the purchase of equipment for franchisees. Massey liked the idea, so they drove to Shelbyville to see the Colonel. It was not an auspicious meeting. The Colonel took one look at Massey and disliked him. Massey developed no more regard for the ill-tempered Colonel.

"I had called the Colonel and told him I was bringing this finance person with me," John recalled. "Maybe that struck him wrong. Jack, of course, was dressed like, acted like, a banker. The Colonel was barging around in his white suit, hollering and mumbling by turns. Maybe Jack made him uncomfortable. At any rate, in a few minutes, even before Jack could suggest some financing to him, he slapped his hand on the table and snapped, 'Let me tell you something right now. There ain't no slick-talking sonofabitch going to come in here and buy my company out from under me. No sir!' Jack and I had not mentioned buying him out. Lord, I had just borrowed enough money to start Porky Pig House."

But apparently the Colonel had been thinking about it. He had had a couple of offers previously but had not taken them seriously. But now for some reason the idea became appealing.

"After that first meeting, the Colonel settled down," said John. "To tell the truth, I think he liked talking to a money man. I think he was sort of confused by all the money he was handling, and here was a man who knew how to do it. Anyhow, Jack and I went back and started talking about it and decided to try to buy him out. We talked about how to approach him, but I had always thought that if you had something to say, the best thing was just to come out and say it. So one day I said to him, 'Colonel, I think you ought to sell us your company.' Well, he blew up, as I expected, cussed and hollered for a while, and finally quieted down and said, 'Well, I don't know. I've been thinking about it and don't see any reason why I should.'"

John Y. Brown the salesman came to the surface. He began by flattering the Colonel, admiring the way he had built his huge company from nothing, then suggested he needed expert help to guide the company through a crucial period. He touched, gently, on the fact that the Colonel was seventy-four years old, with arthritis and failing eyesight, and needed to take better care of himself. Brown noted that Sanders could have a heart attack; then what would become of his beloved company? Who would see that it was not torn apart by squabbling franchisees? Who would see that the Colonel's high standards of service, quality, cleanliness were carried on? Salesman Brown began to sell his vision to the promoter.

On the other hand, Brown continued, why not sell to him and Massey— for a price that the Colonel himself set as fair and proper, one that would ensure that the Colonel and his family had no financial cares for the rest of their lives. Brown and Massey would put together a management team to guide growth, which would free the Colonel to do what he did best— promote the company, act as its goodwill ambassador, be its image, and ride herd on the franchisees to see they followed his rules.

"There is no reason in the world why you should be bothering with cookers and that sort of thing," John told him. "Anyone can do that. You are one of the greatest salesmen in the world. You belong in front of the public. I'll put you there and make you a rich man to boot."

The Colonel sneered. He stomped and grumbled and cursed. But then he grew silent and said nothing. John had reached the heart of vanity.

A few days later, John said to him, "Why don't we go down to Nashville and talk to the men at Third National Bank?" Surprisingly, Sanders agreed. "So we went down and had lunch, and after lunch sat around, waiting for someone to make an opening. I think the Colonel was mulling it over. He had a chance for some big money. He remembered the time he turned down good money for the court at Corbin and saw the value fall next to nothing. He was thinking about those things. And then, all of a sudden, about the way I expected, he said, 'Well, I've been giving this some thought, and I think two million sounds about right.'"

Brown, Massey, and the bankers huddled for a few minutes, then went back and told the Colonel two million sounded about right to them too. The Colonel said he would not sign before he had talked to Pete Harman and Kenny King, his early franchisees. Both Harman and King agreed, and both offered to buy into the company for $5,000. "So we had a contract," said John. "We paid him $5,000 down. I had to come back to Louisville and borrow $10,000 to buy my share." Under the formal agreement signed on February 18, 1964, the Colonel was to receive $2 million for Kentucky Fried Chicken, Inc. In addition, the Colonel would be made a director of the new company and would be employed at a salary of $40,000 a year (later raised to $125,000) to act as public relations man and goodwill ambassador, to appear on TV commercials, to open outlets, and to publicize the company image. John knew that the Colonel was "not just the image; he was the company." The contract not only persuaded the Colonel to sell but also gave Brown the combination of image and product that paved the way to success.

The Colonel did not sell everything. He kept the rights to Canada and England, gave the rights to Florida to his daughter and her husband, and let Pete Harman keep the rights to Utah and Montana.

The Colonel stayed on, but the methods drastically changed. Franchises were sold, not given on a handshake, and operated under strictly controlled conditions. In the future, all new outlets would be freestanding red-and-white striped buildings, designed primarily for take-out orders, but with small counters where diners could stand. Brown and Massey hired a management firm to instill greater efficiency and uniformity in company operation. But John's primary plan included getting the Colonel on national television.

"He wasn't just somebody an ad man had made up, like Aunt Jemima or Betty Crocker. He was a real human being, colorful, attractive, persuasive. My job was to get him before the American people and let him sell his own product."

He did the job well, getting the Colonel on such popular shows as *What's My Line?*, *I've Got a Secret*, and the Johnny Carson and Merv Griffin shows. The Colonel even appeared in a movie, *The Loudmouth*, starring Jerry Lewis. And he loved performing before a national audience. He was a natural and, as John Brown noted, "Every time the Colonel was on one of those shows, our sales jumped. It really put us on the map." But John knew they could not depend indefinitely on free advertising, so in 1965 he asked all franchisees to donate $25 a month toward a national advertising campaign. The next year he asked for $50. This enabled him to initiate, among other advertising messages, the "finger-licking good" TV commercial featuring the Colonel.

"He just had a knack for the camera," John said. "He knew exactly what he wanted to do and did it. No one was going to make him do a bad commercial. One day, this rather effete type said to him, 'Colonel, will you please just read your lines like you're supposed to?' The Colonel looked at him for about five seconds and said, 'Son, if you'll just sit down and shut up, I'll change this thing so it's fit to read. And then I'll read it.' He was as much at home in front of a national TV audience as he would have been back in Corbin with a two-dollar dinner customer."

The image caught on, the chicken sold—it was, after all, good chicken, the best most people had ever tasted. Furthermore, it took a dish that had formerly been a Sunday dinner treat and put it on the everyday table. As the era of fast food and takeout spread across the South and the nation, Kentucky Fried Chicken roared along with it. But there were bumps in the road. Massey and the Colonel did not like each other, and the Colonel grew incensed when Massey decreed that company headquarters would be in Nashville, Tennessee, not Kentucky. "This ain't no goddam Tennessee Fried Chicken," he bellowed. "No matter what some slick, silk-suited sonofabitch says." Brown did not like the idea, either, but under an agreement between the two men, Massey controlled 60 percent, Brown 40 percent of the company, and Massey wanted company headquarters near his home.

But the trouble really stemmed from the fact that the Colonel could not let go. Maureen McGuire tried to convince him that it was a big, new company requiring new ways. He did not agree. "They don't need to do things any new way," he said. "This thing is growing so fast, if they let it alone it will run over them."

The Colonel caused trouble in small ways and large. On one occasion, when he and John Y. were in New York to make TV commercials, the Colonel spotted a fortune-teller's place as he wandered around during a filming break; remembering his previous horoscope, he went in. John almost suffered a seizure when, on the flight home, the Colonel confided that he was quitting the company. The fortune-teller, he revealed, had told him that he was not happy in his present job and that he should quit and go into something new. When they got home, John called a man in New York who went immediately to 57th Street and spoke with the fortune-teller. She promptly called the Colonel and told him she had made a mistake in his horoscope. "She said the stars said I had worked out my differences and should stay with my present job," he said.

Aside from bringing order and efficiency to a ramshackle management structure, John Brown's greatest contribution to the company was the tact and patience with which he treated the Colonel. This was partly because he knew he needed the older man, but partly, too, because he truly liked him. "It wasn't easy," he reminded critics, "for him to sit back and watch other people take over the company he had built and run it the way they wanted to and not the way with which he had made it a success."

The Colonel's simmering resentment boiled over at the worst possible time—the 1967 company convention in Miami. John had worked hard on a speech that would be the convention climax, and he sat nervously waiting for the Colonel to finish what was supposed to be a brief statement of welcome. It turned out differently.

"I suddenly realized that he wasn't making any welcoming speech," Brown said later. "He was making a tense, bitter attack on the new owners and their methods. I couldn't believe it. He said we had forgotten the people who had made the company in the early days, squeezing money out of them, making them pay a percentage of revenue where he had charged them only a nickel. Said we were ruining the company. That the food wasn't as good as it had been. That we had let quality slip. Here, in what was supposed to be our hour of victory, our symbol, our leader, had turned on us."

But John Brown showed the quick mind that had spurred company growth. Dripping sweat, robbed of his speech, he got up and in twenty minutes removed all doubt about whose company it was.

"What you have just heard," he said, "shows why we are one of the great companies of the world, and why it is going to be even greater. This man here," he added, "is an artist, and like all great artists, is a perfectionist. He founded this company on the belief that if you give your customer the best you can, you will prosper. What we represent is the Colonel's dream. It really is a dream, and it is up to us to make that dream come true. It may be that in our drive to organize this fast-growing company along the lines of efficiency that are fair to everyone, we have somehow slipped from following your standards, Colonel. But let me say this: When you sold this company to us, you asked us to be fair and honorable, and we have been. We haven't had a single lawsuit. There isn't a single person who can say we haven't honored every promise, every contract. If there is anyone here who feels he has been treated unfairly, we haven't heard of it."

At this point the Colonel jumped to his feet, grabbed the microphone, and shouted, "All right! All of you who think you haven't been treated the way you ought to be, raise your hand!"

Not a hand went up. There was not a sound in the huge hall. The Colonel hesitated for a minute and then sat down. From then on, it was John Y.'s company.

"Most of the people knew what had happened," said Brown. "They knew it was hard for the Colonel to see the company slip from him. The man had had a dream, he had realized it, and then he had sold it, and he wanted it back. They were embarrassed for him, but they still loved him. The next morning the Colonel came up to me and said, 'Well, John, you did a good job last night.' He knew he had been wrong, but there was no talk of quitting. But that cut the cord. From then on it was ours."

The Colonel's discontent may have been fed by the fact that so many people got rich from KFC when, in 1966, it went public. They were getting rich off of his work.

"I didn't want to go public just then, but Jack was pushing it, so I yielded," said Brown. "We went up to New York and met with Goodbody and Company, and they agreed to put us on the New York Stock Exchange. We had to sell half of our stock to have enough to market. The Colonel was very funny about stock. When he sold out, we gave him half a million and stock for a million and a half, with the stock as collateral. Well, when we went public, we needed that stock, but he balked, although he told everybody that the stock would prove as valuable as toilet paper. He finally said we could have it and sell it, but we'd have to give him the rights to Canada. Which we did. No trouble about it."

The stock opened at 15 and went to 100 the first day, and the Colonel saw the great mistake he had made in not accepting the offer of ten thousand shares from Brown and Massey. But there were bright moments too. On the day the stock was offered, the Colonel, along with Brown and Massey, walked onto the floor of the New York Stock Exchange, and trading stopped while everyone on the floor stood and applauded the man in the white suit, a high moment for the farm hand from Henryville.

Another satisfying moment came in 1969 when John Y., after Jack Massey's resignation, announced that company headquarters would be moved to Louisville. But the company was not just growing; it was diversifying. John Brown, for instance, built a big, white Colonel Sanders Inn. When it showed promise as a moneymaker, he decided it should be the first of a chain. The idea did not work, however, and was abandoned. He had the same experience with H. Salt's Fish and Chips and sold it. And he faced for the first time serious competition to Kentucky Fried Chicken. A Texas chain, Church Chicken, began making inroads on KFC with Crispy Chicken.

The Colonel threw a fit when Brown proposed to offer a new, crispy chicken as well as the Colonel's traditional recipe, but he eventually decided he liked it. But his connection to KFC lessened. He still did the white-suit commercials, but after the big, colonial headquarters opened in Louisville, with his office prominently just inside the front door, he resigned from the board of directors. There were no differences, he explained to reporters. He just did not feel that he had the competence to help run a big business like KFC.

He still spent a lot of time with children and was active in the March of Dimes. "No matter how his arthritis was hurting him," John Brown said, "he'd bend over and shake hands with a child or pat one on the head. He just loved children. He gave the profits from his Canadian franchises to charity."

As he approached eighty, the years rested seriously not only on the Colonel but on officials of KFC. "Nobody knew how long he might last," said John Brown. "He could become incapacitated, even die." Some thought that in Jim Sanders, the Colonel's nephew, they had the answer. "He was smart, looked quite a bit like the Colonel, and he had charm. I could see two men instead of one walking through the airport. Get on TV and get that much more free press."

It did not work. Jim was managing the Colonel's Shelbyville Restaurant, one of the Colonel's and Claudia's retirement undertakings—and a successful one—but he agreed to give it a try. He made a few public appearances. Newsmen covering his appearances commented on the likeness. But in the end, headquarters did not think the Colonel could or should be cloned. "I let some old maids talk me out of it," John Brown said later. "I think the idea would have panned out. The Colonel didn't object."

It is likely that the Colonel was looking for someone to share the load. He kept a schedule remarkable for a man of eighty, with more than a hundred appearances a year for company functions. Sanders became a fixture at the Kentucky Derby and in the Pegasus Parade. And he often visited the Kosair Children's Hospital, cursing with embarrassment when he emerged wet-eyed.

He and Claudia were traveling more now. When he was eighty, the two of them took a trip to Egypt, Russia, and the Holy Land. The Holy Land fascinated him. On September 3, 1970, he and Claudia were baptized in the Jordan River. It was the realization of a dream of Harland Sanders. Despite his temper, profanity, adulteries, and petty meanness, the Colonel was basically religious. He knew little about the Bible, his faith springing from total acceptance of the tenets of right and wrong. Sin, damnation, salvation. He became friends with Billy Graham and Jerry Falwell, and he believed that when he died he would go to heaven or hell according to the way the Lord added up his accounts. His baptism in the Jordan and his walk along the path Jesus took to Golgotha were a moving, cleansing experience.

Colonel Sanders had no cause to be restless or unsatisfied, but he was. He had begun an empire that had spread to forty-eight countries, with more than three thousand outlets. He was many times a millionaire, as were more than three hundred people who had followed him into Kentucky Fried Chicken. Happily married, popular, famous, known throughout the world, he had his office walls adorned with pictures of him with the great and powerful. What else did he want? Not money. He had more than he wanted. What he really wanted was to live, preferably forever. He had always been a vital, tough, muscular, virile, active man who loved life and the living of it. And now he saw the sun moving toward the horizon.

He tried all sorts of things to make time slow down, if not stand still. He went to Duke University for a rice diet and lost fifty pounds (he was badly overweight and would not rein in his appetite). He tried copper bracelets, megavitamins, hot soaks, hyperbaric oxygen tanks. His hopes flared anew with each rumor of a new cure for arthritis or hormones that would slow the deterioration of the body. But he could not stop the clock. His slowly failing eyesight caused doctors to tell him to quit driving. He fumed mightily but eventually hired a driver. And eyesight was not the worst of it. In 1972, one doctor mused, "I saw him sporadically . . . mostly because of his diabetes, and he said, 'Doc, I'll make you a contract. I want you to keep me alive 'til I'm ninety.' I said okay. It became sort of a joke. He was a fascinating man. Later on, I got this call, I think it was from Thailand, and he said he had found this doctor who had a wonderful herb medicine that would keep you young. I asked him if he saw any old people around, told him to bring a sample home, and if we found it wouldn't hurt him, he could take it. By the time he got home he had forgotten about it."

But there was some apparent mental slippage. For no visible reason, he blasted Brown and Massey in an interview with a Chicago reporter for "doing me out of my stock" and referred to them as "a bunch of sharpies." During a business trip to Chicago in December 1972, he told a reporter that the gravy served by KFC "tasted like wallpaper paste." He liked fried chicken all right, he added, but "I'd run my legs off for a good limburger on rye. You can't get good limburger in Kentucky."

Feeling time's passage, in April 1973 he picked out his grave site in Louisville's Cave Hill Cemetery. In the center of a granite portico stood a two-foot bronze bust sculpted by his daughter. The Colonel assured newsmen that he was not planning to use it anytime soon. "I'm just asking seventeen and a half more years," he said.

While this was going on, Claudia announced that she and a partner would begin franchising the Colonel's Lady Dinner House restaurants. On returning from an Asian trip, however, the Colonel learned that Heublein Inc., to which KFC had been sold in 1973, did not intend to allow the franchise. The Colonel blew up, and in 1974 he and Claudia filed suit against Heublein for $122 million. John finally talked the Colonel out of it, reminding him that if the case went to court, he, John, would be forced to testify against him because "we had made the contract and he knew what was in it." Later the Colonel denounced, in no uncertain terms and in the presence of a newspaper reporter, the food in another KFC outlet. The owner took exception and promptly sued the Colonel for libel—unsuccessfully.

In 1976 the Colonel testified before the House Select Committee on Aging, declaring that retirement was a terrible thing. "I'm dead against it," repeating that "a man will rust out quicker than he'll wear out. You've got to stay alive to live." In 1978 he and Claudia dedicated

KFC's Colonel Sanders Museum just off the lobby of the Louisville headquarters. In a glass case, small and awkward, was the first pressure cooker he used, and on the walls were plaques and honorary degrees that he, a sixth-grade dropout, had been awarded. They testify to the will of the man.

The Colonel continued to speak freely—and controversially. In 1979 John Brown divorced his first wife, married former Miss America Phyllis George, and decided to run for governor of Kentucky. The Colonel refused to endorse him and, when he won, refused to attend the victory party, saying he saw no reason to "go down there and let those damn fools blow cigarette smoke in my face." But at Derby time, he attended the traditional dinner given by the Loyal Order of Kentucky Colonels and, to the surprise of almost everyone, insisted on going to the Governor's Derby Breakfast. Governor Brown bustled around the old man as though he were a favorite uncle, and gradually the Colonel unbent. "I think that, toward the end, the Colonel realized how much John meant to him," said an assistant.

A week after the Derby, the Colonel went to the doctor, complaining of chest pains. He had pneumonia and responded well to medication. About the time he was getting well, he said he had to get out and go to Las Vegas for the KFC convention. The doctor advised strongly against it, but the Colonel was adamant. It was like a homecoming—all the old familiar faces were there—but it came at a price. The Colonel soon entered Louisville's Jewish Hospital with pneumonia. And on the afternoon of June 10, specialists told him he had leukemia. The Colonel accepted it calmly and said he wanted merely to make his ninetieth birthday.

He did. KFC and friends threw a massive party, and a crowd of ten thousand cheered as the Colonel made his way to the balcony, waving. The next day he drew another whistling ovation when he appeared to light the eight-foot birthday cake. The crowd, estimated at thirty-five thousand, gave a huge cheer. Some two months later, however, he again developed pneumonia and was listed in critical condition.

The Colonel rallied somewhat but seemed to respond only to his wife. For the next twenty days he seldom spoke. Improving, declining, as though borne on the waves of time, he slipped slowly downhill. Claudia remained in his room during the day, but after he dropped off to sleep she left and was driven home. On the final morning, the doctor asked him how he was feeling. "About the same," he said, adding that he had slept well but did not want any breakfast and just wanted to rest. There was nothing to do but wait. At 7:40, as daylight was breaking, the nurse found Colonel Harland David Sanders dead.

NOTE

Quotations in the chapter are from a series of interviews the author conducted with Harlan Sanders, John Y. Brown, John Y. Brown Jr., Edward T. Breathitt Jr., various individuals in Corbin, employees and officials of Kentucky Fried Chicken, and some of Claudia Sanders's friends. Several general conclusions come from the author's own interactions with the Colonel. Those sources are cited more fully in the author's biography of Harlan Sanders and in several articles in the *Louisville Courier-Journal Magazine*.

SUGGESTED READINGS

Harrison, Lowell H., and James C. Klotter. *A New History of Kentucky*. Lexington: University Press of Kentucky, 1997.

Howorth, Lisa. "Colonel Harland Sanders." In Charles Reagan Wilson and William Ferris, eds., *Encyclopedia of Southern Culture*. Chapel Hill: University of North Carolina Press, 1989.

Pearce, John Ed. *The Colonel*. Garden City, NY: Doubleday, 1982.

Sanders, Harland D. *Life As I Have Known It Has Been Finger Lickin' Good*. Carol Stream, IL: Creation House, 1974.

Vezeau, Jeannie. "(Col.) Harland David Sanders." In John E. Kleber, ed., *Encyclopedia of Louisville*. Lexington: University Press of Kentucky, 2001.

10

Blanche Terry and the White Knights of the Ku Klux Klan

Christopher Waldrep

In August 1955 fourteen-year-old Emmett Till of Chicago was visiting relatives in Mississippi. As he left a store, the African American youth offended a young white woman there. The incident cost him his life. Two white men killed him, tied his body to a cotton gin fan, and tossed it in the river. Though later identified, the men were found not guilty by an all-white jury.

Every site in every town and every city in the South would be a battleground in the emerging struggle for civil rights, and every person, young and old, male and female, black and white, would be a part of that struggle. Blanche Terry represents the dilemmas individuals faced at the local level, and how decisions made there would, one after the other, start to bring about broad change over the region. At first glance, Blanche Terry's life appeared typical for the time. She had married early, worked—as thousands of southern women did—in a factory, and seemed southern to the core—and was. But when the Till murder sparked her son's anger over racial injustice, she began to understand the issue also. More and more she saw the restrictions her society placed on women, and she began to take more control of her own life.

Terry's personal battlefield was the cafeteria in her factory. When the company integrated it, she continued to eat lunch there. She led no marches, made no speeches, offered no programs. She just set an example—she continued to eat lunch there. Ku Klux Klan actions and community pressures drove her coworkers away, yet, despite her husband's losing his job, despite the threats and violence, she persisted. Such actions, by thousands of virtually unknown individuals, showed that integration could occur and that not all supported the resistance led by the KKK and others. Blanche Terry simply showed the courage to live her convictions, and more and more southerners did the same over time, breaking down the racial barriers that had so long existed.

Christopher R. Waldrep is Jamie and Phyllis Pasker Chair of History at San Francisco State University. In addition to articles in the American Historical Review, *the* Journal of American History, *and the* Journal of Southern History, *he has written* Night Riders *(1993),* Roots of Disorder: Race and Criminal Justice in the American South, 1817–1880 *(1998), and* The Many Faces of Judge Lynch: Extralegal Violence and Punishment in America *(2002); he has also edited (with Donald Nieman)* Local Matters: Race, Crime, and Justice in the Nineteenth-Century South *(2001).*

One great irony of twentieth-century American history is that no region of the nation changed as much as the white South, the same part of the country most determined not to change at all. Shortly after the mid-twentieth century white southerners turned away from the extralegal violence they had tolerated for generations, seeing in it the specter of anarchy. This shift does not mean that whites immediately repudiated their racist mind-set. It does mean that a majority of the white population came to perceive the Ku Klux Klan and similar vigilante groups as a threat to order. After 1965, all over the South, police departments disentangled themselves from their erstwhile allies in the Ku Klux Klan. Racial violence did not entirely disappear, of course. But its toleration by the bulk of the white population did.[1]

How this change-resistant society changed is a great historical question. Obviously a large part of the answer lies in the civil rights movement, an extraordinary grassroots campaign for freedom mounted by courageous people against terrifying odds. Historians have not yet satisfactorily explained what revitalized the civil rights movement in the 1950s, although many point to changes wrought by World War II and the Cold War culture that followed. It can be argued that white change resulted from black agitation for freedom. As civil rights workers pressed for freedom, their racist tormentors engaged in violent excesses that sickened the mass of public opinion.

The story of one woman's encounter with the White Knights of the Ku Klux Klan can never definitively answer questions about the influence of the civil rights movement on the thinking of ordinary white southerners or explain why white southerners proved as receptive to it as they ultimately did. Blanche Terry's experiences in Vicksburg, Mississippi, do suggest that white southerners acted in a complex network of social contexts. Neither World War II, the Cold War, nor even the civil rights movement fully explain why white southerners were ready for change in the 1960s.

Nine days before her sixteenth birthday, Blanche Smith married Ray Terry in Vicksburg, Mississippi. In the nineteenth century, southern women

Blanche Terry. *Courtesy of Christopher Waldrep*

tended to marry young. Some historians as well as contemporary observers theorized that southern men deliberately chose younger women in order to dominate their mates more easily.[2] This idea probably does not explain Blanche's twentieth-century marriage. Blanche married a man only a little older than herself, engaging in what was, in a sense, her first serious act of rebellion against her father, a Vicksburg veterinarian. "Back then," Blanche remembered later, "all you had to do was lie and tell the justice of the peace that you were eighteen."[3] No one checked, and the marriage license cost just three dollars. Neither Blanche nor Ray told their parents about their marriage until Ray had found a job in a local bakery.

When Blanche and Ray married, it was 1937. Vicksburg in the 1930s was a troubled place. People whispered about the terrible power the Ku Klux Klan wielded with city officials. Tensions existed between the town's Catholic and Protestant populations as well. Control of the town seesawed between Catholic and Protestant white leaders, and blacks had no hope of electoral power. Ethnic problems aside, economically the city was a wreck. The federal government operated a Civilian Conservation Corps (CCC) camp on the site of Vicksburg's Civil War battlefield in an effort to relieve widespread unemployment. Men went to the CCC camp for training as guides, telling tourists about the great Civil War siege that made Vicksburg famous. At least one historian now argues that the New Deal disappointed white southerners, leaving them skeptical about government just as the civil rights movement, with its demands for government intervention, got started.[4] Perhaps some southerners came out of the Great Depression and New Deal disenchanted with government, but not Blanche. The CCC, Blanche firmly said in 1997, "was a great thing and something they should have today."

Blanche considered herself and her family southern to the core. Her mother had told her that Blanche's great-grandfather John McGuiggin died fighting for the South. In fact, authorities had convicted him of selling forged passes to escaping slaves. After the Union Army liberated McGuiggin from jail, he went to work for the U.S. Army and died in the service of the United States. But Blanche knew none of this as she entered the workforce. She thought her ancestor had died fighting for the Confederacy.

Three years into her marriage, Blanche went to work in a clothing factory, M. Fine and Son. She and Ray lived with her father and had a two-year-old son, Ray Jr. When she became pregnant with twins about four years later, Blanche quit her job with M. Fine and Son but soon realized she had to return to work. In 1946 she entered Vicksburg's garment industry, getting a job in a dress factory. She may not have noticed it at the time, but looking back she observes that the bosses were all men. Some women instructed operators in sewing, but men made all the decisions.

As she worked in these garment factories, Blanche realized that women faced an even rougher time than the men. "If the husband left," Blanche said later, "you didn't make much money and the alimony was—forget that." Women, in short, got only what they worked for. Older women abandoned by their husbands, or widowed, faced age discrimination. Some businesses did not like to hire women over forty, even when they had to support children as well as themselves. So some women lied about their ages to find work. In addition to being divided along gender lines, the factory was strictly segregated. Only white women worked on the cutting floor. Black women carried bundles of finished dresses.

The Terrys earned enough money to send their son, Ray Jr., to the local Catholic school, taught by the Sacred Heart Brothers. In Ray's senior year at the Catholic high school, whites near Money, Mississippi, murdered a young black visitor from Chicago, Emmett Till. The case caused a sensation, especially after an all-white jury acquitted the two men charged with the crime. On January 24, 1956, *Look* magazine published an article by William Bradford Huie based on interviews with the two acquitted defendants. Now that they had been tried and found not guilty, the two had nothing to fear from the criminal justice system. They freely confessed their crime to Huie, who published their justification for their crime in *Look*.

One of Ray Jr.'s high school teachers brought Huie's *Look* article to class. The boys had long since dismissed their teacher as a "nigger lover" and Ray Jr., along with the other boys, argued against using Emmett Till as evidence that segregation and racism promoted violence. More murders took place in Chicago in a week than in Mississippi in a year, Ray insisted. Every teacher hopes to say something to a student that will make a permanent mark on the world by changing that student's life. On that January day in Vicksburg, Ray Jr.'s teacher said, "Terry, whatever you think of Emmett Till, he was a child and whenever a child is murdered it raises national indignation."[5] The words resonated with the young southerner. Emmett Till had been a child, living through an experience universal to all people, regardless of color. From that moment on, Ray began to listen more critically to what his parents and other adults said about race. While Ray Jr. had no luck persuading his father to rethink his white supremacist beliefs, his mother listened and seemed to absorb what he was saying.

At the same time Ray began to rethink his own and his parent's racial attitudes, Blanche increasingly asserted herself, insisting she would have a home. When Emmett Till died, the Terrys lived in a house rented from Blanche's father. Her husband was indifferent; he did not want to be responsible for the taxes and insurance. Ignoring Ray, Blanche searched Vicksburg for a house, finding one owned by a woman wanting $500 down and $65 a month for eleven years. It was a nice house for the money,

Blanche decided, and she liked the fact that she could finance so much of the cost. Blanche did not have $500, but she and Ray together had $500 saved in a Christmas Club account at their bank. Without telling her husband, she used that money for the down payment.

With her husband opposed to the purchase, Blanche had to wait until he was out of town and call on his brother and her sister to help with the move. While Ray Terry was in Port Gibson on the beer truck he operated, Blanche moved into her new family home.

Not long after Blanche installed her family in the new house, the roof started leaking. "Oh, boy," Blanche said later, "he hit the ceiling. So I knew I had to work then, go back to work." Westinghouse had put in a new plant in Vicksburg, manufacturing fluorescent light fixtures. When Blanche realized she needed money for a new roof, the Westinghouse plant was laying off workers, not hiring. Blanche went anyway. "I have got to have a job," she told the Westinghouse man. He answered that Westinghouse was in a layoff and not hiring. Blanche persisted, "I've got to have a job. I went and moved my family in a house and it's leaking." Blanche stubbornly refused to move from the office until she got the job. She worked at Westinghouse for nine and a half years.

Working there allowed Blanche to put a new roof on her house, but the factory job itself proved to be terrible. Blanche toiled all day winding capacitors. Used to working with her hands from her time in the dress factory, Blanche quickly learned how to meet production quotas an hour before her shift ended. Westinghouse sent a time-study man and soon the company increased production. "If I'd been smart," Blanche said later, "I would have slowed down." The speeded-up assembly line made it tougher on all the workers to make the new minimums. In Blanche's view, it mattered that the "time-study man" was a man. "All the men down there were the chiefs, and all the women were the Indians. We were the Indians and they were the chiefs." Blanche never fully understood why she became more critical of Mississippi's patriarchal system. After World War II and Rosie the Riveter, increased female assertiveness was in the air by the late 1950s and early 1960s. Talking to her son was beginning to raise doubts about Mississippi's racial hierarchy and hierarchy in general. And from her teenage years on, Blanche did not see herself as second-class. She just was not that kind of person.

As Blanche Terry began to question Mississippi's male-dominated, racist order, most white Mississippians remained militantly determined to maintain segregation. When rumors circulated that a Vicksburg high school teacher named Joe Ed Price had made critical remarks about segregation in his classroom, the Mississippi State Sovereignty Commission sent detectives to investigate. The investigators interviewed the school superintendent and Price's principal. The principal confirmed that he had received a report that Price had once told students he would not mind teaching an integrated class. The principal told the Sovereignty Commission men that after a parent complained about Price, he began secretly monitoring Price's history class over the school intercom, listening for "disloyal" statements. The school superintendent told the detectives that "if I find he leans toward integration, I will not need the Sovereignty Commission in order to get rid of him."[6] Reassured that the administrators had the situation under control, the investigators went back to Jackson and filed their report.

Even as state government officials tried to squelch anyone "agitating" for integration, vigilante groups organized and expanded. The Original Knights of the Ku Klux Klan formed in 1960, organizing in Shreveport, Louisiana. According to the FBI file, on February 15, 1964, two hundred members of the Original Knights defected from that organization to form the White Knights of the Ku Klux Klan in Mississippi. Within a year the White Knights boasted over a thousand members in the Magnolia State. Led by imperial wizard Sam Bowers, operator of the Sambo Amusement Company in Laurel, the White Knights became the dominant Klan faction in Mississippi, violent and dangerous. Bowers told his followers that he had secret information that African troops planned to invade Mississippi from Cuba. He reported that the federal government planned to nationalize Mississippi's National Guard, immobilize it, and turn the state over to the Negroes. Only the Klan would resist such an invasion, Bowers announced, advising his followers "to be smart and move or be right and fight."[7]

Bowers directed most of his venom against blacks, but he also disliked Jews and "Papists, because they bow to a Roman dictator."[8] In Vicksburg, persons of Irish descent formed a significant portion of the population and the Catholic Church constituted an important social force. In the nineteenth century slave owners had feared local Irish might form an alliance with the slaves and foment an uprising. After the Civil War, reformers hoped to recruit the local Irish population over to the side of black rights, but the Irish proclaimed themselves white and joined white conservative "redeemers" to impose segregation. The Irish became so white and so southern that Blanche Terry's mother changed the color of her great-grandfather's Civil War allegiance from northern blue to southern gray.

Determined to use violence to end the civil rights movement in Mississippi, Bowers directed his followers to collect armaments and ammunition. He taught his followers that the Klan had four projects: (1) threatening telephone calls or visits; (2) burning a cross, usually on private property; (3) beatings or floggings, arson, wild shooting into property, and bombings; and (4) extermination.[9]

The White Knights had a presence in Vicksburg. Through 1964, Vicksburg Klansmen were active, beating black families for hosting civil rights workers, shooting into businesses, and firebombing a house used by civil rights workers. By April 1965, FBI agents had identified Howard Lee Miller Sr. as the White Knights' "exalted cyclops" in Vicksburg. The FBI had infiltrated the White Knights with informants who described Miller as a "'wild talking' individual." When they learned that the exalted cyclops had received training in explosives in the army, FBI officials forwarded his name to the Secret Service, to be placed on a special watch list of dangerous persons.

In such an atmosphere, Westinghouse officials did not buck the system. Black workers did not work on the assembly line. Instead, they "fed the line," bringing lead and other materials to assembly line workers who made the lights. Water fountains and restrooms had signs designating certain facilities for "colored" and others for "white" workers. The cafeteria had two doors, side by side. One door had a sign marked "colored" and the other, "white." Inside the cafeteria a wall segregated white workers from blacks.

As Blanche labored on the Westinghouse assembly line, Americans elected their first Catholic president, John F. Kennedy, who won, in part, because of support from black voters. Once in office, Kennedy disappointed some civil rights organizations when he refused to push Congress hard for a new civil rights law. Kennedy did not want to offend southern Democrats and understood that southern segregationists dominated both houses of Congress. Nonetheless, there were things Kennedy could do. Through his executive powers he could attack segregation around the margins. In 1961, Kennedy established the President's Committee on Equal Employment Opportunity, chaired by his vice president, Lyndon Johnson. This committee's best-known initiative called on government contractors to sign voluntary agreements promising to improve their racial policies. This program, Plans for Progress, led Westinghouse to take down the cafeteria wall separating the races in its Vicksburg factory. As Johnson's assistant, George Reedy, hopefully observed, the Plans for Progress promised actual benefit for black citizens.[10]

William Provance, a mechanic, headed the International Brotherhood of Electrical Workers (IBEW) local chapter at the Vicksburg plant where Westinghouse had "integrated" its cafeteria. There was a moment at the end of the nineteenth century when black and white laborers joined together in biracial unions, especially in Richmond, Birmingham, New Orleans, and other southern cities. The 1893 depression crippled this experiment in racial harmony, though it did not end it altogether. In the twentieth century, union organizers found that white workers could be motivated to unionize in the hope of striking against the employment of blacks. Employers often used rural blacks as "scabs" or strikebreakers, inflaming racial tensions between white and black workers. Unions became a tool not to create racial harmony but to promote white superiority. By the time Blanche joined the IBEW, biracial unionism was not even a distant memory.[11] The IBEW staunchly championed white supremacy. They were the same as the Ku Klux Klan, Blanche later observed, "but I didn't know it at the time." Provance went from one portion of the factory to the next, instructing all white workers to boycott the "integrated" cafeteria.

In the capacitor room where Blanche worked, the women discussed what to do after Provance relayed their union's directive. The woman working next to Blanche asked if she would continue eating in the cafeteria. Blanche had been listening to her son talk about civil rights ever since the Emmett Till murder, more than five years in the past by the time Provance made his announcement. At the same time, Blanche doubted her fellow workers would buy an argument for civil rights. Instead, Blanche pointed out that the company cafeteria provided a good lunch for forty cents. "He doesn't pay for my dinner," Blanche said after Provance disappeared out the door. "I'm going to the cafeteria." Saying it out loud made her even more resolute. "Sure," she said again, more loudly this time, "I'm going to the cafeteria." The women in the capacitor room all agreed to continue patronizing the cafeteria.

Blanche and the other women from the capacitor room sat at the same cafeteria table where they had always eaten, and the black men continued to sit in their customary space. A wall once separated the two groups. Now an empty space served the same purpose. White workers sat at the same tables in what had once been the "white" section of the dining area and blacks sat at "their" tables. Very little had changed, except symbolically.

Still, the symbolism mattered. Friction grew between workers boycotting the cafeteria and Blanche's group. The company had taken down the wall to please the government, but its primary concern, unsurprisingly, was the continued operation of the plant without discord and tension. Herman Vavra, Westinghouse personnel manager, met with Blanche and other workers still eating in the cafeteria. "You girls," he accused, "kind of agitate this thing." "We're not doing anything!" Blanche shot back, "We're just going in there to eat! I am not going to have them run us out of that cafeteria. That's stupid!"

As the company put pressure on Blanche to back down, Provance and other IBEW leaders looked for ways to coerce the women continuing to use the cafeteria. Women with unionized husbands were easy targets. One woman had a husband in the plumbers union. Her husband quickly found he could not get work. She and her husband had five children to feed. She stopped eating in the cafeteria. Another woman's children became ill; their water tank had been poisoned. She stopped eating in the cafeteria as well. Others found dead animals in their mailboxes, left there as a threat. They also quit the cafeteria. Another woman stopped after a sniper shot at her teenage son.

"So, first thing you know, eventually, I was the only one on our time period going in there," Blanche related later. Jim Sullivan, the operator of the cafeteria, lost money now that almost every white worker boycotted it. Westinghouse decided to keep the cafeteria open and covered Sullivan's losses.

As pressure on Blanche increased, Westinghouse decided to desegregate its assembly line. Vavra hired two black women not to feed the line but to work on the assembly line itself. This action violated white space. On June 12, 1965, the White Knights of the Ku Klux Klan for Province 9, which included Warren County and Vicksburg, met. Province Giant J. K. Greer called the meeting to order. The Vicksburg exalted cyclops offered a prayer. According to the FBI informant in attendance, the assembled White Knights first discussed the value of propaganda in fighting school desegregation in the Natchez area before turning to the Westinghouse problem. "The meeting ended," according to the informant, "with a general round table discussion some of which evolved around the hiring of Negroes by the Westinghouse Plant at Vicksburg, Mississippi." Perhaps this was only desultory conversation. The FBI's informant was unable to reveal to his FBI handlers what specifically the Klansmen planned to do about Westinghouse. If the White Knights did not decide what to do about Westinghouse at this meeting, however, they soon did.

Seven days later someone hurled three Molotov cocktails into Vavra's garage, which damaged two of Vavra's automobiles. Newspaper reports observed that Vavra was personnel manager at the plant, "which has in recent weeks been hiring some Negroes." Nonetheless, Warren County Sheriff Vernon Luckett told reporters that he had no clue as to the motive for the attack.

Bowers's "project 1" authorized threatening phone calls. On a Sunday afternoon, Blanche got a call from the woman with whom she rode to work. Someone had called to tell her that if Blanche was in her car Monday morning, her car would be blown up. The woman was embarrassed but told Blanche she could no longer drive her to work. She stressed she had two grandchildren in her house, and she could not risk their lives. That same day Blanche got a similarly threatening call from a man. Speaking in a low voice, he threatened to burn her house down. "You and who else?" Blanche retorted and slammed down the phone.

Despite her bravado, a worried Blanche called the FBI office in Jackson. The FBI had opened this new field office the year before, and it was the largest in the nation. Civil rights workers called the summer of 1964 "Freedom Summer" and targeted Mississippi for a voter registration drive. College students rendezvoused at Miami University in Oxford, Ohio. After training in nonviolence, they fanned out across Mississippi, setting up "freedom schools" to teach Mississippi blacks how to read and write and then register to vote. The Council of Federated Organizations (COFO), an alliance of civil rights organizations, coordinated the effort. In addition to bombing the Vicksburg COFO house, Vicksburg Klansmen also called civil rights workers on the phone to harass them with insulting and threatening language.

The most violent episode during Freedom Summer took place on the other side of the state from Vicksburg, in Neshoba County. Sam Bowers relied on Edgar Ray "Preacher" Killen as his recruiter in Neshoba County. On June 21 the Neshoba County Klan, in coordination with the local sheriff's department, murdered Andrew Goodman, Michael Schwerner, and James Chaney. The FBI launched a major effort to find the bodies and then prosecute the killers. Blanche's son Ray had, by this time, joined the Justice Department's Civil Rights Division and worked on the Neshoba County case. During its investigation into the kidnapping and murder of these three civil rights workers, the FBI had 153 agents working out of its Jackson office.

The agent Blanche spoke with identified himself as John Thomas. You are going to get more phone calls, he warned. Things are going to happen. Thomas was not wrong. Only later did she realize that the first caller was the head of the Vicksburg Ku Klux Klan. Thomas instructed Blanche to listen carefully to the calls, focusing on background noises. She should keep a log of the calls, Thomas said, because they would follow a pattern.

A woman called Blanche, cursing. Blanche listened carefully to the sounds of children in the background. Remembering who in the prosegregation crowd had small children, Blanche addressed her caller by name. "You better get off this phone and tend to those kids," Blanche warned, "or they're going to turn out just like you." This time the caller, not Blanche, slammed down the phone.

The next caller was the wife of Vicksburg's top Ku Klux Klansman, Howard Miller. A shop steward in the union, Gladys Miller had a low voice that Blanche recognized. Blanche listened to the threatening call; by now she made it a point never to hang up first. Once the caller gave up, Blanche looked up her phone number and called her tormenter back. "That was you that just called," Blanche accused. The shop steward hung up the phone.

Klan violence escalated. On June 26 a fire exploded inside Vicksburg's Jitney Jungle store. The heat from the flames was so intense that it melted the glass in parking meters across the street. An FBI informant later reported that the White Knights stole explosives from seismograph crews who stored primer cord, dynamite, and electric blasting caps in their trailers. The crews parked their trailers at least a mile from any occupied residence, the informant explained, making them vulnerable to burglary. Another informant claimed Vicksburg Klansmen had access to plastic explosives from Louisiana.

On July 28 the mutilated body of James Lamar Studdard turned up behind the Illinois monument at the Vicksburg National Military Park. Because officers found Studdard's body on federal property, the FBI claimed jurisdiction and assigned eight agents to the case. Within three days the FBI told reporters that they were working on "something concrete" and were "making headway in our investigation." FBI agents learned that Klanswomen, at least some of whom worked at the Westinghouse plant, had stationed themselves across the street from a black brothel. The Klanswomen had spotted Studdard, a white man, patronizing the brothel. Prodded by their wives, male White Knights had warned Studdard and the police had arrested him, but Studdard persisted in patronizing the black brothel. Despite the initially optimistic reports, by August newspapers reported that the trail was growing cold. Newspaper reports suggest that the FBI decided that the Vicksburg White Knights called on Alabama Klansmen to murder Studdard. FBI agents had begun to interview suspects in Alabama.[12]

In the midst of this violence, Blanche drove herself to the Westinghouse plant. She traveled down lonely stretches of Highway 61 South through wooded areas ideal for ambush. She continued to make this drive even after the Klan's threatening phone calls began specifically mentioning her lonely drive and promising to "get" her before she got to work. Blanche was determined to show no fear. Her husband started keeping a gun next to his bed. Alone, unarmed, threatened by the Klan, Blanche Terry kept driving to work and kept eating in the cafeteria. Blanche now thinks that her childhood friendship with exalted cyclops Howard Miller explains why the Klan did not assassinate her as she drove up and down Highway 61. "We played together as kids," she remembers. "I had never done anything to Howard. That was one reason I wasn't physically harmed."

Ray Terry worked as route manager with a local wholesale beer distributorship. After the Klan started its campaign of harassment against Blanche, area managers representing the two major beers sold through the business visited the company to inquire about the reduction in sales of their products. The only explanation the owner and Ray could offer was that the sales decrease was associated with Blanche's troubles with the Klan. Both the beer company men asked Ray to urge his wife to stop going to the cafeteria. Ray Terry had no enlightened feelings about the "coloreds." Nevertheless, he told the beer company men he had no intention of trying to tell his wife what to do. The company owner announced he would remain neutral by retiring and selling the company. Ray Terry lost his job after sixteen years of service, working his way up from salesman to route manager. It had been the best job he had ever had, and he earned a respectable income.

At the same time, the U.S. attorney general hired Ray Jr., a student at Loyola University in New Orleans, in the Honor Law Graduate program, open only to the best law students in the country. Just as the Klan stepped up its harassment of the Terrys, the *Vicksburg Evening Post* ran a story announcing that their son had joined the Justice Department. Ray Jr. now believes that news of his joining the Justice Department further enraged Vicksburg Klansmen.

Blanche and Ray had purchased a new car just four months before the trouble started. A yellow Ford Galaxy, it was their first new car. Blanche realized that her husband suspected the Klan might do something to their car. Ray, after all, had his own sources into the Klan hierarchy—his father was a member. Ray had the car simonized—coated with a heavy wax—and took out vandalism insurance. One morning Ray called, "Get up and come look at your car!" Acid had been thrown over the car and had eaten the yellow paint off it. Blanche remembered later that it looked like someone had thrown a bucket of white paint over it.

On October 21 agents of the FBI confronted the Vicksburg exalted cyclops, Howard Miller, at his home. The agents advised the cyclops of his right to an attorney and that anything he said might be used against him in court. Asked about the firebombing of Vavra's garage, Miller insisted he knew nothing about it except what he read in the newspapers. The FBI also wanted to know what Miller knew about the murder of Lamar Studdard. Again the cyclops claimed he only knew what he read in the newspapers. But Miller could not resist adding that he had heard that Studdard had patronized two black prostitutes a week or two prior to his death. Aware that the FBI had access to Vicksburg Police Department records, Miller volunteered that he had called local police to complain about Studdard's fraternization with black prostitutes. Any white man patronizing black prostitutes should be arrested, the cyclops said, and ought to be whipped.

The FBI agents told Miller that they knew he was the exalted cyclops of the White Knights of the Ku Klux Klan of Mississippi. Miller must have made a sarcastic retort, as the FBI report of the interview states that the cyclops answered that he had "likewise heard this information only a couple of days before and was glad to hear it." He was not in the Klan, the head of the Ku Klux Klan in Vicksburg lied. He was a Mason and a member of the Order of the Moose. Only after their interview did the FBI learn that Miller had ordered a printer to prepare one hundred "wanted posters" for the civil rights leader Martin Luther King Jr., and also for Paul Johnson, Paul Barrett, Marion Brown, and Jack Smith.

Three and a half months after his interview with the FBI, the exalted cyclops of the Vicksburg White Knights suffered a massive heart attack.

Some in Vicksburg whispered that his confrontation with the FBI had led to the heart attack. The FBI was planning to prosecute him, some said. Justice Department lawyers came to Vicksburg to interview witnesses in preparation for a court case. The Justice Department, Vicksburgers whispered, wanted to prosecute Miller for violating the civil rights of Blanche Terry and for income tax evasion. He had been buying white sheets at the Dollar Store, making them into Klan costumes and selling them at a profit without reporting the income.

If the Justice Department ever planned such a prosecution, it dropped those plans after the cyclops suffered his heart attack. FBI agents reported to Washington that the exalted cyclops was unable to work because of his heart problems. In September 1966, FBI informants reported that Miller had not stepped down but that since his heart attack, "things have quieted down considerably in that area." The White Knights were no longer active around Vicksburg. In 1968 the FBI closed its file on the exalted cyclops. His health was so poor he could no longer hold a job, agents noted. In 1971 the former exalted cyclops of the White Knights died. His tombstone includes an inscription that seems ironic in light of the Klan's terror campaign in Vicksburg: "He built a monument of love in the hearts of all who knew him."

After the Klan hurled acid on her car, Blanche Terry continued working at Vicksburg's Westinghouse plant and eating in the cafeteria. Gradually others rejoined her. Today the factory is closed. Blanche's son is retired from his job in the Justice Department. Blanche managed the gift shop at Vicksburg's Old Court House Museum for thirty-five years, working there until 2003. In 1988, when a former field director of the National Association for the Advancement of Colored People ran for mayor of Vicksburg, becoming the city's first black mayor, Blanche Terry supported him. Blanche Terry died November 9, 2004.

Vicksburg has elected a black mayor and numerous black officials. Much has changed since the 1960s, when merchants hesitated to integrate their businesses for fear they would be firebombed. Historians now attribute much of this improvement to "local people," folks living in Mississippi before the arrival of civil rights workers from the North. Blanche Terry's decision to turn away from Vicksburg's racist tradition can be traced to no single variable. But gender obviously played an important role, as Blanche became more critical of the role men played in her life. And sensational civil rights murders, especially the death of Emmett Till, clearly helped awaken the Terrys to contradictions in their society. These cultural shifts in fundamental attitudes and thinking run deeper than Cold War politics or social changes prompted by service in World War II. It may well be that such cultural shifts largely account for the dramatic transformation of the South's traditional attitudes toward race relations.

NOTES

1. Michal R. Belknap, *Federal Law and Southern Order: Racial Violence and Constitutional Conflict in the Post-Brown South* (Athens: University of Georgia Press, 1987), 229–51.
2. Bertram Wyatt-Brown, *Southern Honor: Ethics and Behavior in the Old South* (New York: Oxford University Press, 1982), 203–5; John Q. Anderson, ed., *Brokenburn: The Journal of Kate Stone, 1861–1868* (1955; Baton Rouge: Louisiana State University Press, 1995), 74.
3. Blanche Terry, interview by author, August 20, 1997. All quotations by Blanche Terry are from this interview.
4. Bryant Simon, *A Fabric of Defeat: The Politics of South Carolina Millhands, 1910–1948* (Chapel Hill: University of North Carolina Press, 1998).
5. Ray Terry Jr., interview by author, August 9, 1996.
6. "Activities of Mr. Joe Ed Price, Teacher at Cooper High School, Vicksburg, Mississippi, reported to be Teaching Subversive Subjects in the School," December 30, 1960, Sovereignty Commission Files, document 2-41-0-25-1-1-1, Mississippi Department of Archives and History, Jackson.
7. *Activities of the Ku Klux Klan Organizations of the United States, Hearings before the Committee on Un-American Activities*, 89th Cong., 2d sess. (Washington, DC: Government Printing Office, 1966), 3:2775.
8. Seth Cagin and Philip Dray, *We Are Not Afraid: The Story of Goodman, Schwerner, and Chaney and the Civil Rights Campaign for Mississippi* (New York: Macmillan, 1988), 265.
9. *Activities of the Ku Klux Klan Organizations of the United States*, 3:2666.
10. Carl M. Brauer, *John F. Kennedy and the Second Reconstruction* (New York: Columbia University Press, 1977), 81, 147–51.
11. Edward L. Ayers, *The Promise of the New South: Life after Reconstruction* (New York: Oxford University Press, 1992), 431–32; Daniel Letwin, *The Challenge of Interracial Unionism: Alabama Coal Miners, 1878–1921* (Chapel Hill: University of North Carolina Press, 1998).
12. *Vicksburg Evening Post*, July 28–31, August 1–3, 1965.

SUGGESTED READINGS

On the role of World War II and the Cold War in the civil rights era, see Mary Dudziak's *Cold War Civil Rights: Equality as Cold War Policy, 1946–1968* (Princeton, NJ: Princeton University Press, 2001); and Thomas Borstelmann, *The Cold War and the Color Line: America's Race Relations in the Global Arena* (Cambridge, MA: Harvard University Press, 2001). See also Philip A. Klinkner with Rogers M. Smith, *The Unsteady March: The Rise and Decline of Racial Equality in America* (Chicago: University of Chicago Press, 1999); and Patricia Sullivan, *Days of Hope: Race and Democracy in the New Deal Era* (Chapel Hill: University of North Carolina Press, 1996).

On the civil rights movement in Mississippi, see Charles M. Payne, *I've Got the Light of Freedom: The Organizing Tradition and the Mississippi Freedom Struggle* (Berkeley: University of California Press, 1995); and John Dittmer, *Local People: The Struggle for Civil Rights in Mississippi* (Urbana: University of Illinois Press, 1994). For John F. Kennedy's reluctance to intervene, see Carl M. Brauer, *John F. Kennedy and the Second Reconstruction* (New York: Columbia University Press, 1977). Michal R. Belknap has more broadly documented the role of the federal government in the struggle, *Federal Law and Southern Order: Racial Violence and Constitutional Conflict in the Post-Brown South* (Athens: University of Georgia Press, 1987). William Doyle, *An American Insurrection: The Battle of Oxford, Mississippi, 1962* (New York: Doubleday, 2001); and Jack Nelson, *Terror in the Night: The Klan's Campaign against the Jews* (New York: Simon & Schuster, 1993), have also looked at violence and civil rights in Mississippi. Seth Cagin and Philip Dray have written about the Neshoba County case in *We Are Not Afraid: The Story of Goodman, Schwerner, and Chaney and the Civil Rights Campaign for Mississippi* (New York: Macmillan, 1988). William Bradford Huie investigated that case as a journalist and authored *Three Lives for Mississippi* (New York: WCC Books, 1965). Florence Mars, a resident of Neshoba County, offers an insider's perspective in *Witness in Philadelphia* (Baton Rouge: Louisiana State University Press, 1977).

A portion of the records of the Mississippi Sovereignty Commission are now open to researchers at the Mississippi Department of Archives and History. A heavily censored record of the FBI's investigation into the Neshoba County murders is available online. I obtained the FBI's file on Vicksburg's leading Klansman through the Freedom of Information Act. The House Un-American Activities Committee investigated the Mississippi Ku Klux Klan. They called leading Klansmen as witnesses, but all the Klan witnesses invoked rights they associated with the Bill of Rights and refused to testify. Nonetheless, committee investigators introduced important information about the White Knights into the public record. See *Activities of the Ku Klux Klan Organizations of the United States, Hearings Before the Committee on Un-American Activities*, 89th Cong., 2d sess. (Washington, DC: Government Printing Office, 1966).

11

Ralph David Abernathy and the Civil Rights Movement

Gerald L. Smith

Ralph Abernathy grew up in a segregated world. As a black man, he could not eat in the same restaurants as whites, could not go to the same hospitals, could not visit the same restrooms, could not swim in the same pools, could not drink out of the same water fountains, could not play on the same sports teams, could not attend the same schools, could not sit in the same places on buses or in theaters, and could not expect the same respect or the same justice. His South told him he was a second-class citizen.

White churches mainly reinforced that color line as they had in slavery times (and also tended to place women in a more subordinate role, as well). Even black churches rarely struck out at that bondage of the soul, for their emphasis on better times in an afterlife tended to lessen social activism. But that pattern was changing, and men like Abernathy helped shape the new religious and racial face of the region.

Black ministers played a major role in African American life and Abernathy and Martin Luther King Jr., among others, sought to reorient church leaders and their flocks to a more activist role. King would argue that segregation scarred the soul of his people and would call on the church to be the conscience of the state. Nonviolent resistance, stressing kindness rather than hate, would be the vehicle to win allies and eventually gain victories for the cause of civil rights and human rights. Yet that success might not have occurred without the dedication and leadership of people such as Abernathy. His life speaks for those quieter soldiers who fought for the cause and reflects both the successes and the tensions within the larger movement. It also shows, once more, the power of an individual in shaping history.

Gerald L. Smith is an associate professor of history and director of the African American Studies and Research Program at the University of Kentucky in Lexington. The author of A Black Educator in the Segregated South: Kentucky's Rufus B. Atwood *(1994) and* Lexington, Kentucky *(2002), he is currently coauthoring a book on African Americans in Memphis with Kenneth W. Goings and coediting volume 6 of* The Papers of Martin Luther King Jr.

On March 12, 1976, nearly 1,000 persons gathered at the Marriott Motor Hotel in Atlanta, Georgia, to celebrate Ralph Abernathy's fiftieth birthday and express their appreciation for his many contributions to the civil rights movement. The occasion, which lasted more than three hours, included remarks from several speakers, the presentation of a plaque from the State General Missionary Baptist Convention, plus $1,200 in cash and a proclamation in honor of Abernathy from Mayor Maynard Jackson. It was a fitting tribute for a man who served on the front line in the fight for racial justice.

Thirteen years later, however, Abernathy did not receive a warm reception from his fellow freedom fighters when he published his autobiography *And the Walls Came Tumbling Down*. Those who once praised his role in the movement offered harsh criticisms of his memoir. The controversy centered on the three pages in the massive 600-page volume that offered details into Martin Luther King Jr.'s intimate relationships with two women on the evening prior to his assassination. Numerous persons questioned Abernathy's decision to disclose such information more than twenty years after King's death. In Atlanta a coalition of King's longtime supporters held a news conference in front of his crypt to criticize how the book distorted King's place in history. Jesse Jackson, Benjamin Hooks, and Andrew Young were among the twenty-seven prominent civil rights leaders who signed a statement questioning Abernathy's health and mental stability and the motives of the book's publisher, Harper & Row. "This is another attempt to diminish the life and work of the only spiritual genius America has produced," read the statement. "It is time for detractors to cease their futile efforts to diminish this legacy that God has given to our time and to all time through Dr. King."[1]

Abernathy lived six months after the publication of his book. He died on April 17, 1990. After having committed much of his adult life to the cause of freedom, he was last remembered as the man who betrayed his best friend, Martin Luther King Jr.

It was a sad twist of history that Abernathy, a leading figure in one of America's greatest movements, died with the tarnished image of a traitor. After all, Abernathy had helped organize the Montgomery bus boycott in 1955. From 1957 to 1968 he was secretary-treasurer of the Southern Christian Leadership Conference (SCLC), a civil rights organization based in Atlanta. He served as first vice president of the organization from 1965 to 1968. Following King's assassination in 1968, he served as president of the SCLC for the next eight years. Abernathy took charge of the organization at a very difficult and challenging period in the history of the civil rights movement. Morale was low, funds were shrinking, and the overall movement was fractionalized. Despite the circumstances, Abernathy remained true to the wishes of his beloved friend, Martin. He was, as the Reverend Hosea Williams, a staff member of the SCLC once said, the "Joshua" to King's "Moses." "We will get to the promised land," exclaimed Abernathy. "It will happen in my time and under my leadership."[2]

Abernathy wanted to prove to white America that the intensity of the civil rights movement would not falter with King's death. He sought to demonstrate to other soldiers in the movement that the struggle would not diminish under his watch. But winning the total confidence of his contemporaries and acquiring the respect of white America would prove to be his greatest challenge. In the public's perception he always seemed to be King's sidekick. Between 1955 and 1968, he led congregational hymns, gave supportive talks, introduced King at rallies, and remained close by as King answered questions at press conferences. But Abernathy never doubted his own leadership skills. Like King, he knew firsthand the sacrifices, struggles, frustrations, and dangers of the movement. He had faced vicious mobs, fire hoses, attack dogs, and death threats. He had stood at King's side in every major civil rights demonstration, leading some people to refer to them as the "civil rights twins." Yet Abernathy never gained a significant place in history. King's intellect, charisma, and oratorical skill overshadowed him at every turn. Abernathy was equally committed to the civil rights movement and had been King's most dependable freedom fighter throughout the dramatic and violent civil rights movement of the 1950s and 1960s. He deserved more.

Born in Marengo County, Alabama, on March 11, 1926, Abernathy grew up on a farm owned by his father, W. L. Abernathy, a successful agrarian who had risen from sharecropping to own more than 300 acres of land in the small town of Linden. Will and Louivery Abernathy had twelve children, with Ralph the tenth and the youngest of seven boys. The Abernathys raised their children in a loving environment and imparted Christian beliefs to them. An influential member of the community, W. L. contributed money to support the all-black high school, Linden Academy, and he served on the school board. He was also chairman of the board of deacons at Hopewell Baptist Church. Louivery was just as hardworking and religious as her husband. Abernathy remembered that his father "was like God the Father. . . . He knew all the answers to the hard theological questions, and he laid down the law. But my mother was more like God the Holy Spirit—full of hope and joy and love."³

Abernathy's religious background proved instrumental in his decision to accept the call to preach. He later claimed he always knew he would be a preacher, but his father had told him that "preaching is not a vocation for a boy but for a man." Abernathy announced his call to the ministry on Mother's Day in May 1948, after both his parents had died. "I chose this particular day in tribute to my mother, who from the beginning had shown me the way to my true vocation."⁴ When Abernathy announced his decision to become a minister at Hopewell Baptist Church, he was only twenty-two years old, but was a mature young man prepared for the responsibilities and challenges that the profession entailed. He had already proven himself to be a leader in the U.S. Army, having been promoted to sergeant during World War II. After the war he had returned to Alabama to complete an examination equivalent to the General Education Degree (GED). Using the benefits of the GI Bill, he enrolled in Alabama State College.

As a college student, Abernathy was active on campus. He participated in dramatic performances and served as the superintendent of the student Sunday school. By his sophomore year he was elected president of the student council and his classmates looked to him to do something about the poor quality of food served on campus. Abernathy led a campus-wide hunger strike in protest of the dining hall. When Alabama State University President H. Council Trenholm asked him to end the strike, Abernathy remained firm in his demand that the students receive better food. Instead of pressing the issue, President Trenholm assured Abernathy that food services would improve. The strike ended. That episode served as a defining moment in Abernathy's life. "This experience," he later wrote, "taught me a lesson that I filed away but never forgot: You can deal with the most awesome authority on an equal basis if the people are on your side."⁵

In spring 1950, Abernathy graduated from Alabama State with a bachelor of science degree. That fall he began working on a master's degree in sociology at Atlanta University. Shortly after arriving in Georgia's capital, he was encouraged by friends to attend Ebenezer Baptist Church to hear the preaching of a young dynamic minister named Martin Luther King Jr. A King sermon impressed Abernathy yet left him envious of King's academic background. The two men exchanged greetings following the service. They met again a few days later at a program on the campus of Spelman College. Over time these contacts grew.

Meanwhile, however, other matters took precedence, for Abernathy had fallen in love with a young woman in Marengo County named Juanita Odessa Jones. The two cultivated the relationship once he completed the course work for his master's degree and returned to Montgomery to accept a position on the faculty at Alabama State in 1951. He also accepted a part-time pastorate position with the Eastern Star Baptist Church in Demopolis, where he preached on the first and third Sundays of the month, and agreed to serve as the acting pastor of the First Baptist Church in Montgomery while that congregation searched for a new pastor. A few months later, to Abernathy's surprise, the members of First Baptist voted unanimously to call him as their new pastor. It was a humbling experience for a twenty-five-year-old who had no formal theological training. But Abernathy was delighted to have the opportunity to become a full-time pastor at the historic First Baptist Church.

On August 31, 1952, Abernathy married Juanita Odessa Jones in the First Baptist Church of Uniontown, Alabama. A teacher at the Monroe County Training School in Beatrice, Alabama, she commuted between Beatrice and Montgomery during the first year of their marriage to be with Ralph on the weekends. As the school term ended, she and Ralph were expecting their first child. Excited church members anxiously awaited the birth. They made gifts and visited the hospital to see little Ralph David Abernathy Jr. But Ralph Jr.'s death shortly after his birth "stunned" Abernathy: "I couldn't believe it. When I got married I prayed to the Lord for one thing: a wife who would be the loving mother of a fine family. I longed for children, and it never occurred to me that I would be denied that one prayer. I thought of that small brown ball, lying in the bassinet, and my heart ached."[6]

The members of First Baptist played a significant role in comforting the family during their tragic loss. Within a few years the Abernathy family included three children, two daughters, Juandalynn and Donzaliegh, and a son named Ralph Abernathy III. But instead of living a quiet and peaceful life, the Abernathy family was at the center of a mass movement for racial justice by the end of the 1950s.

Montgomery, Alabama, was in the heart of the segregated South. Rigid racial lines limited opportunities for education, employment, and decent housing for African Americans. They were expected to accept a restrained quality of life separate and unequal to that enjoyed by their white neighbors. But whites would learn that blacks would not remain docile and indifferent to the conditions under which they lived. In 1955, African Americans constituted close to 40 percent of the population in Montgomery and worked primarily in service and common labor occupations. Public school teachers and faculty members at Alabama State College represented most of the African American professional class in the community.

In spring 1949, Mary Fair Burks, chair of the English Department at Alabama State, organized the Women's Political Council, which addressed political and civic issues affecting the lives of African Americans. It encouraged African Americans to register to vote, pay their poll taxes, and vote on election day. In 1954 the council focused on the segregated city buses. As Montgomery city officials discussed the possibility of increasing bus fares, the council brought to their attention the unequal treatment African Americans experienced on the buses. The law required blacks to sit in the back of city buses and surrender their seats to whites when the bus became full. Additionally, African Americans had to pay their fare at the front of the bus, step off the bus, and reenter at the back of the bus to take a seat. The fact that all the bus drivers were white was an additional insult. They used derogatory language toward blacks, passed up black passengers, and at times even drove away once blacks had paid their fare and were walking to the rear of the bus. Outraged by these conditions, a few blacks had challenged the system, but their cases did not attract broad community support. That attitude changed on December 1, 1955.

Rosa Parks, a forty-two-year-old black seamstress, left work and boarded a bus to go home. As the bus became crowded she refused to give up her seat to a white passenger. Her defiance of the law led to her arrest, although she was a respected member of the African American community who had been active in the National Association for the Advancement of Colored People (NAACP). When E. D. Nixon, past president of the state and local branches of the NAACP, learned of her arrest he encouraged her to test the legality of bus segregation in Montgomery. Jo Ann Gibson Robinson, president of the Women's Political Council, and Fred Gray, a local black attorney, believed the legal case could be best supported by a local bus boycott. Robinson prepared a leaflet calling for a one-day boycott of all city buses in support of Parks's legal case. Meanwhile, E. D. Nixon phoned local ministers to seek their support for the boycott of the Montgomery city bus lines and to encourage them to attend a meeting at Martin Luther King's Dexter Avenue Baptist Church. Ralph Abernathy was among the ministers Nixon called. As secretary of the Baptist Ministers Conference and a graduate of Alabama State College, Abernathy was an informed and respected member of the African American community and, at that time, better known than King. In 1954, when King had accepted the pastorate at Dexter, he and Abernathy became friends and spent time together, discussing black social problems in Montgomery. The bus boycott provided them with an opportunity to address an important issue confronting the African American community.

Following the initial meeting of community leaders in regard to Parks's arrest, Abernathy and King revised the Robinson flier to include an announcement about a mass meeting scheduled at the Holt Street Baptist Church for December 5. Meanwhile, Abernathy and other ministers encouraged everyone to participate in the one-day boycott. Their efforts were successful. The majority of African Americans who lived in Montgomery refused to ride the bus. They walked, rode in private cars, or boarded taxis driven by black drivers who charged only a dime. According to Jo Ann Robinson, "That day was rough on the bus drivers. They complained to the police department that they were being 'persecuted and molested' in various places by colored children who ridiculed them and stuck out their tongues at them as they passed by."[7]

In the midst of the boycott, community leaders met at the Mt. Zion African Methodist Episcopal (AME) Church to establish an organization to discuss the segregated busing issue with city officials. Those present approved Abernathy's recommendation that the organization be named the Montgomery Improvement Association (MIA). King was elected president of the group and Abernathy was appointed to chair the resolutions committee.

As time for the 7:00 P.M. meeting on December 5 neared, the black community readied for mass action. When King and Abernathy approached the Holt Street Baptist Church, they saw several thousand people outside the church unable to get inside the sanctuary. This crowd was an exhilarating sight for the two ministers to witness. Both men would play significant roles at the gathering and had been giving thought to their presentations.

Following singing and scripture reading, King spoke first. "We're here this evening for serious business," he noted. "We're here in a general sense because first and foremost, we are American citizens and we are determined to acquire our citizenship to the fullness of its meaning."[8] In a sixteen-minute statement, King gave the boycott historical, democratic, and spiritual meaning. His statement evoked an overwhelmingly enthusiastic response. Rufus Lewis recalled, "This was the time that the people were brought face to face with the type of man that Martin Luther [King] was—not only the people who came to the mass meeting, but those who nominated him, too. It was astonishing, the man spoke with so much force."[9]

As chair of the resolutions committee, Abernathy followed King's speech by introducing the MIA's resolutions. They asked African Americans to stay off the buses until an agreement with the city had been reached. Private car owners and employers were asked to support the boycott and be mindful of the transportation needs of those participating in the demonstration. In closing, Abernathy said: "We have not, are not, and have no intentions of using any unlawful means or any intimidation to persuade persons not to ride the Montgomery City Lines Busses. However, we call upon the conscience both moral and spiritual, to give your whole-hearted support to this undertaking. We believe we have a just complaint and we are willing to discuss this matter with the proper officials."[10] The crowd unanimously supported the resolutions Abernathy presented.

Following the rally, Abernathy and King mailed the MIA's demands to city officials. Specifically, the MIA demanded seating on a first-come, first-served basis, courtesy from white drivers toward black customers, and the employment of black drivers on predominantly black bus routes. White officials were not interested in compromising with the MIA, however. Racial segregation had deep roots in Alabama and whites were determined to maintain the customs and traditions they inherited from the past.

Realizing the fierce opposition they confronted, the MIA prepared to meet the transportation needs of the African American community. At first black taxi cab companies offered discounted fares to riders, with MIA contributions making up the difference in cost. However, the city put an end to this practice by requiring all taxis to collect a minimum charge that was higher than ten cents. Private car pools then became the main source of transportation. Drivers at pickup and dispatch stations, scattered throughout the community, took people to work and picked them up in the afternoon.

The success of the boycott led Police Commissioner Clyde Sellers to launch a get-tough policy in January 1956. Sellers ordered his police to "break up" African Americans who congregated in white neighborhoods after work waiting for their ride home. In addition, police stopped black motorists randomly, interrogated them, and ticketed some for questionable traffic violations. While some members of the white community supported the boycott, the vast majority did not join the movement. Whites threw potatoes, apples, and rotten eggs at black pedestrians, insulted them verbally, and squirted them with water and urine to discourage the demonstrators.

Committed to a nonviolent protest, African Americans refused to retaliate. However, tension rose in the black community when King's home was bombed on the night of January 30, 1956. His family escaped harm but their lives were clearly in danger. Both the Kings and the Abernathys received threatening phone calls on a regular basis. In fact, the Abernathys received so many calls that their neighbors helped with answering the phone and other volunteers watched their home. With each passing month the boycott became more intense. Whites were determined to defeat the movement. In February, Abernathy, King, and a number of ministers were indicted for violating an Alabama law that prohibited boycotts. That action brought more national attention to the boycott. But African Americans would not give up. When white officials refused to place Parks's case on the court docket, attorneys for the MIA got five African American women to file a suit in federal district court against the city of Montgomery and the state of Alabama. In the case of *Browder v. Gayle*, the plaintiffs claimed that racial segregation in public transportation violated their Fourteenth Amendment rights. On June 5, 1956, a panel of three federal judges heard the case and sided with the plaintiffs. Both the city and state appealed the decision. But six months later the Supreme Court upheld the lower court's decision, giving the MIA and the movement a huge civil rights victory.

The Montgomery bus boycott catapulted Martin Luther King Jr. into the national spotlight. His photo graced the cover of *Time* magazine in February 1957, and a comic book, *Martin Luther King and the Montgomery Bus Boycott,* was published in his honor. As the spokesperson, King captured the media's attention because of his commitment to nonviolence and his ability to articulate the movement's objectives.

Beginning with the Montgomery boycott, it was evident that Abernathy would play a different role in the movement than King. He became King's most trusted adviser and the presiding official at mass meetings, always performing his duties with unique sensibilities. For example, one night in Montgomery at the close of a mass meeting, Abernathy drew laughter and approval from the crowd when he announced that the next gathering would be held at the Day Street Baptist Church. "If I can't see you there, I'll see you in the city jail." "You know," he continued, "they have on the car tags 'Heart of Dixie.' Well *let's walk until Dixie has a heart.*" These remarks reflected Abernathy's courage and determination. "As an operator," wrote historian Lawrence Reddick, "Abernathy had a boldness that King lacked. At times he would push when King would hesitate. Sometimes at committee meetings, he appeared to sleep, but whenever the talking was over and the time for deciding came, he would come to life and often take over putting the motions and beating down the minor objections."[11]

Early on the morning of December 21, 1956, Abernathy joined King and others on a nonsegregated bus ride through the streets of Montgomery that further inspired the movement for civil rights. Local leaders and demonstrators in other southern cities were encouraged by what they witnessed in Montgomery. Reverend C. K. Steele in Tallahassee, Florida, and Reverend Fred Shuttlesworth in Birmingham, Alabama, stood at the forefront of movements in their respective cities. By 1956, Reverend Abernathy was part of a nonviolent team of experts who visited other trouble spots in the South to teach protesters the philosophy of nonviolence. Northern activists associated with the NAACP and other civil rights groups observed closely the activities taking shape in the South. Ella Baker, an organizer of NAACP branches; Stanley Levison, a white attorney and fund-raiser from New York; and Bayard Rustin, executive director of the War Resisters League, became particularly interested in the southern movement. The three had formed In Friendship, a New York–based organization that provided financial support to the Montgomery bus boycott. King and Abernathy met with Rustin, Levison, and

Baker, who suggested ways of expanding the Montgomery movement throughout the South. The two ministers also maintained a close relationship with other southern black leaders.

With the support of Steele and Shuttlesworth, the MIA, under King's leadership, announced that a Southern Negro Leaders Conference on transportation and nonviolent integration would take place at Ebenezer Baptist Church in Atlanta, Georgia, January 10–11, 1957. Participants were invited to come and discuss shared problems and possible strategies to unite their efforts to overcome racism and discrimination. But in the early morning hours of the day the conference was to begin, Abernathy received a telephone call from his wife informing him that their home and church had been bombed. Although no one was injured, Abernathy and King rushed back to Montgomery to comfort city residents and survey the damage. King returned to Atlanta the next day to participate in part of the conference. The sixty ministers from ten southern states and twenty-nine communities agreed to send telegrams to President Dwight D. Eisenhower, Vice President Richard Nixon, and Attorney General Herbert Brownell, urging them to be more supportive of civil rights issues.

In February a follow-up meeting in New Orleans further coordinated and unified the efforts of southern black leaders. At this meeting the group officially formed the Southern Leadership Conference to raise funds and coordinate local civil rights movements. King was named president and Abernathy was elected treasurer of the organization, later renamed the Southern Christian Leadership Conference. Closely tied to the black church and led mostly by ministers, the SCLC did not recruit individual members but instead offered memberships to churches and community organizations. Local organizations looked to the SCLC for encouragement, guidance, and financial support. Reverend Wyatt T. Walker, executive director of the SCLC in 1960, remembered that local groups appreciated the influence and leadership of King and Abernathy. According to Walker, "They wanted Martin and Ralph [Abernathy] to come. 'Cause they knew they could get the folk; you can't do anything without the folk. And Martin and Ralph could get the folk."[12]

In a two-year period, Abernathy and King were at the forefront of a growing national movement for civil rights. "We knew that we had developed into symbols," remembered Abernathy.[13] Their civil rights activities also brought increasing threats against their lives. On September 17, 1958, Reverend J. Raymond, pastor of Second Baptist Church in Los Angeles, wrote both Abernathy and King to suggest that they leave Montgomery and seek employment elsewhere. He advised Abernathy to consider taking a pastorate at a church in New York since he "all but" needed a bodyguard.[14] But Abernathy was committed to remaining in the South and fighting for racial justice. On Sunday, April 27, 1958, King and his congregation joined Abernathy and his members for the rededication services of the First Baptist Church in Montgomery, which had been bombed the previous year. King presided over the program. In a letter to church officers, Abernathy expressed his gratitude to King and the members of the Dexter Avenue church. He wrote, "We stand willing and ready to do whatever we can to assist you and your Pastor."[15] Clearly, the relationship between Abernathy and King was evolving along with the movement.

Abernathy and King held each other in high esteem. In August 1958, King recommended that Abernathy be appointed chairman of the Social Action Commission of the National Baptist Convention. In a letter to Dr. J. H. Jackson, president of the convention, King wrote that Abernathy was "uniquely qualified to fill this post. He has proven his social concern through his work in the Montgomery Improvement Association and throughout the South. He is a marvelous organizer, an indefatigable worker and an able interpreter of the social gospel."[16] Despite King's strong endorsement, Jackson later replied that he was not able to offer the position to Abernathy because he had already made a "tentative agreement" with someone else. Still, King's respect for Abernathy was noteworthy, and the two men would remain extremely close friends even after King moved to Atlanta.

On November 29, 1959, King informed the members of Dexter that he would be resigning as pastor and moving to Atlanta, where the SCLC was based. The decision had been a difficult one. But the work of the SCLC and other demands on his schedule made it increasingly difficult for him to pastor the church. With King's resignation, Abernathy became president of the Montgomery Improvement Association. Abernathy's work and commitment to the bus boycott made him the most likely candidate to assume the leadership role in Montgomery. That he was from Alabama and had established a relationship with local leaders only affirmed that he was the best person to succeed King. Moreover, Abernathy's position with the SCLC would enable African Americans in Montgomery to maintain a close connection with the Atlanta-based civil rights organization.

When King left Montgomery, it was an "adjustment" for him and his friend Abernathy. "We had formed a close friendship that both of us depended on for strength and inspiration," recalled Abernathy. "We were in the habit of seeing each other frequently, and on those days when we couldn't get together, we usually talked with each other on the telephone. . . . We had both gotten used to this closeness, and only when the time drew near for the Kings to leave did I really consider what their departure would mean to me personally."[17] Once he had relocated, King began talking to Abernathy about moving to Atlanta. Abernathy was reluctant to move but King was sure that one of the churches in the city would extend him a call to become pastor. Meanwhile, the SCLC, along with the Congress of Racial Equality (CORE) and the Student Nonviolent Coordinating Committee (SNCC), advocated voting rights and the desegregation of public accommodations throughout the South. It was no surprise that as the movement expanded new challenges emerged.

In February 1960, King was charged with perjury and tax evasion by white leaders in Alabama. Bayard Rustin organized the ad hoc Committee to Defend Martin Luther King. With headquarters in the Harlem Labor Center, the committee worked to raise $200,000 to defray King's legal fees. In order to gain support the committee purchased newspaper advertisements. On March 29, 1960, Rustin wrote an ad for the *New York Times* headlined "Heed Their Rising Voices." He criticized "Southern violators of the Constitution" for their personal attack on King, and he signed Abernathy's name to the advertisement without getting his consent to do so, which led to a major problem. L. B. Sullivan, a Montgomery police commissioner, filed a libel suit against the *New York Times* and included Abernathy and three other clergymen whose names were listed in the newspaper ad in the action. A friendly southern court awarded Sullivan $500,000 in damages, and in 1962 the Alabama Supreme Court upheld the lower court's rulings. The case created major financial problems for Abernathy as other white Montgomery officials filed similar suits. Abernathy's automobile was seized, and the rest of his property was being considered for confiscation. Not until 1964 did the U.S. Supreme Court reverse the lower court's rulings. By then, Abernathy was deeply entrenched in the civil rights movement.

As a committed disciple of nonviolent direct action, Abernathy was a strong supporter of the freedom rides that began in May 1961. Organized by CORE, the freedom rides involved two interracial groups riding in buses through the South to protest segregation in interstate transportation. White resistance sought to end the movement but Abernathy and Juanita encouraged the demonstrations by sheltering freedom riders in their Montgomery home. On Sunday evening, May 21, more than 1,000 people gathered at Abernathy's church for a rally in support of the freedom riders. During the course of the rally a white mob formed outside the church and threatened persons on the inside. Abernathy, King, and other civil rights leaders managed to maintain calm among rally supporters until National Guardsmen arrived to bring the situation under control. Some whites expressed concern that the protests were embarrassing the United States at the height of the Cold War. When a reporter asked Abernathy about the demonstrations embarrassing President Kennedy, Abernathy replied, "Man, we've been embarrassed all our lives." The response was direct and to the point. It was Ralph Abernathy in raw form. Whereas "King would strike a deft, graceful jab . . . Abernathy slugged and walloped," remembered one observer.[18]

In 1961, Abernathy accepted the pastorate of the West Hunter Street Baptist Church in Atlanta, Georgia. The move reunited the two leaders in the same city. It also allowed Abernathy to work even more closely with the SCLC. His experience and contribution would be valuable in the continuous protests taking place in the South.

In the early 1960s black newspapers reported on various local demonstrations against segregation and discrimination in employment. In support of such actions, Abernathy and the SCLC went to Albany, Georgia, in December 1961 to aid a local coalition of African American organizations known as the Albany movement. Dr. William Anderson, president of the organization, phoned his college friend Abernathy to see if King would come and participate in a rally. Both Abernathy and King offered their support, with much enthusiasm.

On December 16, Abernathy, King, and Anderson led 250 people in a march to city hall. But police arrested the marchers because they did not have a permit to march downtown. The arrests were the beginning of a bad experience for the SCLC. Over the next several months, Abernathy and King tried desperately to bring national attention to the movement in Albany. But the local sheriff, Laurie Pritchett, was careful not to attract press attention. He discouraged the use of force when arresting demonstrators. In the end, Albany did not achieve the gains Abernathy and others had sought. By mid-1962, SCLC leaders were deeply embroiled in conflicts with members of the Albany movement and the Student Nonviolent Coordinating Committee. These controversies, and other problems, made it difficult to create a unified movement. Protest efforts failed to break down racial barriers in Albany.

The SCLC did not give up on nonviolence and continued to promote voter registration. It also began a new project called Operation Breadbasket in the fall of 1962. Abernathy led this program in Atlanta. Originally organized by ministers in Philadelphia, it aimed at increasing employment opportunities for African Americans at companies that produced goods purchased by black consumers. Abernathy's group focused first on the baking industry in Atlanta. And in 1963 his committee successfully convinced five different bakeries to expand opportunities for African Americans.

However, it was challenging for Abernathy to pastor a church and maintain a strong commitment to the SCLC. He needed and wanted to be in his pulpit as pastor of West Hunter Street each Sunday, and at times he had to choose between going to jail or being at his church. His dilemma was most evident in April 1963 during the demonstrations in Birmingham, Alabama. Rigid lines of racial segregation had deep historical roots in Birmingham. Public Safety Commissioner Eugene "Bull" Connor was determined to maintain racial barriers. But the SCLC was even more determined to achieve a major civil rights victory in the city, following the disappointing outcome in Albany. Black leaders believed Birmingham would offer a different experience because of the presence of the Alabama Christian Movement for Human Rights, which was an SCLC affiliate led by Reverend Fred Shuttlesworth. They were right.

On April 3, 1963, black college students held sit-in demonstrations at several Birmingham stores. A few days later the media focused on Birmingham when Bull Connor used police dogs to disrupt a civil rights demonstration. Americans observed the brutality of the police action on the evening news. As protests escalated, white city officials managed to get a state court injunction banning further demonstrations. King had to decide whether or not to obey the injunction. Cognizant of the federal government's important role as an ally against the police action, King did not want to jeopardize this support. But he had been criticized by other demonstrators for not violating a similar injunction during the Albany campaign. In order to maintain support for his leadership, King knew he had to violate the injunction and go to jail. Other members of the SCLC opposed this decision, especially when they learned there was no bail money available to get those arrested out of jail.

Abernathy had gone to jail with King on several occasions, but even he was reluctant to support King's decision this time. Abernathy had planned to preach at his church Easter Sunday and was not comfortable with the idea of having to invite a guest preacher because he would be in jail in Birmingham. On April 11, King sat in Room 30 of the Gaston Motel in Birmingham trying to convince the SCLC staff to support his decision. Clearly he had made up his mind to go to jail. After a lengthy discussion, Abernathy agreed to go with him. His decision ended the debate. Publicly Abernathy may have seemed to have a servile role in the movement, but his thoughts and actions in closed sessions with King and the SCLC staff proved persuasive. On April 12, Good Friday, Abernathy and King led fifty other demonstrators in a protest march in Birmingham. They went to jail for violating the court order and remained there eight days before they posted bond.

Abernathy and King's incarceration kept the media spotlight on conditions in Birmingham. Upon their release from jail, protesters continued their demonstrations. More than a thousand young people were arrested. Businesses in Birmingham experienced significant financial losses as a result of the boycotts and demonstrations. These actions led to a major civil rights victory in Birmingham. On May 10 the city agreed to begin the process of desegregating public accommodations and hiring black store clerks in downtown stores. Not all welcomed the announcement. A bomb exploded at the Gaston Motel in the suite in which Abernathy and King had been staying; nevertheless the incident did not distract them from pressing onward.

FBI surveillance of civil rights activities did not make the struggle for equality any easier. Abernathy referred to a surveillance transmitter or bug as a "doohickey" and would delight King and others in the movement by speaking into the device as though "Mr. Hoover" was at that moment listening to their conversations. Despite these difficulties, however, Abernathy and King continued to work toward the dream for equality they shared. They traveled around the country giving speeches and raising money for the SCLC. Following the Birmingham demonstrations, the SCLC joined other groups in planning the historic March on Washington in 1963. The organization also led demonstrations in Danville, Virginia, and St. Augustine, Florida. In 1965 it pushed for black voting rights in Selma, Alabama. Similar to past experiences in other southern cities, strong white resistance to black equality made Selma, the seat of Dallas County, another major battleground for civil rights.

On January 25 demonstrators lined up outside the Dallas County Courthouse to register to vote. An altercation ensued between Sheriff Jim Clark and Annie Lee Cooper. Remaining true to the spirit of nonviolence, King and other men watched as Clark beat Cooper. That night during a rally at the Brown Chapel, King asked Abernathy to serve as the principal speaker. King realized that Abernathy had the uncanny ability to calm people who were angry and frustrated, using words they could relate to and appreciate. Abernathy was at his best during the evening program. Pointing to a radio antenna on the pulpit, Abernathy told the audience that the police had warned him to be careful about what he said and were listening to his message. "They forgot that Ralph Abernathy isn't afraid of any white man, or any white man's doohickey either. In fact, I'm not afraid to talk to it man to man." At that moment, Abernathy picked up the antenna and yelled, "Doohickey hear me well!" The crowd roared with shouts and laughter as Abernathy spoke to the antenna.[19] He had successfully renewed their confidence and hope in the face of difficult circumstances. The incident did not seem like much at the time but within the larger context of the struggle, Abernathy's spirit and loyalty to King significantly stabilized the movement. When King needed someone he could depend on, he turned to Ralph Abernathy.

The movement in Selma continued in spite of severe beatings and massive arrests, and culminated with a dramatic march from Selma to Montgomery. On August 6, 1965, President Lyndon Johnson signed the Voting Rights Act, which strengthened African American voting rights in the South. Black voter registration in the South had increased more than 20 percent by the end of the 1960s.

With each major civil rights battle, King knew he faced extreme danger. He mentioned the possibility of his being assassinated to Abernathy. He even informed Abernathy that he wanted him to become president of the

SCLC should he be killed. King later formalized his idea at the SCLC's board of directors meeting in Baltimore by recommending that Abernathy be appointed vice president at large, making Abernathy his successor. The board approved King's recommendation but had serious doubts about Abernathy taking charge of the SCLC. Staff members did not believe Abernathy possessed the leadership skills to lead the organization in the event of King's death. He was not known as an intellectual, and critics said he was envious of King, especially after King won the Nobel Peace Prize in 1964. Some of King's associates believed Abernathy was recommended in order to appease his desire to be recognized on the same level as King. Stanley Levison believed King had to offer the position to Abernathy. "Martin found himself unable to give Ralph a piece of the Nobel Prize which Ralph was demanding, so therefore he had to promise him he could be his heir. Otherwise, Ralph would have gone berserk with envy."[20] In his own defense, Abernathy said that King believed "if there was any one person who could really keep the team together, then it was me."[21]

On April 4, 1968, Abernathy's leadership confronted its most difficult test. Martin Luther King Jr. traveled to Memphis, Tennessee, to support the sanitation workers strike and was shot as he stood on the balcony of the Lorraine Motel. Abernathy cradled his friend in his arms as he lay dying. King's assassination devastated Abernathy. "I felt that we would be assassinated together because we were together all the time," said Abernathy. "I thought that we might go to the car and get in the car and turn the switch on and we would be blown up. Or somebody would bomb the hotel. I just could not imagine living a day without Martin Luther King, because we were inseparable."[22]

At the time of King's death the SCLC was in the midst of assembling a Poor People's Campaign to organize people to go to Washington, DC, to lobby Congress to feed the hungry and provide better employment and housing for its poverty-stricken Americans. With King's death this massive campaign became Abernathy's primary focus. The plan called for the poor to live on the lawn of the Washington Monument in housing made of plywood and canvas in order to demonstrate their economic plight. Organizing the effort proved to be an overwhelming task for Abernathy and the SCLC. By early June crime and rainy weather conditions had ruined the intentions of Resurrection City. Moreover, Abernathy's plans encountered organizational and financial difficulties that turned the demonstration into a fiasco.

Between 1968 and 1976, Abernathy campaigned successfully for the rights of hospital workers in Charleston, South Carolina, spoke out against the Vietnam War, and lobbied for school desegregation. Still, he did not enjoy the level of respect within the SCLC that had been accorded to King. Differences among SCLC supporters emerged and financial contributions declined in early 1970. Clearly Abernathy's best years with the organization had occurred during King's lifetime.

Together, Abernathy and King embodied a public spirit that represented the virtues of the movement. Hosea Williams was the SCLC's mobilization director in 1968. He recalled fondly the relationship between the two men: "They were just the greatest team, and Ralph was the unsung hero of the civil rights movement. Martin would not make a decision without him. He trusted Ralph like he trusted Jesus. . . . Ralph gave him confidence, security, a strong soul to lean on. On the other hand, he gave Ralph his brilliance, his eloquence and intellectual depth, that charisma the white press is always talking about."[23] According to one of King's aides, "Abernathy was the glue for Martin King's soul. Every Christian has to have a pastor." Abernathy assumed this role in King's life. He "gave him counsel, he gave him solace, he gave him perspective."[24] In doing so, Abernathy committed his life to the civil rights movement. Regardless of Abernathy's decision to include intimate portrayals of his best friend's life in his memoir years later, the bond he and King shared at the height of the twentieth-century civil rights movement is forever embedded in history.

NOTES

1. *New York Times*, October 13, 1989.
2. Charles Moritz, ed., *Current Biography Year Book* (New York: Wilson, 1968), 1.
3. Ralph Abernathy, *And the Walls Came Tumbling Down: Ralph David Abernathy, An Autobiography* (New York: Harper & Row, 1989), 12.
4. Abernathy, *And the Walls Came Tumbling Down*, 12, 80–82.
5. Abernathy, *And the Walls Came Tumbling Down*, 67.
6. Abernathy, *And the Walls Came Tumbling Down*, 109.
7. David J. Garrow, ed., *The Montgomery Bus Boycott and the Women Who Started It: The Memoir of Jo Ann Gibson Robinson* (Knoxville: University of Tennessee Press, 1987), 59.
8. Stephen Oates, *Let the Trumpet Sound: The Life of Martin Luther King Jr.* (Chicago: Mentor, 1982), 66.
9. Oates, *Let the Trumpet Sound*, 68.
10. Stewart Burns, *Daybreak of Freedom: The Montgomery Bus Boycott* (Chapel Hill: University of North Carolina Press, 1997), 93.
11. Lawrence D. Reddick, *Crusader without Violence: A Biography of Martin Luther King Jr.* (New York: Harper, 1959), 117–18.
12. Aldon Morris, *The Origins of the Civil Rights Movement: Black Communities Organizing for Change* (New York: Free Press, 1984), 92.

13. David J. Garrow, *Bearing the Cross: Martin Luther King Jr. and the Southern Christian Leadership Conference* (New York: Vintage, 1988), 289.
14. Clayborne Carson et al., eds. *The Papers of Martin Luther King Jr.*, vol. 4, *Symbol of the Movement, January 1957–December 1958* (Berkeley: University of California Press, 2000), 496–98.
15. Carson et al., *Papers*, 413–14.
16. Carson et al., *Papers*, 462–63.
17. Abernathy, *And the Walls Came Tumbling Down*, 190–91.
18. Robert Weisbrot, *Freedom Bound: A History of America's Civil Rights Movement* (New York: Norton, 1990), 60; Reddick, *Crusader without Violence*, 118.
19. Oates, *Let the Trumpet Sound*, 327.
20. Garrow, *Bearing the Cross*, 417.
21. Adam Fairclough, *To Redeem the Soul of America: The Southern Christian Leadership Conference and Martin Luther King Jr.* (Athens: University of Georgia Press, 1987), 257.
22. *Atlanta Constitution*, November 25, 1977.
23. August Meier and Elliot Rudwick, eds., *Black Protest in the Sixties* (Chicago: Quadrangle, 1970), 285–86.
24. Garrow, *Bearing the Cross*, 366.

SUGGESTED READINGS

Most encyclopedias of the modern civil rights movement include biographical information on Ralph Abernathy. For a more detailed perspective of Abernathy's life, read his memoir, *And the Walls Came Tumbling Down* (New York: Harper & Row, 1989). Abernathy recalls the major civil rights demonstrations of the 1950s and 1960s while offering a personal reflection of his relationship with Martin Luther King Jr.

Two excellent sources on the Montgomery bus boycott are Stewart Burns, *Daybreak of Freedom: The Montgomery Bus Boycott* (Chapel Hill: University of North Carolina Press, 1997); and David Garrow, ed., *The Montgomery Bus Boycott and the Women Who Started It: The Memoir of Jo Ann Gibson Robinson* (Knoxville: University of Tennessee Press, 1987). Both books provide an overview of bus segregation in the city of Montgomery and discuss the African American community's response to this discriminatory system.

The archival Records of the Southern Christian Leadership Conference, 1954–1970, is a wonderful collection of primary sources, including some of Abernathy's correspondence, speeches, and sermons. Adam Fairclough writes an insightful chapter on Abernathy's term as president of the SCLC in *To Redeem the Soul of America: The Southern Christian Leadership Conference and Martin Luther King Jr.* (Athens: University of Georgia, 1987).

For good discussions of the civil rights movement, read Taylor Branch, *Parting the Waters: America in the King Years, 1954–63* (New York: Simon & Schuster, 1988); Aldon E. Morris, *The Origins of the Civil Rights Movement: Black Communities Organizing for Change* (New York: Free Press, 1984); and Robert Weisbrot,

Freedom Bound: A History of America's Civil Rights Movement (New York: Norton, 1990).

The best discussions of Abernathy and King's relationship are included in Stephen Oates, *Let The Trumpet Sound: The Life of Martin Luther King Jr.* (Chicago: Mentor, 1982); David J. Garrow, *Bearing the Cross: Martin Luther King Jr. and the Southern Christian Leadership Conference* (New York: Vintage, 1988); and Paul S. Good, "No Man Can Fill Dr. King's Shoes—But Abernathy Tries," in *Black Protest in the Sixties*, ed. August Meier and Elliot Rudwick (Chicago: Quadrangle, 1970), 284–301.

12

Bill Henry Terry Jr.: An African American's Journey from Alabama to Vietnam and Back

David L. Anderson

Over the years, southerners have readily exhibited a martial spirit, bringing one author to call the land "the militant south." In conflict after conflict, year after year, the numbers of those serving from the region have exceeded what would be expected for a population of such size.

When the fighting in Vietnam escalated in the 1960s, once more southerners went off to fight—only in this instance, and for the first time, they did so in a major conflict in a fully racially integrated army. The battles in Southeast Asia also took place as an expanding civil rights struggle was occurring in the United States.

Those two issues met in the person of Bill Henry Terry Jr. When he joined the army, he sought to make that choice his career. After all, the armed forces had already begun to represent one of the most integrated parts of American society. He hoped to find success there. Terry never realized that dream.

At the same time he served, debate erupted over whether the poor and disadvantaged bore a disproportional part of the fighting and the dying. Young men from rural Appalachia and the urban inner city both seemed to be represented in large numbers in the list of the dead, at least initially. Such perceptions only added to the growing disenchantment with the war. Yet, in the South, a larger portion of the population continued to favor the conflict than did the nation as a whole. In the decade of protests over women's rights, civil rights, and Vietnam, closure to such issues came hard. Bill Henry Terry Jr. would bring about some change, though only in death.

David L. Anderson is dean of the College of University Studies and Programs at California State University, Monterey Bay. He is president of the Society for Historians of American Foreign Relations (SHAFR) for 2005.

Professor Anderson is the author or editor of eight books, including Trapped by Success: The Eisenhower Administration and Vietnam *(1991),* Facing My Lai: Moving Beyond the Massacre *(1998),* The Human Tradition in the Vietnam Era *(2000), and* The Vietnam War *(2005).*

The fourth of nine children, Bill Henry Terry Jr. was born February 23, 1949. His family lived on the south side of Birmingham, Alabama, at 501 First Street South, about ten or twelve blocks from Elmwood Cemetery. Billy was educated in Our Lady of Fatima Catholic School and public schools and completed the eleventh grade at Ullman High School. Rather than enroll for his senior year, however, he enlisted in the army and entered active duty on September 23, 1968.

For the nineteen-year-old Terry, the decision to choose the service over school made sense in his circumstances. Although he could have avoided being drafted for another year if he had remained in school, he faced a high probability of being called up as soon as he had his diploma. Going to college and thus obtaining a further educational deferment was out of the question. He could not afford college, and furthermore, he had other financial responsibilities, for he had married in June 1968 and had a son, Patrick, in August. To support his young family, he worked at odd jobs as a laborer, in a clothing factory, and at a service station. He also made some money as an unlicensed barber, a trade he had learned from his father, Bill Sr. Consequently, with a young wife and a baby to support and facing the draft if he did not return to school, Terry enlisted.

Although his enlistment was, in part, "draft induced," that is, prompted by the likelihood of conscription because of high Vietnam War draft calls, Terry had additional reasons for volunteering. He intended to make a career in the military, following in the steps of his older sister, who was already in the army. He believed the service offered genuine opportunity for a young African American to finish his education while also providing income and benefits for his family. It would also enable him to fulfill a desire to see the world.

For most recruits in 1968, however, the opportunity for world travel meant a trip to Vietnam, and in this, Terry was no exception. He went first to Fort Polk, Louisiana, for basic and advanced individual training (AIT), and on February 14, 1969, he completed the AIT infantry course. The notation on his training certificate read "RVN Oriented," which indicated that he was destined for combat duty in the Republic of Vietnam. He commenced his tour of duty in Southeast Asia on March 6, 1969.

Terry was an infantryman in Company D, Second Battalion, Third Infantry Regiment, 199th Light Infantry Brigade. Ironically, the brigade commander was Brig. Gen. Frederic E. Davison, only the third African

American general in the history of the army and the first to lead an infantry brigade in combat. At the time he received his well-earned star in September 1968, Davison had declared that he wanted "his men to go home feeling they have done something and that black and white alike they have been treated fairly by the army."[1] On June 19 the brigade moved to the area around Xuan Loc in Long Khanh Province. After less than four months in combat, Terry was killed in action on July 3 during a search-and-destroy operation. His wife received the standard telegram of notification and sympathy four days later. In its bureaucratic formality, the wire said only that her husband was killed "while on a combat operation when a hostile force was encountered."[2] No death certificate was issued, and his family never learned the precise place or circumstances of his death. Three other standard forms eventually were given to the family: DD Form 1300, Report of Casualty (a minimal statement confirming Terry's death and length of service); a posthumous promotion to the rank of corporal; and a certificate of honorable service.

According to military unit records now available, the fighting in which Terry died was intense. At about 11:40 A.M. on July 3, his company was moving through dense forest toward a helicopter pickup zone northwest of Xuan Loc. They literally walked into the middle of a well-concealed North Vietnamese Army base camp and immediately came under heavy fire from machine guns, automatic weapons, and snipers. U.S. casualties mounted quickly. Company C of the Second Battalion worked its way through the jungle to provide covering fire for Company D. Both companies then pulled back about 250 meters, allowing U.S. tactical aircraft and artillery to pulverize the enemy camp shortly before 9:00 P.M. Terry and several other soldiers were reported missing and possibly killed during the fighting, and it was not until noon the next day that their bodies were recovered. Company D suffered nine men killed and twenty-two wounded in the battle.

Corporal Terry's body arrived back in Birmingham under military escort about a week after his death. Elmwood Cemetery had been advertising plots for sale, and after going to Vietnam, Terry had written his family that, if he was killed, he would like to be laid to rest in this beautiful and prestigious burial ground. His wife, Margaret Faye Terry, later recalled that "at the time we all thought of it as being a joke, something to pass the time, to make a letter longer." Sometime in June, however, another letter arrived from her husband, saying that "if I should die over here in Nam I want to be buried in Elmwood."[3] When that tragic possibility became reality, the family tried to make the arrangements. They knew that the cemetery was for whites only, but they went to Elmwood, accompanied by the military escort officer, in the belief that their situation surely would be different. The Elmwood manager turned them away, saying that racial covenants in the deeds of the other plot owners legally prevented him from selling to the Terry family.

Interment took place with full military honors on July 19 in the all-black Shadow Lawn Cemetery, but soon afterward, Billy Terry's widow and his mother, Jimmie Lee Terry, went to see the parish priest, Fr. Eugene Ferrell. "I just didn't feel right about it," Margaret Terry recalled. The white minister of a predominantly black congregation, Ferrell described his reaction: "It seemed a really very simple thing. He had died for his country, and he should have the right to be buried wherever he wanted."[4]

Father Ferrell contacted the NAACP Legal Defense and Education Fund, which helped the family file a class-action suit in federal district court. The plaintiffs asked the court to order Elmwood to sell burial plots in its public cemetery to any citizen, regardless of race or color, and to declare null and void the racial covenants in the existing lot deeds. Such a ruling would be precedent setting. In a previous incident in 1966, the public cemetery in the small community of Wetumpka, Alabama, had refused to bury Jimmie Williams, an African American and Green Beret paratrooper killed in Vietnam. The white elected officials of the town declared that the black sections of the only cemetery in town were full and suggested a pauper's grave as an alternative. Williams's mother responded that her son "did not die a second class death" and "he didn't die a segregated death and would not be buried in a segregated cemetery."[5] He was laid to rest with full military honors at the nearest integrated burial site, the Andersonville National Military Cemetery in Georgia.

In death, Billy Terry had been thrust into the front lines of the civil rights struggle then under way in the United States, even though, as a friend of his remembered, "Billy never really got too much interested in the marching and the other civil rights things. He was always working at some job or another and never had much time for that, I guess."[6] His case attracted national press coverage. Catholic priests, organized by Father Ferrell, held prayer vigils in Birmingham and Washington, DC, and Ferrell also led a group of clergy who asked President Richard Nixon to urge Elmwood to change its policy.

Because both sides acknowledged the facts, the briefs submitted in the case of *Margaret Faye Terry, etc., et al. v. the Elmwood Cemetery, et al.* and the judge's ruling focused on the Thirteenth Amendment and the Civil Rights Act of 1866, which declared African Americans free and entitled to the same rights of property as white citizens. The plaintiffs' brief cited precedents from cases involving property, discrimination, and grave sites. The defendants' response simply quoted Elmwood's rule, established in 1954, that "cemetery lots shall be owned only by human beings of the white and/or Caucasian race and the said lots shall be used only for burial of human bodies of the white and/or Caucasian race." The defendants further denied that "refusal to grant interment rights at Elmwood Cemetery constitutes a badge and incidence of slavery" unlawful under the Thirteenth Amendment and the Civil Rights Act of 1866.[7]

The constitutional arguments clearly favored the plaintiffs, and the cemetery's attorneys almost seemed to welcome a court ruling that would free Elmwood from an untenable legal position. The seventeen-page memorandum of opinion issued by Judge Seybourn H. Lynne, as prepared by his clerk Robert L. Potts, was a virtual history of civil rights legislation. Lynne decided entirely for the plaintiffs, declaring that Elmwood was legally obligated to sell burial plots without regard to race or color. The cemetery agreed to comply voluntarily with the ruling, and thus, no injunction was issued.

On January 3, exactly six months after Terry's death, his body was exhumed from Shadow Lawn and reinterred, with full military honors, in Elmwood. The ceremonies included a brief memorial service in Our Lady of Fatima Church, where he had been confirmed at age twelve and where his mother was an active parishioner. The flag-draped coffin was then transported in a hearse to Elmwood, followed by twelve hundred mourners singing "We Shall Overcome." Many residents of Terry's poor neighborhood watched from their yards and porches as the procession passed. At the cemetery a ten-man military honor guard led by a white chaplain and a black major fired the salute, played taps, folded the flag, and presented it to the widow. "This is not really a funeral march," Father Ferrell exclaimed in his eulogy. "This is a victory march for Billy and for truth and right."[8] The priest captured the symbolism of the moment when he observed: "We, the white race, have a lot of atonement to make to this young man, for we have discriminated against him from the cradle to the grave. . . . When he had done his best for his country, his country was still doing its worst for him."[9]

Tragic ironies such as the case of Bill Henry Terry Jr. pervaded America's war in Vietnam. Lyndon Johnson and other U.S. leaders repeatedly justified military intervention there as necessary to defend hallowed American principles of freedom, democracy, and self-determination. Yet for Americans at home as well as for the Vietnamese, the U.S. attempt to force its will on Vietnam undermined these noble ideals. Among the threats to America's governing principles, racism and economic discrimination in U.S. wartime policies were especially troubling.

Some racial and economic groups in the United States appeared to pay an exorbitantly high share of the personal costs for the war. Selected government statistics suggested that the percentage of Hispanics among the fifty-eight thousand American war dead far exceeded that group's percentage of the population, and African American deaths early in the Vietnam War were reported to be double the relative proportion of blacks in the population. Conversely, middle-class and college-educated whites were greatly underrepresented both in the casualty totals and among the force of two million American servicemen who went to Vietnam.

Paradoxically, the inequities in Vietnam military service emerged just as the civil rights movement was beginning to remove some of the legal and social discrimination that had long oppressed African Americans. The connection between the war and the black struggle for equality appeared so clear to Martin Luther King Jr. that he joined the antiwar movement and declared the war's conduct to be a grave injustice and danger to black citizens. As soon as President Johnson launched an American ground war in Vietnam in 1965, it was evident that the military escalation threatened LBJ's ambitious domestic program, the Great Society. The president saw this peril clearly and lamented, in his earthy style, "If I left the woman I really loved—the Great Society—in order to get involved with that bitch of a war on the other side of the world, then I would lose everything at home. All my programs. All my hopes to feed the hungry and shelter the homeless. All my dreams to provide education and medical care to the browns and blacks and the lame and the poor."[10] Still, Johnson plunged the nation into the carnage of Vietnam, believing that the world's most powerful democracy had to oppose communist totalitarianism in Asia. Speaking for the intended beneficiaries of the president's domestic plans, King's Southern Christian Leadership Conference (SCLC) charged that the "promises of the Great Society top the casualty list of the conflict."[11]

The SCLC's use of the casualty metaphor was pointed. Even as the $20 billion annual expenditure on the war drained resources from poverty programs and saddled all Americans with growing inflation, young black men were dying in large numbers in combat. In 1966, *Parade* magazine reported that 50 percent of the men in the airborne and other elite fighting units were black soldiers. Although Department of Defense officials could not immediately confirm the racial composition of individual units, they did acknowledge that 15 percent of all the soldiers in Vietnam were black. Other reports showed that 20.7 percent of the army's 1965 casualties were black. At that time, blacks made up only 11 percent of the U.S. population and 13.5 percent of the 19- to 25-year-old segment, so the death rate clearly posed a disturbing issue of "representativeness."[12]

Because of the attention given to the 20 percent black casualty rate early in the fighting, that figure was cited repeatedly even after the war. If accurate, it would mean that 11,000 names on the Vietnam Veterans Memorial are those of black GIs. (In fact, the total is 7,257, or 12.5 percent of all deaths throughout the war.) In 1966 the percentage of black deaths was 20.8, but that number dropped to 13.4 in 1967 and was below 10 for each year after 1970. The high initial numbers reflected the nature of the army in 1964 and 1965. Elite combat units, the first to be deployed, were primarily composed of regular enlistees, not draftees. Many of these soldiers were minorities who, like Terry, saw the military as providing a better economic opportunity than civilian society. At the time of Terry's death the reenlistment rate for blacks was twice as high as that for whites in all the services and three times higher in the army, indicating the career orientation of minority troopers. Meanwhile, the dramatic rise in draft inductions, from 106,000 in 1965 to 339,000 in 1966, changed the racial composition of the combat units. Although there were racial and social inequities in the draft itself, the larger manpower pool and the assignment of 45 to 50 percent of draftees to Southeast Asia eventually brought the racial percentages in the units in Vietnam into closer proximity to the composition of the general population.

Statistics for Hispanic GIs somewhat paralleled those for blacks. Some authors claimed that Spanish-surnamed soldiers made up almost 20 percent of all Vietnam casualties. In fact, however, only about 4.9 percent of the names on the Vietnam Veterans Memorial are distinctively Spanish, which approximates the 4.4 percent of the 1970 census that was Latino.[13] Still, the 20 percent figure, which was derived from an analysis of war dead from California, Texas, New Mexico, Arizona, and Colorado, was close to correct for those states and almost double the percentage of Hispanic citizens in that region.

The high number of blacks in the army before draft calls were increased and the even higher number in the all-volunteer army in the post-Vietnam years presented two related possibilities: (1) that the military offered more attractive socioeconomic opportunities to minority youth than did society at large, and (2) that the army was largely a poor man's institution. Even with high wartime draft calls, this pattern persisted. Assuming that a college degree indicated middle-class status or a potential for middle-class income, it was significant that only 4.9 percent of enlisted men at the end of 1969 had degrees. College students received draft deferments, but few entered the service after graduation. Only 2 of Harvard's 1,200 graduates in 1970 went to Vietnam, for example, and only 56 went into the service at all.

Statistics alone do not tell the whole story. Using quantitative analyses, many sociologists support the contention made in Pentagon studies that discrimination in the military was more often socioeconomic rather than racial and that poverty, not race, was the dominant characteristic shared by most Vietnam casualties. This generalization must be used with care because race consciousness remained strong among the minority poor, who suffered under the twin burdens of poverty and color. Puerto Rican congressman Herman Badillo from New York found it "repugnant and fallacious" to contend that economic incentives made "the risk of injury or death so overwhelmingly attractive to young Blacks and Puerto Ricans" that they would want to be "the white man's killer."[14] Other minority observers questioned the use of statistics to define fairness because that suggested quotas, which bureaucrats had often applied in the past to limit minority access to opportunity. Despite the "concern" she heard professed about the high percentage of poor and blacks in the military, black congresswoman Shirley Chisholm perceived a possible racist fear "of a whole army of black men trained as professional soldiers."[15]

The historical record resounds with the rhetoric of black voices condemning the racism that permeated American society, including the military. In Vietnam, minority spokespersons contended, black men fought to impose "democracy" on a nonwhite Asian people while the black GI was denied the full benefits of democracy at home. The emphasis on the race of the enemy was new, but the rest of the complaint was old and all too familiar. During the Civil War, former slave Frederick Douglass proclaimed that he would willingly "march to the battle field" if he would have "a government that recognizes my manhood around me, and a flag of freedom waving over me!"[16] "The American Negro . . . is more than willing to do his full share in helping to win the war for democracy," W. E. B. Du Bois wrote during World War I, "and he expects his full share of the fruits thereof."[17]

These pleas went unheeded, and black veterans suffered at home under the same burden of Jim Crow segregation and racial oppression as others of their race. From the early days of the Republic, it was standard military policy to use black troops primarily to meet wartime manpower needs, to assign them to support (not combat) roles, to place them in segregated units under white officers, and to deny them command of white troops. In World War II, this institutionalized racism remained entrenched. Blacks fought valiantly in segregated units, yet no black GI received the Medal of Honor during the war (although there had been black recipients in earlier wars). The brutal racism of the Nazi enemy, the postwar rhetoric about freedom versus communist tyranny, and the insistent demands for justice from black leaders, however, finally brought change. In 1948, President Harry Truman ordered the integration of the armed forces. The process started slowly, but by the early 1960s, as the civil rights movement battered down barriers at lunch counters, bus terminals, and polling places, the U.S. military was the most integrated institution in the nation. And by earning high efficiency ratings, many blacks had achieved positions of genuine authority, especially as noncommissioned officers.

In 1965 Johnson's land war in Vietnam brought the first truly integrated conflict in U.S. history. Terry went to Southeast Asia when the American deployment was at its peak of 540,000 troops. Blacks constituted 10.7 percent of that number and 13.5 percent of the combat deaths in 1969. In the initial troop buildup, black fighting men seemed to follow the traditions of their predecessors in earlier wars. They were eager to prove their manhood and their patriotism. One young marine, Pfc. Reginald "Malik" Edwards, later recalled that he enlisted in the service for a job but chose the corps because "the Marines was bad." Once in training, he encountered racial slurs, but that did not deter his desire to fight the Vietcong: "I knew Americans were prejudiced, were racists and all that, but, basically, I believed in America 'cause I was an American."[18]

Edwards served in Vietnam with valor, reenlisted, and rose to the rank of sergeant, but in 1970 the corps booted him out with a bad conduct discharge for repeated fighting in retaliation for what he considered racial harassment. He joined other black veterans in the Black Panthers. "We figured if we had been over in Vietnam fighting for our country, which at that point wasn't serving us properly, it was only proper that we go out and fight for our own cause," he explained.[19] This embittered Blood, as black GIs began to call themselves in Vietnam, expressed forcefully a spreading black belief that the war was not their war. In a 1970 poll, 57 percent of black respondents favored U.S. withdrawal from Vietnam, compared to 37 percent of whites.

Initially, black leaders were reluctant to break openly with Johnson on the war because he was a valuable ally in their struggle for civil rights legislation. They also hesitated to appear disloyal in wartime and thus reverse their hard-earned gains in civic respectability. King expressed doubts about the war as early as March 1965, but he finally decided "to break silence" on April 4, 1967. In a stirring address at the Riverside Church in New York City, this Nobel Peace Prize laureate lamented the casualties, underfunded poverty programs, and recent outbreaks of urban violence. He joined his hallmark appeal for nonviolence at home with a plea for peace abroad. Declaring himself a brother to the poor of America and Vietnam, he castigated the U.S. government for brutalizing the downtrodden of both nations while defending a corrupt regime in Saigon. The United States was on the wrong side of the world revolution and needed, he urged, to make "a positive thrust for democracy."[20]

King's voice added stature to the growing antiwar movement, which, in 1967, many Americans still considered a radical fringe. Some journalists suggested that the minister had fallen under communist influence, but King's rhetoric was relatively mild. He stopped short of terming the war overtly racist and did not call for a communist victory, as did some white extremists. Black moderates Ralph Bunche and Roy Wilkins criticized King for merging the peace and civil rights movements. Black Power advocate Stokley Carmichael of the Student Nonviolent Coordinating Committee (SNCC) welcomed King's speech, but he, too, rejected a coalition with antiwar activists. SNCC leaders viewed the peace movement as "basically all-white" and something to which they could not relate. Carmichael's racial separatism led him to characterize the draft, for example, as "white people sending black people to make war on yellow people in order to defend the land they stole from red people."[21]

Shortly before his murder in 1968, King reflected on the "tragedy" of military service for young black men. He expressed faith in the initial sincerity of the proponents of the Great Society. But he believed the war prevented its realization, and that failure left closed many doors to education, training, and dignity for the poor. Meanwhile, young black males risked death in the military because "life in the city ghetto [or] life in the rural South almost certainly means jail or death or humiliation. And so, by comparison, military service is really the lesser risk." America was not a venal nation, King argued, but it was complacently blind to "habitual white discrimination." "Was security for some," he asked, "being purchased at the price of degradation for others?"[22]

In 1966 the Johnson administration created a remarkable program—Project 100,000—that addressed the tragedy of which King spoke. Its implementation, however, validated the minister's concern about equity. As touted by Secretary of Defense Robert McNamara, the program was designed to "salvage the poverty-scarred youth of our society" for military service and "for a lifetime of productive activity in civilian society."[23] The plan called for inducting 100,000 men a year (through the draft or enlistment) out of the 600,000 who failed annually to qualify under previous mental and physical induction standards. These men were some of the nation's poorest, least-educated, and most disadvantaged youth, but the Pentagon claimed the project would benefit them because it would "spread more equitably the opportunities and obligations of military service."[24] The plan also expanded the available manpower pool for the war—a fact readily admitted in military circles but not specifically designated as a program objective.

Project 100,000 was schizophrenic. Ralph Nader's Center for Study of Responsive Law termed it hypocritical in a report entitled "How the Great Society Went to War."[25] The initiative was simultaneously a Great Society effort to rescue "the subterranean poor" and a guise for filling the ranks in an increasingly questionable war with men who had little voice and few means to resist. McNamara and Clark Clifford, who became defense secretary in 1968, boasted that 40 percent of the men in the program were black, 60 percent had less than a high school education, and over half were unemployed or earning less than sixty dollars per week when inducted. Other statistics showed that 96 percent of them graduated from basic training (compared to 98 percent for all troops), and that, after the first sixteen and a half months, 91 percent of those in the army had received excellent conduct and efficiency ratings. Billy Terry fit this profile. The underside of Project 100,000 was revealed in an October 1967 *Washington Post* article: "Secretary of Defense McNamara has ordered the armed forces to accept some misfits and dropouts . . . so President Johnson won't be forced to widen the draft or call up the reserves during the 1968 election year."[26]

From the outset of the war, Johnson had purposefully sought to contain political repercussions by relying on the draft and enlistments rather than a mobilization of reservists, but his motive for developing Project 100,000 was not simply political expediency. The administration's leaders were part of the generation that had promoted the integration of the military as being good for the nation. Moreover, Johnson's personal stamp was on the civil rights laws of 1964 and 1965. McNamara had established federal civil rights protection for service personnel when outside military installations, and Clifford had been one of Truman's advisers who helped craft the executive order integrating the armed forces. Thus, these officials saw military training as beneficial to young black men, and each had personally aided in the African Americans' fight for the right to fight.

Respected social scientists in the 1960s also championed the benefits of military service for minorities. The planners of Project 100,000 drew explicitly on the work of Daniel Moynihan, the sociologist who, with Nathan Glazer, coined the term *ethnicity* in his studies of New York City. As assistant secretary of labor, Moynihan helped produce influential socioeconomic studies on young men disqualified for military service and on the black family. These reports argued that the young black male stood only to gain in self-esteem and skills from military service. Separate research outside the government similarly concluded that integration of the armed services had brought about "a marked and rapid improvement in individual and group achievement."[27]

These strong theoretical arguments make it difficult to characterize Project 100,000 as purposefully exploitative, but other studies conducted at the time and later revealed that the plan was a mistake of large proportions. "The main thing Project 100,000 seems to have done," Representative Chisholm observed, "was to ease the pressure of the draft among the white middle class."[28] In 1967, as the Pentagon began full implementation of Moynihan's recommendations on recruiting poor and minority soldiers, the National Advisory Commission on Selective Service issued a report entitled *In Pursuit of Equity: Who Serves When Not All Serve?* This investigation confirmed the high black casualty percentages. It also found that blacks accounted for only 1.3 percent of local draft board members but made up 16 percent of draftees. Minorities faced serious institutionalized racism, not just the socioeconomic hurdles that Moynihan highlighted.

The armed forces had data, especially from World War II, that also predicted many problems with Project 100,000. Candidates for the program had an Armed Forces Qualifying Test (AFQT) rank of Category IV, indicating a score of 10 to 30 out of 100 on the preinduction mental examination.

(Billy Terry had an AFQT score of 20.)[29] Although a few Category IV new standards men (NSM)—as they were called—were later found to be retarded, most scored low because of a lack of education. Many read at or below the sixth-grade level. Experienced military trainers knew that it was inadvisable to try to make soldiers of such men, especially during wartime.

Project 100,000 ended in 1972 as military manpower needs declined and the program experienced mounting problems. Many NSM never received the remedial help, especially with reading, that the program had promised. Those training centers that did attempt to accommodate the needs of the NSM experienced marked cost increases. The NSM also had a high rate of recycling through training and of medical discharges. Commanders found a high absence rate among low-ability soldiers, and in the army, there were twice as many disciplinary actions and courts-martial in this group as among other men. In 1974, President Gerald Ford established a clemency board for draft and military absence offenders, and almost one-third of the military applicants were Category IV men, who would not have been in the service without Project 100,000. A follow-up study of the NSM, completed in 1990, found them worse off in terms of employment, education, and income than disadvantaged youth who never served.

William P. Bundy, one of Johnson's officials who helped shape Vietnam policy, has advised historians to compare the chronologies of the Great Society and the Vietnam War. This juxtaposition reveals the difficulty inherent in the Johnson administration's attempt to expand citizenship rights to more Americans at the same time that combat service was increasing citizenship costs. Yet the traditional linkage between military service and citizenship rights remained strong in the Pentagon rhetoric about a young man's military obligation and even in the arguments of some minority spokespeople. As late as 1971, with the war continuing and with growing controversy surrounding casualty figures and Project 100,000, the NAACP complained that AFQT scores were still being used to deny blacks "opportunity" in the armed forces.

For military service to convey civic opportunity, however, the mission assigned the armed forces must itself be honorable. This reality was central to King's indictment of American purposes in Vietnam. He could not join with Douglass and Du Bois and argue that for blacks, the risks of combat were a high but reasonable price to pay for respect. King contended that black casualties and the demise of the Great Society were unacceptable consequences of an immoral policy in Asia. In his view, the Vietnam War was a violent colonial conquest unbefitting the democratic principles of the United States.

Although the overall casualty figures for blacks and Hispanics were not as extraordinarily high as some critics claimed, minority opposition to the war mounted faster than did that of the white majority. The explanation rests, in part, on the fact that some inequities did occur, as reflected in the high percentage of black deaths early in the war, the high casualty rate among Hispanics from the U.S. Southwest, and the dashing of hopes raised by the Great Society. Project 100,000 illustrated the problem. Johnson's aides initially congratulated themselves on the number of poor blacks being helped by the program even as black leaders saw it as the latest example of minority manipulation by the white power elite. Combined with a history of discrimination, these realities caused minorities to perceive that they bore an unfair burden, regardless of what the actual data revealed. Adding to the distrust was the violence of the war itself, in pursuit of vague objectives in a place little understood by most Americans. The Vietnam War did not necessarily produce the tension and distrust within the United States, but the pressures of this controversial military operation revealed the depth of such preexisting pathologies.

The leaders of the Athenian democracy "adopted bad policies at home and in the empire," Thucydides recorded twenty-five hundred years ago during the Peloponnesian War, and "this failure did harm to the city in the conduct of the war."[30] The Vietnam experience underscores a timeless reality that foreign policy and all good public policy must serve the domestic interests and internal welfare of the nation and all of its citizens.

Bill Henry Terry Jr. was a good citizen. He came from a close-knit, churchgoing, hardworking family. Despite his youth and his humble circumstances, he was trying to be a good husband and father and a responsible adult. He was caught in a social web of race and class that actually made volunteering for almost certain assignment to a brutal and dangerous war appear to be a good choice. His gamble cost him his life, but in death, he still contributed to society and his family. Through the courage of his wife and mother and the responsiveness of Father Ferrell and the legal system, Terry's simple request for a dignified burial helped end one of the morbid legacies of Jim Crow racism—segregated cemeteries. It was also a significant step in giving African American soldiers proper recognition of their service and sacrifice. In later years Billy Terry's veteran's benefits enabled his son Patrick to attend college. Terry's short life left a lasting legacy.

NOTES

1. Clipping from *Chicago Tribune*, September 16, 1968, in "Scrapbook," Box 2, Organizational History, Second Battalion, Third Infantry, Records of the United States Army Vietnam, Record Group 472, National Archives, College Park, Maryland.

2. The author thanks Margaret Terry for her generous assistance in providing copies of this telegram and other personal documents related to her husband's military service.
3. Margaret Terry, letter to author, March 2, 1998.
4. Quoted in James T. Wooten, "Black Soldier Buried among Whites," *New York Times*, January 4, 1970.
5. Quoted in James E. Westheider, *Fighting on Two Fronts: African Americans and the Vietnam War* (New York: New York University Press, 1997), 73.
6. Quoted in Wooten, "Black Soldier Buried among Whites."
7. Answer of Defendant, the Elmwood Cemetery Corporation, in case file of *Margaret Faye Terry, etc., et al. v. the Elmwood Cemetery, et al.*, Records of Alabama, North District, Records of District Courts of the United States, Record Group 21, National Archives—Southeast Region, East Point, Georgia.
8. Quoted in Wooten, "Black Soldier Buried among Whites."
9. Quoted in Westheider, *Fighting on Two Fronts*, 74.
10. Quoted in Doris Kearns, *Lyndon Johnson and the American Dream* (New York: New American Library, 1976), 263.
11. Quoted in David J. Garrow, *Bearing the Cross: Martin Luther King, Jr., and the Southern Christian Leadership Conference* (New York: Morrow, 1986), 470.
12. *Congressional Record*, House, 89th Cong., 2d sess., July 18, 1966, 15,232–33.
13. The analysis of the Vietnam Veterans Memorial is my own count of the distinctively Spanish surnames in *Vietnam Veterans Memorial Directory of Names* (Washington, DC: Vietnam Veterans Memorial Fund, 1989). About 2,900 of the 58,219 names on the memorial are Spanish. Of the 2,900, about 1,800 were from the five southwestern states and represented 17.3 percent of the deaths from those states. Some of those with Spanish surnames were tribal American Indians; see Tom Holm, "Forgotten Warriors: American Indian Servicemen in Vietnam," *Vietnam Generation* 1 (Spring 1989): 58.
14. Congress, House, Committee on Armed Services, *Extension of the Draft and Bills Related to the Voluntary Force Concept and Authorization of Strength Levels: Hearings before the Committee on Armed Services*, 92d Cong., 1st sess., February 23–25 and March 1–5 and 9–11, 1971, 600.
15. House, Committee on Armed Services, *Extension of the Draft*, 670.
16. Frederick Douglass, "Pictures and Progress: An Address Delivered in Boston, Massachusetts, on 3 December 1861," in *The Frederick Douglass Papers*, ed. John W. Blassingame, 5 vols. (New Haven, CT: Yale University Press, 1985), ser. 1, 3:468.
17. Quoted in Bernard C. Nalty and Morris J. MacGregor, eds., *Blacks in the Military: Essential Documents* (Wilmington, DE: Scholarly Resources, 1981), 88.
18. Wallace Terry, *Bloods: An Oral History of the Vietnam War by Black Veterans* (New York: Random House, 1984), 6, 8.
19. Terry, *Bloods*, 13–14.
20. Martin Luther King Jr., "A Time to Break Silence," in *A Testament of Hope: The Essential Writings of Martin Luther King, Jr.*, ed. James Melvin Washington (New York: Harper & Row, 1986), 231–44.
21. Quoted in Charles DeBenedetti, with Charles Chatfield, *An American Ordeal: The Antiwar Movement of the Vietnam Era* (Syracuse, NY: Syracuse University Press, 1990), 158–59, 172–73.

Bill Henry Terry Jr.: An African American's Journey   207

22. Martin Luther King Jr., "A Testament of Hope," in Washington, *A Testament of Hope*, 326–27.
23. Robert S. McNamara, address to the National Association of Educational Broadcasters, November 7, 1967, "DOD Integration 1967" file, Office of the Secretary of Defense Historical Office, Washington, DC (hereafter cited as OSD Historical Office).
24. Office of Assistant Secretary of Defense (Manpower and Reserve Affairs), *Description of Project One Hundred Thousand*, April 1968, OSD Historical Office.
25. Paul Starr, with James F. Henry and Raymond P. Bonner, *The Discarded Army: Veterans after Vietnam* (New York: Charterhouse, 1973), 185–97.
26. *Washington Post*, October 23, 1967.
27. Charles C. Moskos Jr., "Racial Integration in the Armed Forces," *American Journal of Sociology* 72 (September 1966): 132–48.
28. House, Committee on Armed Services, *Extension of the Draft*, 671.
29. Bill H. Terry Jr., Enlisted Qualification Record (DA Form 20), courtesy of Margaret Terry.
30. Thucydides, *The Peloponnesian Wars*, trans. Benjamin Jowett, revised and abridged with an introduction by P. A. Brunt (New York: Washington Square, 1963), 83.

SUGGESTED READINGS

In addition to the sources cited in the notes, information on the demographics of those who served in Vietnam is found in Lawrence M. Baskir and William A. Strauss, *Chance and Circumstance: The Draft, the War and the Vietnam Generation* (New York: Vintage, 1978); Gilbert Badillo and G. David Curry, "The Social Incidence of Vietnam Casualties: Social Class or Race?" *Armed Forces and Society* 2 (May 1976): 397–406; and Neil D. Fligstein, "Who Served in the Military, 1940–1973," *Armed Forces and Society* 6 (Winter 1980): 297–312. For statistics on minority participation in the war, see Martin Binkin and Mark J. Eitelberg, with Alvin J. Schexnider and Marvin M. Smith, *Blacks and the Military* (Washington, DC: Brookings Institution, 1982); Ralph Guzman, "Mexican American Casualties in Vietnam," *La Raza* 1 (1970): 12–15; and U.S. Department of Defense, *U.S. Casualties in Southeast Asia: Statistics as of April 30, 1985* (Washington, DC: Government Printing Office, 1985).

Index

Page numbers in italic indicate pages with photographs

Abernathy, Donzaliegh, 177
Abernathy, Juandalynn, 177
Abernathy, Juanita Odessa Jones, 176–77
Abernathy, Louivery, 175–76
Abernathy, Ralph David: autobiography of, 174; birth of, 175; and civil rights movement, 178–89; death of, 174; religious life of, 176–77, 185
Abernathy, Ralph III, 177
Abernathy, W. L., 175–76
Adams, Charles Francis, 48–49
African Americans, xiii–xiv, 19–28, 39–41, 48–61, 72, 76, 80–88, 163, 170–89; and Vietnam, 198–205. *See also* civil rights movement; slavery
agriculture, xiii, 2, 21, 24, 38–39, 55–57
Alabama, 2, 91, 107, 131, 168, 175–84, 186–87, 194–97
Alabama State College, 176–77
Albany (GA), 185–86
Allen, Mel, 107
The Americanization of Dixie (Egerton), xv

American Journal of Sociology, 52
American Labor Education Service (ALES), 117
Anderson, Eleanor Copenhaver, *113*: birth of, 114; career of, 114, 116–25; death of, 124; description of, 115–16; education of, 115
Anderson, Sherwood, 114–15, 123
Anderson, William, 185
And the Walls Came Tumbling Down (Abernathy), 174
Appalachia, xiv, 19–28
Arkansas, xiv, 91–92, 94, 98, 107, 119–21
Armstrong, Louis, 85
Atlanta, 32–34, 36, 38–44, 174, 176, 185
Atlanta Constitution, 5–6, 32
Atlanta University, 176
Atlantic Monthly, 39

Badillo, Herman, 199
Bailey, Thomas Pearce, 49
Baptist Church, 86, 175–78, 181–85
Barbati, Ona May Stewart Leddington, 138, 141, 144, 146

Barber, Red, 107
Beavers, James L., 40
Bennett, Zachariah (Black Zack), 26; estate of, 23–24; monument of, 20–25; reputation of, 21–22
Bethesda (TN), 20–28
Bethesda Presbyterian Church, 20, 22–24
Birmingham, 186, 194–97
Blattner, Buddy, 106
Blight, David W., xiii
blues, 79–80, 82–87. See also music
Bowers, Sam, 163, 167
Broaddus, Margaret Ann Sanders, 130–132, 139
Broaddus, William, 131
Browder v. Gayle, 180–81
Brown, John Y., 140, 145
Brown, John Y. Jr., 145–55
Brown, Sterling A., 87
Bryn Mawr College, 115, 117–18
Burks, Mary Fair, 177

Calvert, David, 69
Calvert, Hester McClain: and agrarian life, 70–71, 76; children of, 69; death of, 77; early life of, 69; everyday life of, 71–75, 77
Calvert, Indiana, 69–70
Calvert, Robert, 69–71, 75, 77
Candler, Asa: and Coca-Cola, 34–35, 44; early career of, 33–34; early life of, 32; as mayor, 40–41; and philanthropy, 36–38, 41, 44; and religion, 33, 36–37, 39, 44; views on women of, 42, 44
Candler, John, 39
Candler, Lucy Howard, 34, 36, 43
Candler, Mae Little Ragin, 43–44
Candler, Martha, 32–33, 42–43
Candler, Samuel, 32–33, 44
Candler, Warren, 32, 36–38
Carmichael, Stokley, 201–2
Carner, Lucy P., 116
Cash, W. J., ix–x
Chandler, A. B. "Happy," 107, 140, 146
Chicago Daily News, 115

Chisholm, Shirley, 200, 203
civil rights movement, 24, 59–60, 108, 158, 175, 177–89, 196, 198
Civil War, x, xiii, 5, 33, 50–51, 160
Clifford, Clark, 202–3
Cobb, James C., xi
Coca-Cola Company, 32, 34–36, 44
Commonwealth College, 112, 120
Completely Queer, 83
Confederate Veteran, 6, 9, 13
Congress of Racial Equality (CORE), 184
Conkin, Paul K., xi
Connor, Eugene "Bull," 185–86
Copenhaver, B. E., 114
Copenhaver, Laura Lu Scherer, 114, 124
Copenhaver, Randolph, 123
Corbin (KY), 136–44
Council of Federated Organizations (COFO), 167
Creedy, Brooks Spivey, 116
The Crisis, 49

Davis, Jefferson, 2, 4–7, 10
Davis, Varina Howell, 4, 7–8, 15n18
Davis, Varina "Winnie," 3; birth of, 4; courtship of, 3, 7–8; death of, 10; image of, 11–13; as symbol for South, 1–13
Davison, Frederic E., 194–95
Dean, Albert, 92, 98
Dean, Alma, 92, 94
Dean, Cora Parham, 94
Dean, Elmer, 92, 98
Dean, Jay Hanna "Dizzy," 93; as announcer, 104–8; death of, 107; early life of, 92, 94; off-field activities of, 95–98, 101, 103; playing career of, 94–104
Dean, Patricia Nash, 97, 103, 107
Dean, Paul, 92, 94, 96, 98, 100–102
deBouchel, Onezima, 43
Degler, Carl, ix
Democratic Party, xv, 2, 41
Dillion, Merton L., 50
Dodd, Myrtle Calvert, 70, 72–75, 77
Dorsey, Tommy, 85–86

Du Bois, W. E. B., 49–50, 52, 54, 57, 61
Dudley, Jimmy, 107
Dunleith (plantation), 50, 52, 55–57, 60
Dunlevy, Dick, 131, 133
Dupree, Jack, 87
Durocher, Leo, 99–100

Emory College (University), 38–39, 44
An Epitaph for Dixie, xvi

Falstaff Brewing Company, 104–107
Federal Bureau of Investigation (FBI), 164, 166–70, 187
Ferrell, Eugene, 196–97, 205
foodways, 72–75, 129, 138, 141–55
Ford, Gerald, 204
Fort Polk (LA), 194
Fort Sam Houston (TX), 94
Fredrickson, Mary Evans, 118
Frisch, Frankie, 100–103

Galilean Children's Home, 139–40
Galloway, Charles B., 37
Georgia, 2, 32–45, 80, 86, 91, 107, 176, 182, 185
Gibson, Robert, 137–38
Gordon, John B., 2, 5
Grady, Henry, viv, 5–6, 32, 40
Grantham, Dewey, xiv
Greeley, Horace, 5
Green, Charles, 85
Greenville Times (MS), 51

Happy John (ex-slave), 80–81
Harmar, Leon "Pete," 143, 145, 148–49
Hays, Amon (Uncle Amon), 23; death of, 27; family of, 25–26; as farmer, 26; and religion, 27
Hays, Esther, 25–27
Hays, George, 25, 28
Hays, Jackson, 25, 27
Hays, Marion, 28
Hays, Oliveve, 26
Hays, Peggy Swinney, 25
health, xv, 71
Henderson, Fletcher, 85
Heublein, Inc., 154

Highland Folk School, 112, 118
Hispanics, 197, 199, 204
Hopewell Baptist Church (AL), 175–76
House Un-American Activities Committee, 123
Houston Buffaloes (baseball team), 95–97
Howard, George, 33–34

industry and commerce, xiii, 31–45, 129–55
In Pursuit of Equity, 203
International Brotherhood of Electrical Workers (IBEW), 164–65

Jameson, J. Franklin, 49
Jervey, Theodore D., 49
Johnson, Lyndon B., xii, xiv, 187, 197–98, 200
Jones, J. William, 5
Jones, Thomas Jesse, 49

Kennedy, John F., 164, 184
Kentucky, x, 91, 119, 133–55
Kentucky Fried Chicken, 143–55
King, Martin Luther Jr., xii, xiv, 169, 174, 176, 178–88, 201–2
Koch, Lucien, 120
Ku Klux Klan (KKK), xi, xv, 123, 158, 160, 163–70

labor, 2, 42, 44, 98, 101, 117–23, 164–65
Ladies Home Journal, 5
Landis, Kennesaw Mountain, 98, 101, 103
Lewis, David Levering, 48
Lewis, Rufus, 179
Look, 161
Louisiana, 91, 194
Louisville (KY), 133, 146, 152
Lynne, Seybourn H., 197

MacDonald, Lois, 116
Margaret Faye Terry, etc., et al. v. the Elmwood Cemetery, 196–97
Marion (VA), 114–15, 124–25
Marion College, 114–15

Martin, Johnny "Pepper," 100
Massey, Jack, 146–50, 152
McClain, Mary A. Strickland, 70
McLennan County (TX), 70–71
McNamara, Robert, 202–3
Medwick, Joe "Ducky," 100
Memphis (TN), 188
Mencken, H. L., xi
Methodist Church, 33, 36–39, 76
Middleton, Haven, 28
Miller, Gladys, 167
Miller, Howard Lee, 164, 167–70
Mind of the South (Cash), ix
minstrel shows, 80–83
Mississippi, 7, 11–12, 48, 50–52, 55–60, 83, 91, 107; in 1950s and 1960s, 157–70
Mississippi, University of, 51
Mississippi Historical Society, 51–52
Missouri, 82, 95–106
Montgomery (AL), 177–84
Montgomery bus boycott, 178–81
Montgomery Improvement Association (MIA), 179–83
Morris Brown College, 41
Moynihan, Daniel, 203
Mullin, Willard, 100
music, 79–88
Muste, A. L., 118

National Association for the Advancement of Colored People (NAACP), 170, 178, 181, 196, 204
Nelson, Lindsey, 107
New Orleans (LA), 50, 82, 131
New York Times, 123, 184
New York World, 8, 100
Nicholasville (KY), 134–36
Nickerson, Edmonda, 13
Norfolk and Western Railroad, 132
North Carolina, 92, 119, 121–23, 140
No Time for Sergeants (Hyman), 94

Oklahoma, 83, 91, 94–95, 107
On Horseback (Warner), 80

Parade, 198
Paramount Records, 84–86

Parks, Rosa, 178, 180
Peer, Ralph, 84
Pemberton, S. J., 34–35
Phillips, Ulrich B., 60
Pinckney, Charles, x
politics. *See also* Democratic Party; Republican Party
Poor People's Campaign, 188
Price, Joe Ed, 162–63
Pridgett, Ella, 80
Pridgett, Malissa, 86
Pridgett, Thomas (brother of Ma Rainey), 86
Pridgett, Thomas (father of Ma Rainey), 80
Project 100,000, 202–5
Provance, William, 164–65
Prudential Life Insurance Company, 133
Pulitzer, Joseph, 6–7, 10

race relations, xiii, 2, 4, 44, 28–60, 112, 121, 161–63, 165, 168, 170, 175
Rainey, Gertrude Pridgett "Ma": death of , 86; description of, 82, 85–87; early life of, 80; marriage of, 80; as singer, 82–87
Rainey, William "Pa," 80, 83
Reconstruction, xiii, 2, 51, 53, 60
Reddick, Lawrence, 181
Reed, John Shelton, x
Reese, Pee Wee, 107
religion, xi, 20–27, 32, 36–39, 44, 117, 119, 121–22, 153
Republican Party, xv
Richmond (VA), 4, 10–11
Rickey, Branch, 95–98, 104
Riis, Thomas L., 81–82
Robinson, Frank, 35–36
Roland, Charles P., ix
A Romance of Summer Seas (Davis), 8
Roosevelt, Franklin D., xiv–xv, 105, 117

St. Louis Browns, 104, 106
St. Louis Cardinals, 95, 106
St. Louis Globe Democrat, 105
St. Joseph (MO) Saints (baseball team), 95–96

Sanders, Clarence, 133
Sanders, Claudia, 139–45, 153–55
Sanders, Harland (Colonel): birth of, 130; death of, 155; early careers of, 130–42; and Kentucky Fried Chicken, 141–55; and religion, 143, 153
Sanders, Harland Jr., 132, 134, 137
Sanders, Josephine King, 132–33, 135, 137–38, 142
Sanders, Margaret, 132, 135–36, 141
Sanders, Mildred, 132–33, 136, 141
Sanders, Wilbert D., 130
Sellers, Clyde, 180
Selma (AL), 187
Shelburne, H. D., 137–38
Shelbyville (KY), 145, 147, 153
Shell Oil Company, 136–38
Shuttlesworth, Fred, 181–82, 186
slavery, x, xiii, 21, 25, 41, 51–53, 57, 60
Sledd, Andrew, 39
Smith, Bessie, 83–84
Smith, Hilda W., 118
Smith, Mamie, 84
South: definition of, x, xii; history and memory in, ix–xi, xiii, 1–2, 4, 8, 10–13, 160; image of, ix, xi
South Carolina, 12, 91, 123, 188
Southern Christian Leadership Conference (SCLC), 174–75, 182–83, 185–89, 198
Southern Music, American Music (Malone and Stricklin), 79
Southern Railroad, 131–32
Southern Summer School for Women Workers (SSSWW), 11, 116, 118–19
Sporting News, 105
sports, 91–108
Standard Oil of Kentucky, 135
The Staple Cotton Review, 51
Steele, C. K., 181–82
Stengel, Casey, 102
Stewart, Matt, 137–38
Stone, Alfred Holt: career of, 51; early life of, 50; and race, 48; views on books of , 49; writings of, 51–55, 57–60
Street, Gabby, 97, 99
Studdard, James Lamar, 168–69

Student Nonviolent Coordinating Committee (SNCC), 184, 201
Studies in the American Race Problem (Stone), 48, 60
Sukeforth, Clyde, 99–100

Tennessee, xi, xv, 12, 19–28, 91, 107, 119, 122–23, 150, 188
Terry, Bill Henry Jr.: birth of, 194; burial controversy concerning, 195–97, 205; death of , 195; military service of, 194–95, 200, 202
Terry, Blanche Smith, *159*; death of, 170; and factory integration, 164–66, 170; and KKK, 166–70; marriage of, 158, 160
Terry, Margaret Faye, 194–96
Terry, Patrick, 194, 205
Terry, Ray, 158, 160, 162, 168–69
Terry, Ray Jr., 160–61, 167, 169
Texas, 8–9, 68–77, 91, 94–96
Theater Owners' Booking Agency (TOBA), 85–86
Till, Emmett, 157, 161, 165, 170
The Time of Man (Roberts), 67
Trenholm, H. Council, 176
Truman, Harry S., 59, 200

United Confederate Veterans (UCV), 5, 9–13
United Daughters of the Confederacy (UDC), 1, 10–11
United States v. Forty Barrels and Twenty Kegs of Coca-Cola, 35

Vavra, Herman, 165–66, 169
The Veiled Doctor (Davis), 8
Vicksburg (MS), 158–70
Vicksburg Evening Post, 169
Vietnam War, xi, 188, 194–205
Villard, Oswald Garrison, 49
Villa Rica (GA), 32–33, 36, 42
Virginia, 4–5, 91, 107, 114–15, 122, 124–25, 187
Voting Rights Act, 187

Waco (TX), 71, 74, 77
Walker, Wayne T., 182

War between the States. *See* Civil War
Warner, Charles Dudley, 80–81
Washington, Booker T., 49–50, 54, 57
Washington Post, 48, 202
Westhampton College, 115
West Hunter Street Baptist Church (Atlanta, GA), 185
Westinghouse plant (MS), 162, 164–66, 168, 170
Wetherby, Lawrence, 142
Wilkinson, Alfred, 7–8
Williams, Hosea, 175, 189
Williams, J. Mayo, 84
Williams, Jimmie, 196

Williams, Miller, xvi
Williamson, Joel, 48
women, 1–2, 4, 8–12, 42–44, 67–88, 114, 117, 120, 158–70
Women's Political Council, 177–78
Woodward, C. Vann, xii
World War II, xiv–xv
Wylie, Harvey, 35

Young Women's Christian Association (YWCA), 112, 119, 121, 124; Industrial Department of the National Board in, 114–18, 120–22, 124

About the Editor

James C. Klotter is the state historian of Kentucky and professor of history at Georgetown College. The author, coauthor, or editor of over a dozen books, he most recently wrote *Kentucky Justice, Southern Honor, and American Manhood: Understanding the Life and Death of Richard Reid* (2003). His other publications include such articles as "The Black South and White Appalachia," *Journal of American History* (1980). He serves as co–general editor of an oral history series that has published five books to date.